For
ALL PEOPLES
and ALL NATIONS

Advancing Human Rights
Sumner B. Twiss, John Kelsay, and Terry Coonan, *Editors*

BREAKING SILENCE
The Case That Changed the Face of Human Rights
RICHARD ALAN WHITE

FOR ALL PEOPLES AND ALL NATIONS
The Ecumenical Church and Human Rights
JOHN NURSER

FREEDOM FROM WANT
The Human Right to Adequate Food
GEORGE KENT

For ALL PEOPLES *and* ALL NATIONS

The Ecumenical Church and Human Rights

JOHN S. NURSER

Foreword by DAVID LITTLE

GEORGETOWN UNIVERSITY PRESS | Washington, D.C.

Georgetown University Press, Washington, D.C.
© 2005 by Georgetown University Press. All rights reserved.
Printed in the United States of America

10   9   8   7   6   5   4   3   2   1   2005

Library of Congress Cataloging-in-Publication Data

Nurser, John, 1929–
    For all peoples and all nations : the ecumenical church and human rights / John Nurser.
        p.   cm.—(Advancing human rights series)
    Includes bibliographical references and index.
    ISBN 1-58901-039-6 (cloth : alk. paper)—ISBN 1-58901-059-0 (pbk. : alk. paper)
    1. Human rights—Religious aspects—Protestant churches—History—20th
century.   2. Ecumenical movement—History—20th century.   3. United Nations.
General Assembly. Universal Declaration of Human Rights.   I. Title.
II. Series.
BT738.15.N87   2005
261.7'09'045—dc22   2004022931

In grateful memory of James Luther Adams and Leslie Hunter, who between September 1957 and December 1958, by teaching me at Harvard Divinity School and ordaining me in the diocese of Sheffield, set the course of my life.

But anyone who has misgivings and yet eats [meat sacrificed at pagan worship] is guilty, because his action does not arise from conviction, and anything which does not arise from conviction is sin. Each of us must consider his neighbor and think what is for his good and will build up the common life.

—Saint Paul, Letter to the Romans (14:23)

I see that if I do not respect in others the rights that I would have them respect in me, I make myself the common enemy of all. This sacred duty, which reason obliges me to recognize, is not strictly speaking a duty of one individual toward another but a general and common duty, just as the right that imposes it on me is also general and common.

—Jean-Jacques Rousseau, Letter on Virtue, the Individual, and Society (1757)

[Recent popes] have repeatedly praised the Universal Declaration and called for its faithful implementation. Like Dr. Nolde these three popes have recognized the centrality of religious freedom. If the right to orient one's life toward the ultimate truth and goodness found in God were denied, all other rights would be hollow.

—Avery Cardinal Dulles, S.J., Letter to Lutheran Theological Seminary at Philadelphia (December 1998)

Contents

Appendixes

Foreword

AN ARRESTING ASPECT of the growing fascination with the role of religion in global politics is the effort to show that however much religion may contribute to violence, intolerance, and discrimination, that is not its only function. Alongside the expanding number of studies purporting to demonstrate the perverse influence of religion on civil war, terrorism, illiberal nationalism, and the like, there emerges a contrasting set of studies endeavoring to exhibit a more constructive, irenic, and tolerant side to the political and diplomatic contributions of religious individuals and groups. Such accounts are commonly described as examples of "religious peacebuilding."

The volume before us clearly falls into the second category. It is the story, compellingly told by John Nurser, of the disproportionate influence of a few committed, persevering, and highly effective religious individuals, along with the supporting groups to which they belonged, on efforts during the 1940s to include and elaborate human rights as part of the United Nations system that was then being created. This contribution was particularly important in formulating what we now call "religious" or "belief rights," namely, those human rights aimed at ensuring tolerance and nondiscrimination regarding the expression and exercise of religious and other fundamental beliefs. For all who celebrate, some fifty-five years later, the significance of that accomplishment for the cause of "freedom, justice, and peace in the world," as the Preamble to the Universal Declaration of Human Rights puts it, this account of a creative and successful act of public intervention by religious individuals and the groups they represented will stand as an inspiring addition to the growing literature on religious peacebuilding.

The acceptance of human rights as a central part of the structure of the United Nations could not be taken for granted at the time. In fact, there was considerable resistance to the whole idea. In the opinion of a congressional member of the U.S. delegation to the founding conference of the UN in San Francisco, human rights "means nothing." If other members of the delegation were more supportive, they were nevertheless initially pessimistic about their prospects, particularly with regard to creating a Human Rights Commission as the indispensable first step to codifying universal human rights standards.

Nurser shows that it was the indefatigable efforts of one of the book's heroes, O. Frederick Nolde, an American Lutheran seminary professor from Philadelphia, and an early proponent of the World Council of Churches, as well as of like-minded colleagues, such as Joseph Proskauer and Jacob Blaustein of the American Jewish Committee, and other mostly religiously motivated participants, that combined decisively to redeem the cause of human rights in a fateful late-afternoon meeting with the U.S. delegation on May 2, 1945. According to the report of one who was there, "it was that afternoon that the Commission on Human Rights was born."

This was a gigantic achievement. It was, after all, the Human Rights Commission, eventually headed by Eleanor Roosevelt, that went on to bring into being the Universal Declaration, and thereby to make way for and inspire a whole array of subsequent human rights documents on civil, political, economic, social, cultural, racial, gender, minority, environmental, and other issues, that today set international standards for what is expected of nation-states, both within and outside their borders. Although these standards are not uniformly enforced around the world, they are more and more taken to comprise the basic international requirements of political legitimacy. It is simply the case now that states found systematically and grossly to violate these standards are regarded as pariahs. Whatever the final accounting of the causes of this revolutionary state of affairs, the crucial contribution of a key group of religious actors appears, thanks to John Nurser's revealing narrative, to have been indispensable.

But that is not all. Nolde and his associates also made a signal contribution to the drafting of what became Article 18—the article on religious freedom in the Universal Declaration—and he influenced other aspects of the document as well. In the fall of 1947, as the Human Rights Commission was struggling to overcome sharp controversies among its members over the meaning and scope of religious liberty, Nolde weighed in actively. In representing the newly formed Churches' Commission on International Affairs, and in reflecting the thinking of key figures in the World Council of Churches (which was still in the process of formation), he presented proposals for wording, some of which were apparently adopted in the final version of the Universal Declaration.

This is a very significant part of Nurser's story, and his discussion of it sheds considerable light on critical developments regarding the general connections between religion and human rights that emerged during the formative period of the late 1940s. Much of the impulse for the protection of religious freedom had originally come from the Protestant missionary movement. Leaders thought of the new postwar international institutions and rights as a means of advancing Christianity. They were frustrated by local resistance in Latin America and elsewhere toward attempts to open opportunities for untrammeled Christian propagation and conversion. On this understanding, the campaign for human rights and religious liberty depended on a particular religious point of view. According to Nurser, this understanding was widely shared among Protestant leaders and church groups, which saw the campaign for human rights as part of a Christian-based crusade.

Such an outlook converged with similar attitudes in other quarters. Some members of the Human Rights Commission proposed that the Preamble to the Universal Declaration should include specific references to the deity and to the spiritual destiny of humankind. Such members, like the Protestant counterparts Nurser discusses, could not imagine that the Universal Declaration might be advanced without an explicit religious foundation.

Interestingly enough, Nolde and some of his associates gradually came to a different view—a view that eventually prevailed. As early as 1944, Nolde concluded that a strongly parochial bias would weaken the appeal of human rights for those who did not share his Protestant outlook, or, for that matter, any religious outlook at all. Having interacted with people of widely divergent convictions and points of view, Nolde arrived at the belief, as he said, that "freedom demands a broader base than can be offered by religion alone," and, moreover, that ideas about extending religious liberty needed to be placed in "a secular context." By "secular context," Nolde evidently meant a common, religiously impartial moral space shared by peoples of very different fundamental commitments and identities.

These were prophetic sentiments, and they conformed to what turned out to be the dominant view in the Human Rights Commission. After heated debate, the commission ruled out all confessional references in the Universal Declaration as being inconsistent with the nondiscriminatory character of human rights. Human beings are held to possess human rights, and to be accountable and obligated to live up to them simply because they are human, *not* because they are Muslim, or Christian, or Buddhist, or Jewish, or Hindu, or a member of any particular religious or philosophical tradition. The whole point of human rights is that they are taken to be binding and available, regardless of identity or worldview.

This does not mean, of course, that people are not free to harbor their own personal reasons—religious or otherwise—for believing in human rights. It only means that such views may not be taken as "official" or in any way binding on others who do not share them. Such is the meaning of religious liberty enshrined in the Universal Declaration. Such, too, is the implied conviction that all religious, as well as nonreligious, individuals and groups are equally free to propound and advocate their point of view, as long as they do not violate others' fundamental rights and freedoms as elaborated in the international documents. This understanding itself is not, to be sure, uncontested. However, it is hard to imagine a solution better suited to reconcile common standards with the world's religious and philosophical diversity.

The connection of Nolde and his associates to these developments reveals an important new wrinkle in the annals of religious peacebuilding. Here are individuals, themselves strongly motivated by religious commitment, supporting and contributing to a set of standards, deemed indispensable for establishing peace and justice around the world, that do not necessarily depend on any particular religious or other point of view. Rather, they depend on a shared moral basis taken to be universally common to all people, a basis Nolde described as "secular"—or perhaps "pluralistic," in present-day parlance. The ultimate, somewhat paradoxical, assumption is that religious people may best contribute to peace, and at the same time most successfully express their own deepest commitments, when they surrender proprietary claims in favor of sharing common ground with others, and thereby create maximum space for freedom of fundamental belief, religious or not.

Both because of the large gap it fills in the story of the founding of the United Nations and the events surrounding the adoption of human rights, and because of the wider message it conveys about religion and peacebuilding, *For All People and All Nations* is an immensely important contribution. We are all mightily in John Nurser's debt.

DAVID LITTLE
Harvard University

Preface

THE IDEA FOR THIS BOOK was born in 1987, after I had eventually published the book on Lord Acton that arose from my Ph.D. dissertation at Cambridge thirty years earlier. But in 1989, while continuing to be a residential canon at Lincoln Cathedral in the Church of England, I launched an organization called "Christianity and the Future of Europe," which became a body-in-association of the national ecumenical Christians Together in Britain and Ireland. It seemed urgent to look at the rapid development of transnational institutions in Europe. I had become convinced that Lord Acton's metanarrative of universal history had had wide influence in the English-speaking world in preparing early-twentieth-century students for human rights as the key to "progress." And I had been impressed while warden of Saint Mark's Institute of Theology in Canberra (1968–74) by the difficulty of getting the states-based churches to think in a wider framework. I hoped that my Australian experience could be helpful as the national churches of Europe (including my own) came—in most cases reluctantly—to relate to a rapidly burgeoning European Community whose established ideology was already human rights.

I had already begun work in the archives of the World Council of Churches and found that its first boxes from the Churches' Commission on International Affairs were full of material relating to preparations by Dr. Fred Nolde, its director, for discussion of drafts of the 1948 Universal Declaration of Human Rights. The work of my small group on Europe took more and more of my time from 1989 and made it impossible to return to this project until my retirement in 1997. But during this period, I had the good fortune in 1990 to be invited to a conference on Acton in Boston. Afterward, I took the opportunity to spend a few days at the Lutheran Theological Seminary at Philadelphia, which had been Nolde's base. The then-dean, Dr. Faith Burgess (whose doctoral work on Fr. John Courtney Murray, S.J., I had found valuable for Acton), was welcoming, She herself had begun to raise consciousness of Nolde's achievement in the community of the Lutheran Seminary from a low ebb. She introduced me to Mrs. Nancy Nolde, still living in the family home and full of life. By the time I was free to return to the project, I had decided to reshape it to explore the contribution of the World Council of Churches to the establishment of a "global order" in the United Nations Organization that would give a new authority to human rights. The decade from the founding of the World

Council of Churches in 1938 to the UN's proclamation of the Universal Declaration of Human Rights in 1948 marks a step change in world affairs.

Although, therefore, this is a distinct story with a dramatic unity, and (due to the circumstances of World War II) largely taking place on the East Coast of the United States, it is of unusually wide relevance. It should be of interest to church historians, political scientists, jurists, and students of international affairs.

Acknowledgments

M ANY PEOPLE have given help with this project; and, in many cases, they have expressed their opinion that addressing this topic was overdue. To a quite extraordinary degree the (still mostly) men whose names appear in this story lived to old age. If I had been free to seek them out in 1988, many who by 1998 had died would still have been alive. It has been moving to talk with those few who remain. My wife and I are grateful. For instance, in April 1998 we drove from Sewanee, Tennessee, to Black Mountain, North Carolina, to meet Paul Limbert of the YMCA, knowing he was then a centenarian, and not expecting much. He turned out to be mobile, articulate, and active in leading courses in the community on international affairs. But he died in December of that year.

I wish to record heartfelt gratitude to the following persons in particular, whose contributions have been foundational. Mrs. Nancy Nolde, Dr. Nolde's widow, and the three surviving children from his first marriage—Mr. Derf Nolde, Ms. Suzanne Nolde, and Mrs. Fredericka Berger—have given their encouragement, unstinting assistance, and warm friendship. Mr. Crispin Rope followed grants from the Mrs. L. D. Rope Third Charitable Settlement for my work on Acton with financial support for this project. Professor Kevin Boyle, the director of the Human Rights Centre (of which I am honored to be a fellow) at the University of Essex, offered me guidance and collegiality as I entered an unfamiliar field. Without my wife Elizabeth's steadfast resolution and editing skills, this vehicle would have run into the sand some time ago. I am grateful, too, to Mr. Richard Brown of Georgetown University Press for his care.

I was privileged to be given special access to the papers of two central players in these events. I wish to thank Mrs. Isobel Metzger, John Mackay's daughter, for her gracious permission to use her father's papers, and also the Reverend William Harris, a student and lifelong friend of Mackay's. I also wish to thank Dr. Habib Malik, the president of the Charles Malik Foundation, for his permission to use his father's papers in Washington, and for the personal kindness he showed in introducing me to them. Mrs. Dorothy Bennett kindly gave me permission to use certain letters of her father, Bishop Ernest Burgmann, and the Australian Student Christian Movement gave permission to use its collection at the Australian National Library.

I wish, too, to express appreciation of the hospitality offered by the following institutions during my research: as visiting scholar, School of Theology, University of the South, Sewanee, April 1998; as visiting speaker at the Nolde Celebration, Lutheran Theological Seminary at Philadelphia, December 1998; as visiting scholar, Human Rights Center, Columbia University, June 1999; as Woods Fellow, Virginia Theological Seminary, Alexandria, September–December 1999; and at Saint Mark's National Theological Centre, Canberra, November 2001.

It is only as the years have slipped by that it has grown on me how significant a story it is that I have been exploring, and how germane the arguments derived from it are to current policy decisions in "church, community, and state" (to cite the title of the Oxford conference in 1937). The following names comprise those whose recollections and reflections have helped construct the following pages. Each deserves a paragraph of explanation and thanks; but that is not possible. Many others have given precious help through friendship and hospitality.

In the United States: Mia Adjali, Michael Battle, Stephen Cary, Avery Cardinal Dulles, S.J., Roy Enquist, Denis Frado, Felice Gaer, Alan Geyer, Mary Ann Glendon, William Harris, Stan Hosie, Glen Johnson, John Kaufmann, Patrick Killough, Clarissa Kimber, Bill and Paula Knipe, Kosuke Koyama, Howard Kuehnle, William Lazareth, Gail Lerner, Paul Limbert, David Little, Bert Lockwood, John Lucal, S.J., Paul Martin, Loren Mead, Randolph Miller, James Phillips, Bob Prichard, Larry Rasmussen, Jack Reumann, Oscar Schachter, Howard Schomer, Ken Senft, Francis Shearer, Louise Shoemaker, Robert Smylie, Max Stackhouse, Betty Thompson, and Robert Traer.

In Europe and Australasia: Paul Abrecht, Andre Appel, Clyde Binfield, Alan and Irmgard Booth, Colin Brown, Keith Clements, Martin Conway, Frank Engel, Dwain Epps, Alan Falconer, James Fawcett, John Garrett, Peter Hempenstall, Peter Leuprecht, Dominique Micheli, Sally Morphet, Joan Lockwood O'Donovan, Philip Potter, Barbara Rees, Marjorie Reeves, Brian Stanley, George Wedell, and Patti Whaley.

Archives and Abbreviations

ARCHIVES

I have worked in the following archives, and I wish to express my thanks for permission to cite material from their collections. In every instance, their staffs were efficient and helpful in suggesting useful leads, particularly when—as was normally the case—I had very little time available. The major collections that I used are very substantial indeed, and it is likely I missed important boxes. I hope this work may stimulate others.

The principal archives that I used are held by the following:

National Library of Australia, Canberra, Manuscripts Division;
Library of Congress, Manuscript Division, Washington;
Lutheran Theological Seminary at Philadelphia, Lutheran Archives Center at Philadelphia;
National Council of Churches Records, Federal Council of Churches Records, Presbyterian Historical Society, Philadelphia;
Princeton Theological Seminary, Luce Library, Princeton, New Jersey;
Franklin D. Roosevelt Library, Hyde Park, New York;
World Council of Churches Library and Archives, Geneva;
Kautz Family YMCA Archives, University of Minnesota, Minneapolis.

I wish to record my particular gratitude to Carmel McInerny, John E. Haynes, Robyn Kulp and John Peterson, Margery Sly, William Harris, John Sears, Pierre Beffa (and earlier Ans van de Bent), and Andrea Hinding, who smoothed my path in the use of their archives.

I also consulted the following libraries and archives:

United States

Carnegie Endowment for International Peace, Washington;
Columbia University, Rare Books and Manuscript Library, James Shotwell Papers;

Harvard Divinity School, MSS and Archives Collection, Papers of Howard Schomer;
Mount Holyoke College, Papers relating to Mary Woolley;
Princeton University, Mudd Library (Oral History Project), Papers relating to J. Foster Dulles;
Stanford University, Hoover Institution, Easton Rothwell Collections and Harold H. Fisher Collections;
Swarthmore College, Peace Collection;
United Nations, Dag Hammarskjöld Library (Oral History);
Union Theological Seminary, Burke Library, Papers of A. L. Warnshuis;
University of Pennsylvania, Biddle Law Library, Papers relating to American Law Institute;
U.S. National Archives II;
Yale Divinity School, Papers relating to G. Coe, K. Latourette, and J. R. Mott.

Other Countries

Christchurch, New Zealand, Anglican Diocesan Archives;
Fondation Jean Monnet, Lausanne, Switzerland, Monnet Papers relating to J. Foster Dulles;
Lambeth Palace Library, London, Papers of George Bell;
School of Oriental and African Studies, University of London, C.B.M.S. Collection;
World's Association of YMCAs, Geneva.

ABBREVIATIONS

Abbreviations used in the text and/or notes:

ALI	American Law Institute
ASCM	Australian Student Christian Movement
CCIA	Commission of the Churches on International Affairs
CEIP	Carnegie Endowment for International Peace
CHR	Commission on Human Rights
CJDP	Commission to Study the Bases of a Just and Durable Peace
CMS	Church Missionary Society
CSOP	Commission to Study the Organization of the Peace
ECOSOC	United Nations Economic and Social Council
FCC	Federal Council of Churches of Christ in the United States of America
FMC	Foreign Missions Conference of North America
ILO	International Labor Organization
IMC	International Missionary Council
JCRL	Joint Committee on Religious Liberty
LTSP	Lutheran Theological Seminary at Philadelphia

NGO   nongovernmental organization
SCM   Student Christian Movement
UN   United Nations
UNCHR   United Nations Commission on Human Rights (see CHR)
UNCIO   United Nations Conference on International Order (1945)
UNESCO   United Nations Education, Social, and Cultural Organization
UNO   United Nations Organization
WCC   World Council of Churches
WSCF   World Student Christian Federation
YMCA   Young Men's Christian Association
YWCA   Young Women's Christian Association

Abbreviations for archives used:

Columbia   Columbia University, Butler Library, J. T. Shotwell Papers
Hoover   Stanford University, Hoover Institution, Easton Rothwell
                Collections
LC, Malik   Library of Congress, Washington, Malik Papers
LC, Oxnam   Library of Congress, Washington, Oxnam Papers
PHS (FCC)   National Council of Churches Records, Federal Council of
                Churches Records, Presbyterian Historical Society, Philadelphia
PTS, Mackay   Princeton Theological Seminary Libraries, Special Collections,
                John A. Mackay Papers
Roosevelt Library   Franklin D. Roosevelt Library, Hyde Park, New York
UN Library   United Nations, Dag Hammarskjöld Library (Oral History—
                Easton Rothwell)
WCC Archives   World Council of Churches Library and Archives, Geneva
YMCA   Kautz Family YMCA Archives, University of Minnesota,
                Minneapolis

Introduction: Revisiting a Myth

In the first decade of the twenty-first century, an alien from one of the fantasy societies in outer space who was making one of her periodic inspections of planet Earth might be persuaded that "human rights" is what holds our world together, our "religion." In Britain, for example, the whole structure of the state's legal system (and even its constitution) has been under detailed reconstruction since the passage of the Human Rights Act of 1998. This process is within a regional frame, to make that system compatible with the provisions of the European Convention of Human Rights of 1950 (whose scope is, however, limited to civil and political rights in contrast to the UN's Universal Declaration of 1948) and with subsequent judgments of the European courts, of both the Council of Europe and the European Union. Admittedly, our alien would not easily come to this conclusion if her one-stop spaceship had landed in a territory governed by one of the many militaristic, poor, corrupt, traditionally theocratic, or Marxist states currently in power.[1] And that in itself should cause us to ask questions.

The topic of this book is how, in the ten years after the founding of the World Council of Churches (WCC), a group of men and women, lay and ordained, from within the Protestant and Anglican Christian traditions of religion was able to play a significant role in including what became a "universal declaration" of human rights within the post–World War II attempt to construct a new order of international affairs in the United Nations. This group described its work in this area as one aspect of an "ecumenical movement" that was also a missionary movement. They saw themselves as midwives at work in a period of change that would be as far-reaching as Luther's Reformation. Indigenous Christian churches—known at the time as the "younger churches"—had taken their place in non-European cultures in most areas of the world. To be "ecumenical" was not only to seek a reunited Christian church but also to see its gospel as requiring conversation with every human culture and, after the 1960s, as having a common concern for our biosphere—integral with any doctrine of creation.

The vocation of these churches was to become the vanguard in the struggle for what their "guru," J. H. Oldham,[2] conceived as a new secular structure for the "good society" that would inherit the fruits of the Christian centuries. They were not alone in the 1930s crisis of international affairs in seeing an effective "global

1

order" as urgent. They saw such an order as, in practice, wholly dependent on the acceptance of a "global ethos." Some, like John Mott before World War I, thought that "the evangelization of the world" to Christian faith in one generation was the only way such an ethos could possibly emerge. It became clear in the 1920s that that was daydreaming. In the turmoil of World War II, the idea emerged (hesitantly and patchily) that such a global ethos could perfectly well be secular.[3] Why should not all religions be prepared to do their work under such a universal rule of life? Concern for religious liberty among ecumenically minded leaders of the American churches broadened in 1944 to fuel a politically sophisticated campaign for human rights as this global ethos. Any universal right of religious liberty had to be seen in symbiotic relation with a bundle of other rights, each requiring the other[4]—together a startlingly fresh interpretation of "Christendom."

Such action beyond what had been thought "appropriate" or "normal" behavior on the part of church bodies came to be surprisingly well accepted in the decade between 1938, when the WCC (provisionally "in-formation") was set up with a nuclear office in Geneva, and 1948, when—the war having ended with victory for the "United Nations"—the WCC was able at last to hold its first constitutive assembly. A few months later, the UN General Assembly promulgated its Universal Declaration of Human Rights.

One of the factors in this ecumenical engagement was that relevant opinion in the Protestant churches was confined by the fortunes of war almost entirely to English-speaking societies across the world and their particular habits of thought and experience. Another factor was the pervasive sense of a culture in crisis throughout the 1930s. In comparison with World War I, it was far easier to see the war against Hitler as involving the honor, and indeed the future, of Christianity itself. Explicitly neo-pagan and anti-Semitic, and with a drive to exploit "lesser" colored races in a worldwide empire, German Nazism had a clear religious dimension. As did Soviet Communism.

A difficulty in understanding this story, now more than fifty years past, is that secular acceptance of organized religious involvement in "politics" or, perhaps better, involvement in such a public constitutional issue, has changed. It remains a question how long-lasting a phenomenon it will be, but there has been pressure, at least since 1960,[5] to label inappropriate and unwelcome any religious contribution (or even language) outside the dimension of private lives and the particular communities of faith adherents. The "public square" should display its nakedness for all to see, and it should be inspected frequently to keep it that way. For instance, the report commissioned by the archbishop of Canterbury on "Faith in the City" and the Catholic bishops' message on "The Good Society" before the British election of 1997 had trouble in being received as properly "religious." And if something "religious" is now to be presented to public life, almost a condition of its being received is that it should come incorporating every flavor of religiosity represented among citizens, including witchcraft. It is a far cry from the beginnings of radio media at the British Broadcasting Corporation in the 1930s under Lord Reith. We have to take account of an established church of "evangelical secularism."

In such a climate, it has become clear that the part played by Protestant groups, but also Catholics and religious Jews, in establishing human rights in international affairs is deeply unwelcome to those who have written on the subject. The picture commonly conveyed is of an initiative by a group of public service jurists working (if doing so within a tradition of ideas from outside their professional training at all) wholly within the *laïque* framework of the French Revolution's Declaration of the Rights of Man. Even individuals well disposed to the Christian tradition assume the essential independence from religious roots of human rights. The London *Times* of June 16, 2003, carried a report on the Warburton Lecture at Lincoln's Inn by Lord Bingham, the senior English law lord. He declared that the "present preoccupation with human rights is not a product of the Bible or of religious belief." Some of those most involved in preparing and putting into effect the human rights revolution of the late 1940s are (often unintentionally) airbrushed out in properly Stalinist style.[6] This results, at a minimum, in tendentious history.

If this book is successful, it will have helped remodel the perceptions and interpretations that exert this control over public language and practice at both the nation-state and international levels. It is, after all, only possible for politicians to offer leadership from within the limits of the language current in their society. In particular, this book prepares the way for a more discriminating assessment of the chameleon web of religions from all six continents that now present themselves in any English-speaking "public square." "Religion" has become a catchall label of a word whose flavor and usage have changed greatly (at least in the West) in the generations since the Spanish civil war ended in 1939 with the victory of General Franco. He had announced his intention of ruling responsible "only to God and to history." Both entities were closely identified by him with the national hierarchy of the Roman Catholic Church, in whose context his interpretation of that intention has not worn well. But it is arguable whether Dietrich Bonhoeffer's contemporary advocacy from the opposite corner—as a German Protestant martyr to Nazism—of a future for "religionless Christianity" has worn better.

What is indisputable in the 1930s and 1940s is the centrality that understanding history's "universal" meaning had for those facing the outbreak of a second world war in their own lifetime. An extraordinary number of studies in history-as-progress were published in the two generations before 1939, and until 1960. The more popular ones—such as H. G. Wells's *Outline of World History* (before him Edward Bellamy's *Looking Backward*)—were read avidly and across the world in English-speaking populations by those whose newly literate grandfathers had fed on the history-as-pilgrimage of God's chosen people in both the Old and New Testaments of the Bible and in *Pilgrim's Progress*. Once the European "discoverers" (the critique of Columbus in 1992 would have been unthinkable fifty years earlier) had done their work, so that by 1890 few spaces on the map were left unwashed in European colors, universal history began to meet new challenges. The genre of such history could be widely rejected as invalid; non-Christians could write it; and it raised difficult questions for all religions. It was the generation in which the sociology of religion and the comparative study of "the idea of the holy" took root.

But the greatest linear macro influence of all in these years was provided by science. Its history was clearly one of incremental progress. Its presence signified the modern world. Nationality, gender, and race were irrelevant. What its relation was to various cultures as defined by their religious matrix was hotly debated. International Marxist socialism, once it had secured a power base in 1917 in the Soviet Union, was able to tap into the authority of science. In the 1930s, it was easily the dominant idea among "intellectuals" across the world. At the micro level, too, Freudian psychoanalysis led its patients to rational self-understanding of their own unreason via history. This as well was popularly received as "science," and therefore as valid across cultures—sufficiently so at least to put aside the provincial "illusions" of Judeo-Christian religion, the sexual guilt it induced, and its social pressures to conform.

To compete, therefore, in the 1930s political marketplace, Christian apologists needed a universalizable vision of the future. It would need to be grounded in a narrative of the past that was as prepared to denounce as an offense to Christ the sufferings induced by laissez-faire capitalism as much as fascist anti-Semitism. The Cambridge historian Lord Acton's lifework before World War I on the outline of a *History of Freedom*, and his *Cambridge Modern History* (which required its contributors to write from a "mid-Atlantic" point of view), had offered a shape to English-speaking history students before World War I that remained potent in urging them as World War II leaders to follow a global human rights norm for both civil and church structures. The need to build a Christian-inspired intellectual system that would not run away from taking account of the scientifically known world and of future time drove some disparate 1930s names, including Frank Buchman, A. N. Whitehead, Christopher Dawson, Jacques Maritain, and Pierre Teilhard de Chardin (the last three of whom, with Acton, were Catholics).

The historical self-consciousness of the English-speaking countries, however, where the principal action during World War II was to take place, was antagonistic to theory. Public opinion was not greatly upset by the corrosive currents from continental Europe. In Britain itself, Macaulay's national "Whig interpretation of history," the tradition of parliamentary government as progress, had been dominant for more than two centuries. Stemming from memories of Magna Carta and the providential defeat of the Spanish Armada, and the victory of the "people's" cause in the English Civil War—sealed by the Glorious Revolution of 1688—it had mutated into the democratic ideology of the American Constitution of 1787. In Britain it had been given a new twist by the rapid expansion of the empire under Queen Victoria to every continent, to take in territories (and above all India) where there were never plans for British settlement. A considerable proportion of those from outside Europe who were prominent in the early years of the United Nations had been educated at the best British or American universities, owning their familiarity with Shakespeare and the Common Law.

But the 1930s were not in any way consensus years. No one (not even the Soviets) was prepared to announce *The End of History*, as Francis Fukuyama did much later. Everything was still to play for. In all the interwar ideologies, "youth" was the arbiter. The fascist theme song was *Giovanezza*. The future and its abundant fountain of technology for all was constantly envisaged, but it had not (except in Hollywood) quite arrived. Even remote colonies had seen airplanes, but very few people had flown. There was little preparedness to entertain what have become "postmodern" relativities and pluralities. So an apocalypse of mighty opposites came easily to be the currency in which both World War II and after it the cold war were paid. In the 1930s it seemed to be an inescapably global zero-sum game of winner-takes-all in which it was clear that national fascisms and international communism were players. It was not clear on what basis there could be other players.

The governing idea of those who shared the leadership of the Life and Work conference on "Church, State, and Community" in Oxford in 1937 was that their Western politico-religious culture could not in conscience just lie down and die, particularly as so much would then be irrevocably lost for so many yet unborn. The church could, by the grace of God, become what it is, an international faith-inspired community more than capable of taking on tribal fascisms and the antipersonal monoliths of state socialism; but it would be a closely run thing. Perhaps those leaders would be grievously disappointed to see the minor part played by the Christian churches as the twenty-first century opens. But, though fascism is not dead, it was defeated in World War II. And after that war, the United Nations system, built across the divide between the United States and the Soviet Union, has seen itself (largely through the will of its less powerful members) come to be perceived as having its Commission of Human Rights (to quote John Foster Dulles) as its "soul." This victory of the personal went as much against the probabilities of 1944 as of 1937.

The first two chapters of this book have a scene-setting character. Chapter 1 draws out the significance of the renewed use of the word "Christendom" as an active element in the decision at the Oxford conference of the summer of 1937, confirmed in the following month by the Faith and Order conference in Edinburgh, to set up a World Council of Churches. There was from the beginning a sense that the ecumenical movement had a properly theological commitment to "global order." It is also important to indicate the wider geographical roots of the policy whose narrative working out is set—necessarily so in the context of the war years—largely within the United States.

Chapter 2 sets out the formative experiences in the life of O. Frederick Nolde before, at the age of forty-two years, he became involved in international affairs. This came about through a sequence of events only possible in wartime. He was not appointed out of a bureaucracy. In fact, he was given extraordinary freedom to develop his vocation as he thought best. It is therefore necessary, if we are to understand his goals, to allot more space to the background of his formation than might otherwise seem appropriate. Nolde came into the narrative of the interplay of institutions well after the curtains had closed on its first act, but he rapidly graduated to a leading role. The dénouement of this drama is inexplicable without him. His personal vision of the task and his particular talents were a necessary condition for the successful inclusion of a mandatory Commission on Human Rights in Article 68 of the UN Charter in 1945, the foundation of the Churches' Commission on International Affairs (CCIA) in 1946, and to the drafting and defense of, in particular, Article 18 of the Universal Declaration of Human Rights in 1948.

Chapters 3 through 10 follow the engagement of the ecumenical churches and missionary societies of the United States with what one of their leading figures, John Mackay, president of Princeton Seminary, called "the churches writing the peace." This narrative ends with the UN General Assembly's passage of the Universal Declaration in 1948, with abstentions but no opposing votes. It was only the end of a beginning for the CCIA. Chapter 11 offers a concluding survey of the significance of this story and the issues with which it was concerned.

There are a number of appendixes containing excerpts from selected documents. Those active in these developments worked in a generation whose clergy were well educated and wrote many words. It is sad that so many powerful and moving reports, speeches, papers, and controversies are only in a handful of libraries, and so are virtually inaccessible. When that is compared with the academic publications of collected papers from early-twentieth-century socialist and literary worthies, the Western world seems to have got its priorities wrong. For it is hard to imagine how Nolde and the church groups he represented could have had a more important impact on the world that has now entered its third millennium.

Finally, it is vital not to give the impression that to recount what happened in the metropolitan centers of Protestantism (in London, Edinburgh, Geneva, Toronto, and the Washington–Chicago–Boston triangle in the United States) had any substantial impact in even English-speaking congregations across the world before World War II. Even at the center, the ideas of the ecumenical leaders were widely regarded as experimental and elitist, and not as binding on the loyalty of ministers of their denominations. The provincial churches of whatever color received, selected, and adapted what came to their attention from the ecumenical leadership. But, as will appear at certain moments even in this quasi-diplomatic narrative, World War II marked a transition to a more multipolar Protestant church consciousness. Through the WCC, the periphery came to make original contributions. For example, few interwar societies were more provincial than the English-speaking states of the Antipodes. Yet in 1943, New Zealand was able to demonstrate a model Campaign for Christian Order to the Princeton Round Table. And Australia emerged as a principal player in the UN Commission on Human Rights starting in 1945. Not least, these so recently peripheral countries demonstrated that they worked with human rights language in their own individual and fresh keys.

NOTES

1. See Kevin Boyle and Juliet Sheen, *Freedom of Religion and Belief: A World Report* (New York: Routledge, 1997).

2. Joseph H. Oldham (1874–1969), was born in Bombay and worked in India with the YMCA after graduating from Oxford. He was executive secretary of the World Missionary Conference at Edinburgh in 1910, secretary of its continuation committee, and was first secre-

tary of the International Missionary Council from 1921. He edited *International Review of Missions* from 1912. In 1934 he was chair of the research committee of the Universal Christian Council on Life and Work, organizing its conference on "Church, Community and State" at Oxford 1937. He had a special interest in Kenya and published *Christianity and the Race Problem* in 1924. He was a significant figure in the preparations for the WCC's First Assembly in Amsterdam in 1948, proposing its key idea of "responsible society."

3. Patti Whaley (recently of Amnesty International) has suggested that "it is instructive to think that it might be more possible to bring about the essence of Christianity by giving up the name and guise of Christianity—that is, by trying to institutionalize the values without cloaking them in specifically Christian identity" (personal communication).

4. This was Nolde's rationale for campaigning for the full package of human rights as necessary for religious liberty.

5. Callum Brown, *The Death of Christian Britain* (London: Routledge, 2001).

6. Even Sir Brian Urquhart, a former undersecretary general of the United Nations and perhaps the most distinguished current commentator on UN affairs, has described the wartime campaign to persuade the American electorate of the necessity for a postwar international organization as purely political, without any reference to the churches' involvement. *New York Review of Books*, January 15, 2004, 8.

$\mathcal{P}$ART I

CHAPTER 1

◆

The Idea: To Universalize "Christendom"

THE REPRESENTATIVES of the ecumenical-movement churches who played a role in ensuring a mandatory place for a Human Rights Commission—and by extension its Universal Declaration of Human Rights (1948)—in the UN Charter (1945) were influenced by a self-conscious tradition of "Christendom" (however much that tradition is now deemed to be unacceptable). However, what was understood by that word bore little resemblance to what followed in fourth-century Europe from the Roman emperor Constantine's conversion to Christianity, or the Christian Church's conversion to Constantine.

What was self-evident in 1945 was that any acceptable system of international affairs, following two world wars in forty years, had to be planned with every human community in mind and could no longer be confined to Western Europe and North America. It was also self-evident that any such "common house" (to use President Mikhail Gorbachev's phrase about the rapidly developing European institutions of the late 1980s) would require, as he said to the Council of Europe in 1989, a framework of shared "public values."

Human rights began to emerge in the 1940s as a candidate for such secularly acceptable "public values." Yet it was surprising that human rights became both (in John Foster Dulles's comment at the time) the "soul" of the UN Charter and again in 1948 the subject, with no dissenting voices, of a reverberating declaration.[1] In each case what seemed so unlikely beforehand was carried forward to conclusion with unforeseen personal enthusiasm taking over (among diplomats of all people!). It appears that nearly all the cultures of the world were able to find significant elements in their pasts to connect to this proposed future.[2]

A practical step along the same human rights lines was taken in 1949 with the establishment of the Council of Europe. The council was set up by the states of Western Europe in which, before Vasco da Gama and Columbus, the spiritual authority of the pope had been acknowledged. This was the old "Christendom," a territory. These nations had shared a common language of literacy and scholarship, a common set of meanings and symbols in the liturgy, common networks of religious orders, a common framework of canon law, and a common "other" in Islam. Since its launch, the council has had its Convention on Human Rights. Its offer of judicial remedy via its Commission and Court at Strasbourg to any citizen appealing against his or her own state on human rights grounds is unprecedented in the history of the modern state.[3]

Christians were active in this remarkable exercise. Many of those prominent in establishing the post–World War II European institutions were active lay Catholics. What is not so well known, and has only recently been shown us by Dr. Zeilstra,[4] is how strongly those Protestant leaders associated with the forming of the World Council of Churches (WCC) in 1938 felt that post–World War II Europe would have to develop such institutions. Its peoples could only find a grounding for such transnational institutions in their common tradition of civilization. Could the by then long-discarded political inheritance of Christendom be used in a helpful way? In the late 1930s American church leaders, too, were impatient—only twenty years after Versailles—that the sovereign nation-states of Europe were again about to unload their endemic internecine wars on the whole of humanity.

A parallel task was for the Christian churches to discover an ecumenical language in which to recognize one another as, by now, a worldwide "family"—a nonterritorial, nonracial, nonpoliticial Christendom. The International Missionary Council's conference in Tambaram in 1938 is a turning point in the twentieth-century history of Protestant Christianity, partly because representatives of the Asian and African "younger churches" (as they were then called) did not hesitate to condemn European missionaries for the damage they had done to, for example, Indian Christian apologetics by their unrepentantly nationalist sectarianism.

Thus, there was a potential linkage in the thinking of reflective Christians in the 1930s between one kind of Christendom and another, looking to future transnational institutions that might (in the concluding words of the New Testament) be "for the healing of the nations." It was impossible in the 1930s to confine any ecumenical policy in international affairs to Europe. The Christian churches had spread into the six continents. Science-based "modern civilization" had developed recognizable settlements and subcultures in every corner of the world. These could, it was thought, come in practice to accommodate individuals from any race or faith tradition, and in principle eventually all the "families of man."[5] The moth-eaten garment of territorial Christendom was in the wardrobe. Why not take it out, dust it, and try it on for size? Three major alterations were needed. First, it had to be universalized. Second, it had to have exclusively lay officers. Third, being by definition a public and legal system, it had to refuse to distinguish between religious faiths. Would it still be a Christian garment? Some impressive leadership figures replied Yes.

This particular subgroup of Protestant Christians worked from a radical reformulation of "Christendom." Any limiting association of a twentieth-century living Christian faith with Charlemagne's continental Europe would have seemed laughable to them.[6] The group's leading members came from the Reformed tradition, which has been transnational, missionary, and lay oriented from its beginning.[7] It was no accident that the birth of public ecumenism took place in Edinburgh, the city of John Knox, at the great international missionary conference of 1910. The conference proceedings were much influenced by a Scots layman with YMCA experience, Dr. Joseph Oldham, who was to become the principal architect of the WCC. He came to prominence when Western Christian leaders had become convinced that they were living in a providential moment.[8] With the application of focused energy and prayer, the ancient hopes of mass conversions into the Christian faith could become expectations. At evening prayers during that conference, even the archbishop of Canterbury had spoken rashly of the possibility that they might be living on the eve of the Kingdom of God's coming on earth.[9] The other world faiths were said to have lost heart. Oldham is associated in ecumenical history with John Mott,[10] an American businessman with his base in student missionary work and the YMCA. His pan-Protestant charismatic advocacy set a tone of high anticipation. His call for "the evangelization of the world in this generation" had been heard in public meetings across the world.

Planning for a transition to such world horizons was not confined to church leaders. The two decades before World War I saw many initiatives designed to further structures of international law and welfare planning and scientific cooperation, even interfaith dialogue. The "father of missiology," Gustav Warneck,[11] had been influential in proposing that civilizing all societies had to go forward as an enterprise of "law"[12] alongside preaching the "gospel" of Christ to them as individual evangelism. These were necessary elements for any reformulation of "Christendom" thinking. The founding fathers of the WCC came to maturity in this period.

No one found it easy to absorb what meaning (or destruction of meaning) the experience of World War I might offer. Things could hardly go on as before (though there is plenty of foundational Christian material to indicate that the best and worst times come in accelerating proximity). Leading Christian figures of the interwar period, such as Paul Tillich and Pierre Teilhard de Chardin, found it possible to use their service in the trenches to deepen their faith. World War I hardened the determination of many church leaders to carry on with what already, before the war, they had seen as necessary tasks. Indeed, the abyss of greed, hatred, and ruthlessness into which the "Christian nations" of Europe stumbled in 1914 provoked an urgent energy. As a member of the U.S. delegation at Versailles, John Foster Dulles had observed the impotence of Christians acting as individuals, even in peacemaking. He and others put their minds to how national churches (and then in the late 1920s, churches acting together across countries) could influence the construction of an international order that had inherent technical quality. If this order were constructed to be subject to periodic revision to take account of changes, and could be recognized on all sides as just, then it might be durable enough to engender an age of peace. Sustained intelligent support from Christian communities could, they believed, be mobilized for what had become a necessary secular task.

The 1910 missionary conference had been an occasion of cusping excitement, with its experience of bonding across boundaries of denomination and nationality. By the 1930s, however, the urgency was fear. Rival faiths had recharged their batteries, and few missionaries could see the hopes they expressed at home "on furlough" as realistic for the area they themselves knew. The most creative missionaries began to dissociate themselves from their mission societies' ways of working. After the war, for instance, a small body in England called the Survey Application Trust (including the World Dominion Press) was endowed with quite substantial funds for research, and to gather and analyze statistics. Mission should, it was now thought, become less enthusiastically amateur.[13] Expatriate laypeople should be recruited for short-term secular professional posts overseas to work alongside indigenous church leaders. Saint Paul seemed to have been altogether more successful with "missionary methods" different from nineteenth-century tradition.[14]

The ubiquitous John R. Mott was chairman and Galen Fisher[15] of the YMCA was secretary in a comparable initiative in New York, the Institute of Social and Religious Research, whose aim was "to combine the scientific method with the religious motive." This institute was associated with the ecumenical Missionary Research Library of the Foreign Missions Conference of North America (FMC), and it was well enough financed to employ twelve staff members. It produced a *World Missionary Atlas*[16] that offered much statistical information, and whose editorial matter had got to the point of apologizing for its incompleteness in not being able to include Catholic material. Mott's preface highlights two consequences of World War I: that it was still disrupting the personal relationships on which sending societies depended and that it had drastically globalized the world through its economic consequences. A substantial section of the *Atlas* is devoted to information about constituent mission societies, including their declared objects. There are revealing turns of phrase. The Board of National Mission of the Presbyterian Church of the United States, for instance, worked "to make America Christian for the redemption of mankind and the friendly service of the world," while the World Student Christian Federation (WSCF) was "to influence students to devote themselves to the extension of the Kingdom of God [the only society using that phrase] in their own nation and throughout the world."

In the 1930s there was recognition that the territory of the old Christendom was itself now a mission field. During the Great Depression, family churchgoing was rapidly losing priority for those who had jobs and had bought a car. For those who had no jobs, and for many intellectuals, actively atheist Soviet Russia was the beacon of hope and the Spanish republican army the only good cause. The people of Germany (and most of their pastors) were newly happy in reconstituting a "folk" past that had scant regard for the Christian centuries. The Latin countries of Europe (with their colonies) had largely accepted "*duce*" figures—Mussolini, Franco, Salazar. These men presided over corporatist one-party regimes with which the Vatican established single-church concordats that were anathema to the Protestant ecumenical leaders. In the East, the Japanese, having seen their proposed antiracist wording of the Versailles treaty rejected, had already begun an aggressive nationalist war in which Geneva conventions were an alien irrelevance. The crisis for Western, politically liberal Christians, whose leaders could remember Edinburgh 1910 vividly, was this time not one of opportunity but of catastrophe.

Protestant academics and church leaders discovered each other as brothers in the ecumenical conferences of the 1920s (often after membership of the YMCA or the WSCF). They went on in the 1930s to commit themselves (and nominally their churches) to organizing a World Council of Churches following two interlocking, but separate, understandings of the word "ecumenical." The Faith and Order strand was concerned to bring ecclesiastical bodies together in theological dialogue; and its hope was to build on contemporary biblical scholarship a platform on which churches could be reconciled in unity, and an altogether more compelling gospel made available for world mission. The Life and Work strand started from the perception that the working life of the "modern" world needed the active personal presence of Christians (only in exceptional cases ordained), and that missionary discipleship required of Christian communities a well-thought-through commitment in service of "the other" anywhere in the world.[17]

The strong points of the ecumenical movement were its willingness to engage with current publicly recognized problems from a theological perspective, its intellectual vigor, its international and interdenominational network of well-placed contacts in the professions (to a growing extent lay, female, and people of color as well as ordained, male, and Caucasian people), and its habit of welcoming a variety of ideas into any discussion. This subculture was exemplified in a recognizable way across the university campuses of the world in branches of the Student Christian Movement (SCM), including its senior and schoolteacher affiliates.[18] On his return from a visit to Australia in 1910, William Temple remarked on the effect these branches were having on intentionally secularist state universities. Among the marvels he had seen there, he said, "the greatest marvel of all is the Australian SCM." In the vast distances of that continent, its annual national conference was a rare opportunity to enjoy being with like-minded contemporaries—whatever kind of Protestant they might be. There were games and Scottish dancing; and marriages were made.

The WSCF subculture had six marks. First was the conviction that the litmus test of a Christian life is an expression of the duty to serve others in love. Second, the modeling of such adult lives was via regular group meetings to read "study guides" (normally on a book of the Bible) and discuss them at length. Third, branches made no differentiation on grounds of denomination, sex, or orientation to ordination. Fourth, student members were wholly responsible for the affairs of the branch. Fifth, through the WSCF's publications, local SCM branches tended to be more aware than their contemporaries of the world church's theologians, and were prepared to cross racial boundaries.[19] And sixth, groups defined themselves as normal young people, open to outsiders and ready to be active with them in bettering society; and, above all, they were not "pious."

But even in the ecumenical movement's most vibrant years, it was a minority concern within the institutions of its member churches, and a peripheral topic within their seminary education. Perhaps it was an impossible dream to build a strong, adequately financed, and coherent "world" organization on the fissile inheritance of the Reformation. Especially was this so when even leading local church members had only fitful news of the project. Such facts make the achievements of the founding fathers of the World Council the more remarkable; and in no area more so than in international affairs.

It has been suggested that the WCC's inner circle, faced in the late 1930s with the odds stacked against the survival of what they saw as advanced civilization and Christianity, took a gamble. They would concentrate what resources they had on careful preparations for a postwar world, assuming that fascisms in Europe and Asia would be defeated. Virtually half the staff of the wartime WCC office in Geneva constituted its Study Department[20] and—together with their correspondent colleagues across the world—they were assigned the topic of a postwar global "order." This included planning church action in the inevitable humanitarian tasks of relief work and relocation of refugees.

In particular, their collaborators from the mission societies hoped that the WCC's work might gather support from many cultures for a postwar "global ethos." Without a quite new foundation in such an ethos, which could sustain human rights and religious liberty, the WCC leaders saw little prospect of any global order.

Within ten years of its foundation, the World Council was rewarded by seeing its gamble come off beyond all expectation. Both in San Francisco at the Conference on International Order and in the drafting of the Universal Declaration of Human Rights, its officers were able to play an influential nongovernmental role in nudging those policies in the desired directions. Those achievements still hold two generations later. It is widely accepted that their abrogation is now unthinkable—perhaps overconfidently so.

THE NEW CHRISTENDOM LANGUAGES

Dr. Joseph Oldham is a principal witness for the claim that a revisionist concept of "Christendom," built on the concept of "the responsible society," was the driving vision for the ecumenical movement in the generation before 1960. He is the only person given a memorial in the Geneva headquarters of the WCC. Immediately after the meeting in Utrecht in 1938 at which a "World Council of Churches–in–formation" was formally set up, he began to draft a short book that was only published in 1940 after the outbreak of war. He titled it *The Resurrection of Christendom*.

His choice of title for this book should be set against the background of Oldham's work as secretary of the Continuation Committee of the 1910 conference and, subsequently, founding secretary of the International Missionary Council in 1921. His biographer, Keith Clements,[21] sees the ideas with which Oldham fired the International Conference on Life and Work at Oxford 1937 as having their origin in his *The World and the Gospel* (1916), a reflection on world Christian mission in the light of World War I. Clements writes: "Crucial for him was the realization, due to the war, that the 'Christian nation' idea of the West was bankrupt, and that Western Christianity itself—that which was sending missionaries to the 'mission fields' in their thousands—had all but lost its credibility and its moral authority for engaging in such an enterprise. The missionary task of evangelizing the whole world remained. . . . But what it *means* to evangelize is to be learned in the daily secular life of Western society, in the call to Christianize social structures and economic life as much as to call individuals to personal faith."[22]

It is not obvious what Oldham meant by such "Christianizing" (which, it is important to point out, was not proposed as an alternative to a "call to personal faith" but in parallel with it). A similar two-pronged strategy characterizes the radical *Laymen's Report* of 1932[23] on overseas mission, which was fiercely criticized by the denominational mission societies.[24] The report was uncomplimentary on what its authors found on their visits into the "mission fields," as to both policy and implementation. Rather, they proposed as their preferred policy orientation for mission the establishment of social structures that expressed the Christian doctrine of humanity. These, in the various regions of the world, would be designed for a democratic lifestyle and openness to Christian activity, rather like the local YMCAs and YWCAs on every continent. These structures could be conceived as mildly socialist engineering for personal life pilgrimages, with much in common with John Dewey's social philosophy in the United States and the Workers' Educational Association in Britain. Garden cities were good examples; experiments in which people, too, might be planted out in beds to flower.[25]

Oldham himself embarked on "Christianizing" in the 1920s with his work on racial discrimination in colonial Kenya.[26] His (very English-establishment) method was to compile and master accurate information, consult "the best minds" (whether Christian or not), and then take those who were to make the decisions to lunch at the Athenaeum Club.[27] As preparation for the thematic sections of the 1937 Oxford conference, he presided over the careful assembling of expert papers from a number of countries, with participants from other countries criticizing the material. This process produced volumes worth publishing in their own right.[28] Perhaps for the first time at an ecumenical conference, non-English-speaking delegates both felt confident they had grasped the thought processes behind what was going to be said and then put faces to familiar names. As one consequence, this conference changed the direction of John Foster Dulles's life. Having been invited to be a plenary speaker on international affairs, he was struck by the personal trust, the informed intelligence, and the buoyancy of this international church gathering. It was a contrast to the depressed and cynical League of Nations meeting in Paris from which he had come,[29] and it made him decide to put his weight behind the World Council of Churches that this conference resolved to establish.

The seventy pages of *The Resurrection of Christendom* are a manifesto more than a treatise. After the WCC opened its Geneva office in 1938, Oldham engineered the setting up in Britain of a Council on the Christian Faith and the Common Life. Oldham's *Resurrection* is directed at this council. He begins with the gravity of the situation: "It is a fact of vast historical significance that in what was once known as Christendom the Christian tradition should be deliberately and publicly repudiated," and "to commit crimes under the pressure of seeming necessity is bad, but to enunciate the doctrine that in the interest of a class or nation all considerations of truth and justice may be ignored is the spiritual death of man." "An effort on a wholly new scale" is urgent, and "those who believe that the welfare of mankind is bound up with the Christian understanding of life must affirm that faith in the public sphere and seek to embody its values in public policy."[30]

If such effort is called for on the national scene, how much more so internationally, where war was again the scene of unchecked evil and suffering? The book ends with chapters on "the task" and "the churches and the new Christendom." Oldham declares it to be "an absolutely vital matter for Christians." He restates his concern that the churches should begin to see effectiveness as a criterion of their action: "All talk about a better society is idle daydreaming till it is translated into public policy. To suppose that we can meet the needs of other men today by individual action, except within a very restricted field, is to be blind to the nature of modern society." He acknowledges his debt to the process thinking of A. N. Whitehead[31] and to his friend T. S. Eliot's *The Idea of a Christian Society* (1939). The need of the moment was for a "social philosophy," which the church (largely through its laity) would need to midwife "in collaboration with those who do not call themselves Christians."

The nub of Oldham's argument—his redefinition of the word "Christendom"—is this: "The Church should make appropriate provision for getting certain things done, which it cannot itself undertake, but which are necessary for its own life and health."[32] This was exactly the point made by Lord Acton when he promoted the advantages for religion of a framework of constitutional political liberty (in his case for the internal health of the Roman Catholic Church).[33] However, most people in the years of the Great Depression were more likely to begin from the need to secure a healthy society than a healthy church. There was much contemporary secular debate, for example, Walter Lippmann's *The Good Society* (1936). But such a society, it was thought, did indeed require what faith traditionally offered—a "community" that could call on God and was undergirded by a narrative and a folk ethos.

There was considerable use of the word "Christendom" in England (not Scotland) in the 1930s. In most cases, it was among individuals from among educated élites, who spoke at conferences and who attended "summer schools." An influence on left and right in common (though not on Oldham) was their interest in medieval society as precapitalist and preindividualist. R. H. Tawney[34] was an important figure, as were T. S. Eliot[35] and Christopher Dawson.[36] At some remove, these ideas were at the root of the post–World War II British welfare state, set out as a war-aim in Sir William Beveridge's *Report* (1942). The annual Anglo-Catholic Summer Schools in Sociology at Oxford attracted an academic and ecclesiastical group that was close to the ecumenically active leaders of the Church of England. It published distinguished authors in its quarterly, which it chose to title *Christendom*. Also, as late as 1946, the telegraphic address of the World Evangelical Alliance was "Christendom. Westcent. London."

These were the years of somewhat simplistic "moral re-armament"—the "Oxford Group"[37]—which had a similar socially élite constituency and shared Oldham's anxieties (but not his dismissal of individualism). In any estimate of twentieth-century Christendom-thinking in England, it is impossible to overestimate the background influence of the middle-class networks based on "public school" educa-tion—fee-paying, games-playing, residential, with a traditional Christian denomi-nation its principal stakeholder. These schools advertised their primary aim as to educate through experience of a "Christian community" (though recognizing that not all their pupils were Christians), with an explicit self-location in a Whig[38] narra-tive of world history that encouraged vocations to serve the world outside Britain.

It is not surprising—as similarly for the Americans—that the British Christian leaders' vision of a post–World War II global order should have been so governed by national experience and mindsets. It is difficult now to realize how big the British Empire was at the outbreak of the war. *The World Missionary Atlas* (1925) gave its area as a quarter of the world's land mass and its infinitely varied population rather more (though over half of these people were in India). A British projection of the future would be different from the American; the Crown held together wildly differ-ent societies, often autonomous or administered by indirect rule. It was multicul-tural, linked largely by language, trade, Common Law tradition, defense, and education.

The United States, however, presented the heart of its national narrative as its break with all that the old European "Christendom" signified. There was to be no church-crowned king; no censorship; no church courts; open access to education; open doors to immigrants; citizen access to certain "human rights"; and above all—recognized at the time as its truly revolutionary character—a veto on any identifi-cation of a particular religious organization with the public sphere. But it is easy to let slip from memory that the state of Massachusetts (with Magna Carta still its coat of arms) was founded in the 1630s precisely for the world to see a "City set on a Hill," as Governor John Winthrop had envisioned. The intention was to show what a real—a Reformed—Christendom would look like, in contrast to the unedifying compromises and hesitations of Old England. Europe was analyzed as having become incapable of advertising a consciously Christian society, wedded to biblical and doctrinal truth, under an effective local church discipline, and ruled by godly leaders. Such a vision had inspired the eleventh-century Pope Gregory VII, the real patron saint of European Christendom, as he inaugurated his own reformation of European culture in the name of the objective *justitia* or "right order" that lies behind Magna Carta. The fathers of the later American Constitution produced a mutation of this, not its denial.[39]

So it is not as curious as at first sight it seems that the quarterly journal founded in 1935 by the American members of "Life and Work," the international "practical theology" group founded by Archbishop Nathan Söderblom[40] at the 1925 Stockholm conference, should have been named *Christendom*. William Temple[41] chose to write articles on the theme of "Christendom" for its first two numbers. It was a journal that helped American Protestant academics and church leaders prepare for the Oxford and Edinburgh conferences in 1937. With the setting up of the WCC in 1938 (which brought Life and Work together with Faith and Order), it continued as its principal American forum. In 1949, when the WCC decided to set up its own *Ecu-menical Review* with the general secretary in Geneva as editor, this was grafted on to the rootstock of the American *Christendom*. By then, in neoorthodox Protestant Europe, the former title could not serve.

It was the Americans within the ecumenical movement who took the lead in exerting a Christian influence on the post–World War II settlement in international affairs. These churches were little influenced by Karl Barth until the late 1940s. The principal Protestant theologian in the life of the YMCA especially, but also in branches of the World Student Christian Federation, was Emil Brunner (1889–1966), who, while no liberal, did demand space for natural theology and its connecting points with revelation.

Although it was an extraordinary blip for an archbishop of Canterbury to have spoken in 1910 of the "dawning of the kingdom of God," it was for generations the small change of American public rhetoric to hold together in discourse the far-off territory of North America, the providential vocation of its Protestant founding churches, its federal constitution, and the recognizable inauguration there of "kingdom of God" elements that in their replication carried the hope of the world's nations. So the "social gospel" of Walter Rauschenbusch (1861–1918) has to be understood in the context of this American variant of "Christendom"; it was not a strange or alien religious movement. And it was enormously influential on the older leaders of American Life and Work ecumenism such as William Adams Brown.

A powerful tradition has seen the field of religion as the American Constitution's primary benefit both to citizens in general and to lay Christians. That has been almost as true for Catholics and Jews as for Protestants. Possibly it will become so for Muslims and others. John Mackay (1889–1983), a platform speaker at the 1937 Oxford conference, constantly used that conference's mantra, "Let the church be the church." In America, a church was free—it was asserted—to take responsibility for its own mission, whether that was deemed to be a success or a failure. Would that were so, it was said, elsewhere in the world.

If rights designated as "human" (though unavailable to black slaves) were protected by the U.S. government, why could such rights not be protected in the case of humans living under other governments? For the missionary societies, this question had a day-to-day urgency. If a missionary overseas is not free to worship and to teach, and those who wish for baptism are forbidden to receive it under pain of loss of property or even of life, to whom could there be an appeal? For any change, would there have to be a revolution or an exercise of external imperial power? What gives freedom its sacred quality in Protestant mission is the space it gives for men and women to respond in personal relationship to the grace of God in the Holy Spirit. How can a missionary not see this as trumping other considerations? This personal freedom is inseparable from community. That community is a manifestation of the church. So, the argument ran, Christians live an ethos that asserts a clear obligation to campaign for, help establish, and defend an order that would provide a civil shield everywhere for both personal and community religious liberty.

Such an order has no place for arbitrary exclusions and derogations. Processes for appeal and enforcement are logically part of it. It was an easy step for mission societies to take to see a form of international court with police powers, and agreed-on definitions (as of religious freedom in Article 18 of the Universal Declaration of Human Rights) as clearly required if any "global order" were to be achieved. This is a variant of Christendom in an unexpected guise, though wholly without any privileged legal status for Christians or official role for church (or any other religious) leaders.

The territorial flavor of the word "Christendom" was still how even "advanced" ecumenical leaders read it with part of their minds. The younger theologians in Europe were uneasy on Barthian grounds. A correspondence in January 1940 between Visser 't Hooft as general secretary of the WCC in Geneva and Van Dusen in New York, chair of the Study Department, illustrates this.[42] Van Dusen criticizes a paper of Visser 't Hooft's, asking: "How can usage of Christendom referring to old Europe be meaningful to Chinese Christians in a World Council of Churches?" and it was absurd to try to construct a Christian contribution to global order on the presumption of worldwide mass conversions. In his reply, Visser 't Hooft agrees: "It is impossible to speak of the present situation as the breakdown of Christendom," and he argues for showing "the kernel of truth in the concept of Christendom, but, on the other hand, to show its unreality if it is conceived as a solid basis on which we can build."

It does, however, remain doubtful whether those American churches that fought such a competent fight to include human rights in the UN Charter, and then to secure what they required in the Universal Declaration of Human Rights, understood that other religions and other Christian cultures might not see the language of the American solution as straightforwardly capable of globalization. Was that language in fact explicable outside Christian tradition? Was it for some churches and on other continents not even a Christianly preferable ordering of public life? Was it appropriate to rest a global ethos on the claims of one religious tradition to a deposit of revealed truth? But to think along such lines was to be forced to give up the long-nourished mission hopes of ecumenically minded Protestants. Even into the early 1950s, many were quite unwilling to accept this. Any move to globalize a public ethos would more and more hazard involving representatives of the traditions of "the other" in its monitoring, teaching, and living development.

Certainly the Catholic Church, the largest church, would have to be involved. No other institution had taken so seriously the new possibility of a worldwide frame for administration in the second half of the nineteenth century. Propaganda Fide was in action generations before the International Missionary Council, with an enviable system of communication, standardization of liturgy, and discipline. The Catholic Church had become a genuinely intercontinental reality.

This was reinforced by the revival of its natural law tradition, given authority by the approval of neo-Thomism in Pius XI's *Studium Ducem* (1923). Important areas of properly theological truths are accessible to human reason as such, from whatever culture. It is hard to exaggerate the revolutionary influence of such reasoning by Jacques Maritain[43] on the Catholic understanding of the word "Christendom" and its estimation of human rights. His *True Humanism* (1937) presented a fresh "personalist" understanding of Catholicism that was read with unusual interest outside church circles and admired as an attractive alternative to "failed secularisms," as he called contemporary materialist and neonationalist ideologies.

Maritain was stranded in New York by Hitler's occupation of France in 1940. His short book, *Droits de l'Homme*, published in 1942 (translated as *Human Rights and Natural Law*, 1943) was a powerful manifesto in the cause of continuing principled resistance to fascism. It was particularly widely read in both North and South America, and influential on wartime State Department thinking. It was a Catholic philosopher's description of the values that should be accommodated by structures of public order. These structures, for all the peoples of the world to inherit over time, could find a place in the salvific metanarrative.[44] To strive to bring such an order into full attainment, and maintain it for the church's own well-being and that of human "blossoming" everywhere, is, he said, to describe "Christendom." A 1940 Harvard doctoral dissertation on "the cultural and political philosophy of Jacques Maritain" was titled "The Ideal of a New Christendom." Whereas the 1940s Protestants derived much of their energy in asserting human rights from promoting freedom of religious choice, Maritain's apologetic (perhaps less dynamic) was based on reason and conscience, from a sense of the dignity of any human being "created in God's image." An advantage of this was its easier recognition across the boundaries of world faiths. And its resonance among the politicians of Latin America was hugely important both in 1945 at the San Francisco conference and in the drafting of the Universal Declaration.[45] Paul VI was Maritain's disciple for thirty years before he became pope in 1963 and took *renovatio* as his theme for the remaining months of Vatican II. From being a concept anathematized by Pius IX a century earlier, human rights became a recurring theological concept in Vatican II documents. Since the 1970s, it has been the leitmotif of John Paul II's papacy, and far more salient in Rome than in contemporary Protestantism.

To round off, the third leg of the stool of Christian tradition, the Orthodox churches, has never been disposed to deny a proper authority in church matters to the heirs of Constantine, whether emperors, czars, or more recently presidents. Enthusiasm for human rights has certainly been less clear-cut than in Western cultures. But there is no questioning the contribution made to the 1937 Oxford conference by the few, but able, Orthodox representatives to the call made there for a new and more Christian world order.[46]

SAN FRANCISCO, 1945 AND AFTER

What the human rights elements in the final UN Charter signified was ground for a fundamental shift in understanding international relations, however slowly and uncertainly that has been reflected in subsequent events. It was a shift to the secular "Christendom" ideas of Oldham and Maritain. These ideas had become absorbed by some leading Protestant circles during the war years.[47]

The Commission to Study the Bases of a Just and Durable Peace in the United States stressed the necessity that any global-order institution replacing the League of Nations should have a "curative and creative" as much as a "security" function. The Sponsoring Powers at Dumbarton Oaks in 1944 had expected a postwar continuation of the UN wartime alliance that would have the permanent members of the Security Council as its key innovation over against the old league. In the pre–cold war months of innocence in 1945, this council was largely envisaged as a compact between the USSR and the United States, empowering them to launch a joint, standing military force ready to overwhelm any new Hitlers who might arise. What emerged was a rather different Security Council, set in the context of an assembly composed of all those states (however small) prepared to make a values commitment to human rights, and of an Economic and Social Council (which was to include a Human Rights Commission) coequal with it in principle, and in its potential for a global ethos significantly greater.

After the world-historical moment when she had shepherded the Universal Declaration to victory at the UN Assembly in December 1948, Eleanor Roosevelt famously spoke of it (as she had done earlier in the process) as a "Magna Carta for mankind." Perhaps this was intellectually careless. The 1215 confrontation with executive political power on behalf of English liberties and of due process was a document incomprehensible outside the old Christendom culture. Its "liberties" protected endowments of delineated space within which to act. The most important reaffirmation of any "liberty" in Magna Carta was religious, that of the church and its clergy—a liberty granted by God himself as the primary element in medieval European Christendom. The Magna Carta strand of liberty had required development before it could be recognized as available to subjects of the Crown who chose to flee England for Massachusetts. To become available to the "mankind" of any faith and no faith, this had to go much further. It was now urgent for some claim to be constructed for individual human beings as such and especially their forms of community (irrespective of states) to enjoy appropriate "liberties."

Such a new claim was advanced with energy by representatives of the ecumenical churches within the Judeo-Christian tradition during World War II, though from within the Judeo-Christian tradition of a single creator God and a metanarrative of his gracious purpose for all humans. Other claims for human rights that take no account of an inescapable presence of God in all human life—as, for example, the *laïque* tradition of 1789—have to look (and be) different, in both theory and practice. They are less potent. And, mirrorwise, any religious faith or institution that takes no account of the Universal Declaration of Human Rights is now much diminished and circumscribed.

NOTES

1. Jacques Delors, the president of its Commission, famously said in 1991 that without a "soul" any achievements of the European Union would be short-lived.

2. However, a cautionary note comes from Philip Rieff: "A universal culture is a contradiction in terms. We Jews of culture are obliged to resist the very idea." *The Feeling Intellect: Selected Writings* (Chicago: University of Chicago Press, 1990), 367.

3. In 1945 it had been the hope of many at the San Francisco conference that access to remedy for rights might become available to individual citizens of all UN member states. In both the UN Commission and Council of Europe negotiations, René Cassin was a central figure. He used his Nobel Peace Prize (given for his work on the Declaration) to endow an International Institute for Human Rights at Strasbourg, the seat of the Council.

4. Jurjen A. Zeilstra, *European Unity in Ecumenical Thinking 1937–1948* (Zoetermeer: Uitgeverij Boekencentrum, 1995).

5. The Soviet approach to rights was self-consciously scientistic, refusing to discriminate on grounds of religion or race.

6. It was Charlemagne's coronation by the pope at Christmas 800 in Rome as Holy Roman Emperor that marked the birth of "Europe-Christendom" (which did not include Britain).

7. Prominent names include (to name only a few) Henry P. Van Dusen, John Mackay, John Foster Dulles, Archie Craig, William Paton, Joe Oldham, Livingston Warnshuis, and Willem Visser 't Hooft. A subgroup are those from Canada whose careers were lived in the United States, including John Humphrey, James T. Shotwell, John T. McNeill, John C. Bennett, and F. Ernest Johnson.

8. Two leading theological ideas in the decade before World War I could be readily conflated. There was the biblically critical progressive liberalism represented by Adolf von Harnack (1851–1930); and there was the focus of Albert Schweitzer (1875–1965) on the imminent coming of the Kingdom of God in Jesus' prophetic consciousness.

9. W. H. T. Gairdner, *Edinburgh 1910: An Account and Interpretation of the World Missionary Conference* (Edinburgh: Oliphant, Anderson & Ferrier, 1910), 43.

10. John R. Mott (1865–1955) became traveling secretary of the student YMCA after evangelical conversion while a student at Cornell University. He was one of the founders of the World Student Christian Federation in Sweden in 1895, and he became its general secretary from 1895 and chairman from 1920 for thirty-three years. Mott chaired the Edinburgh conference (1910) and was closely associated with the International Missionary Council (IMC). He was an indefatigable traveler throughout Asia and Africa and had contacts throughout the world. At the WCC's Amsterdam Assembly Mott, then eighty-three years of age, preached at the opening service and became, uniquely, the WCC's honorary president.

11. Warneck (1834–1910) was the first in the world to hold a chair in missions—at the University of Halle. His *Outline of a History of Protestant Missions* was translated and published in Edinburgh (1901). In it he wrote (p. xi): "I understand by missions the whole operations of Christendom directed towards the planting and organization of the Christian Church among non-Christians, that is, their Christianization." Joseph Oldham was a pupil of Warneck's.

12. A. R. Vidler, an early member of Oldham's discussion group, The Moot, and later Dean of Kings College, Cambridge, wrote *Christ's Strange Work* (London: Longmans, Green and Co., 1944).

13. For the Survey Application Trust see David M. Paton, ed., *Reform of the Ministry* (London: Lutterworth Press, 1968), 59–84. This body was influential in the ecumenical movement until c. 1960. One of its leaders was Sir Kenneth Grubb (1900–80) who became chair of the council (and for a few months in 1946–47 the first director) of the WCC's Commission of the Churches on International Affairs.

14. A prophetic figure (both for the 1920s and again in the 1960s) was Roland Allen (1868–1947), author of *Missionary Methods: St Paul's or Ours?* (London: R. Scott, 1912). His later work was supported by the Survey Application Trust.

15. See chapter 4, note 16, in the present volume.

16. Harlan P. Beach and Charles H. Fahs, eds., *World Missionary Atlas* (New York: Institute of Social and Religious Research, 1925). The copy in the WCC library shows signs of much use.

17. Lesslie Newbigin, originally a Presbyterian, but later a bishop in the Church of South India, became the leading Protestant mission figure of the late twentieth century—he was secretary of the IMC in 1959, and on the IMC's merger with the WCC in 1961 he became director of the WCC's Commission on World Mission and Evangelism until 1965. In the 1980s, he was anxious to counter the postmodern attack that religious vocabularies' sole meaning is the exercise of power; and he claimed that, uniquely, the working out of Christian faith is in its serving of the "other."

18. In North America, the corresponding associations were the Inter-Collegian and Inter-Seminary movements.

19. T. Z. Koo, a familiar figure in ecumenical circles before the war, made a return visit to the Australian state capitals and to New Zealand in 1941. The Perth SCM branch persisted from 1937 to 1940 (when Subrij Thacore arrived) in its invitation to host an Indian SCM student for a year. National Library of Australia, Engel Papers, box 6.

20. The chair of the Department's Council was Professor Henry Pitt Van Dusen, a notable president of Union Theological Seminary, New York. Its staff—two of the five in the Geneva office—were a German, Hans Schönfeld, and a Swede, Nils Ehrenström (who continued from the previous Life and Work office).

21. Keith Clements, *Faith on the Frontier* (Edinburgh and Geneva: T. and T. Clark, 1999).

22. Clements, *Faith on the Frontier*, 135.

23. *Re-Thinking Missions: A Laymen's Inquiry after One Hundred Years* (New York: Harpers, 1932). This was always referred to as the Layman's Report. The authorship was given as "The Commission of Appraisal, W. E. Hocking, Chairman." William E. Hocking (1873–1966) was a key member of virtually all significant committees of the Federal Council of Churches, including the Commission to Study the Bases of a Just and Durable Peace, from the late 1920s until the mid-1940s. In the mid-1920s, he was the principal influence on J. H. Oldham; and Charles Malik came from Lebanon as a research student to study under him at Harvard in 1932. Howard Schomer was Malik's classmate then and recalled Hocking's energetic opposition to Nazism (personal communication). The "Directors" of the Inquiry comprised a chair and four members from each of seven American denominations. The fifteen commission members, three of them women, with strong links to the YMCA and to the World Student Christian Federation, spent some months in a variety of "mission-fields" on a "fact-finding mission."

24. Max Warren (1904–77) illustrated this understanding of mission in his widely read *C.M.S. Newsletters* in the post–World War II years. Warren, like Grubb, was an Irish Anglican, who from 1942 to 1963 was general secretary of the Church Missionary Society. He was also secretary (1944–46) of the ecumenical British Committee on Religious Liberty that related to government on these issues at the time of the UN San Francisco conference and liaised with the American Joint Committee.

25. Cp. T. J. Gorringe, *A Theology of the Built Environment* (Cambridge: Cambridge University Press, 2002). This interprets Saint John's Gospel—that Jesus "came that they may have life, and have it abundantly"—to assert that spiritual and artistic experience are necessary parts of any fully human life and, therefore, a right.

26. J. H. Oldham, *Christianity and the Race Problem* (London: Student Christian Movement, 1924).

27. This is perhaps the best-known of the "gentlemen's clubs" around Saint James's Square in London; and it traditionally draws its membership from university dons, clergy, and civil servants.

28. Seven preparatory volumes were published by George Allen & Unwin, London 1937, under the conference title *Church, Community, and State*. The first, *The Church and Its Function in Society,* was coedited by Oldham and W. Visser 't Hooft (who was to become the founding general secretary of the WCC), and reprinted in 1938. An eighth volume, the report of proceedings (*The Churches Survey Their Task*), was published immediately after the conference.

29. Dulles's son (now a cardinal), Avery Dulles, S.J., accompanied his father to this league meeting, and he recalls his anxiety then about the direction of world affairs. They had lunch at a sidewalk café with Jean Monnet (the father of the post–World War II European Union), who had been an equally alarmed colleague of Dulles at Versailles, and discussed what they might do to confront the crisis (personal communication).

30. Clements, *Faith on the Frontier*, 5. On the wider contemporary discussion, see also the chapter "1940 and 'Christian Civilization'" in Keith Robbins's *History, Religion, and Identity in Modern Britain* (London, Hambledon Press, 1993).

31. Whitehead and Hocking were Charles Malik's principal teachers at Harvard.

32. Clements, *Faith on the Frontier*, 67.

33. See J. S. Nurser, *The Reign of Conscience: Individual, Church, and State in Lord Acton's History of Liberty* (New York: Garland Press, 1987). Acton, a faithful lay Catholic, was in his middle years obsessed by the problem for liberty posed (unavoidably) by a hierarchical clergy in an institution with no limiting forces: "Power tends to corrupt and absolute power corrupts absolutely."

34. Tawney (1880–1962) was professor of economic history at the London School of Economics and Political Science and a founding figure (with Archbishop William Temple) in the Workers' Educational Association. Social equality was important to him. His work on the connection between *Religion* [specifically Calvinism] *and the Rise of Capitalism* (London: John Murray, 1926) was specially influential.

35. Eliot (1888–1965) was from a New England (originally Unitarian) family. He settled in England in 1914, and he rapidly established his position as a nonbelieving avant-garde poet and literary editor. But in 1928 he declared his mature position now to be "classicist in literature, royalist in politics, and anglo-catholic in religion." He was a core member of Oldham's group, The Moot.

36. Dawson (1889–1970) was a lay Catholic cultural historian who pioneered the academic study in England of "Europeanness" (q.v. *The Making of Europe* [London: Sheed & Ward, 1932]) and its roots in medieval Christendom. In 1943 he was a leading member of the "Sword of the Spirit" group of Catholic intellectuals that (for a short time) succeeded in getting permission for the Lord's Prayer to be said by Catholics together with other Christians. His final post was as first holder of the chair in Roman Catholic Studies at Harvard Divinity School.

37. Although the Oxford Group was held at some distance by the ecumenical leaders, there was considerable overlap in that they were concerned with the same issues. Frank Buchman, its founder, had even been a student at the Lutheran Theological Seminary at Philadelphia. The principal American contact of Bishop Moyes, who came as an Australian delegate to the Princeton Round Table in 1943, was with Sam Shoemaker, rector of an Episcopal parish in New York and a Buchmanite. Moyes, "My Confessions: An Australian Remembers," vol. 1, p. 85 (manuscript; copy by courtesy of Monica M. Moyes, Armidale, New South Wales, Australia).

38. This is an adjective that became common in eighteenth-century English politics to signify a narrative of modern history. The Glorious Revolution of 1688 was seen as a turning point for the "progress" and "liberty" of humankind in general. It was not a consciously egalitarian movement. Its classical writer was Macaulay. Acton's *Lectures on Modern History* (London: Macmillan & Co., 1906) can be seen as a subtly modulated updating of this approach, which took favorable account both of America and of Catholicism. The generation of professionals involved in English-speaking discussions of public affairs between 1930 and 1950 would almost certainly have been required to study Acton's text at school or college.

39. Calvinistic Protestantism left both modern Britain and the United States with a peculiar sense of national vocation. Cp. Clifford Longley, *Chosen People: The Big Idea That Shapes England and America* (London: Hodder and Stoughton, 2002).

40. Söderblom (1866–1931) became archbishop of Uppsala in 1914. He was much exercised by the difficulty experienced by separated churches in being of service to the European world

of World War I. His theological interests were in Ritschlian ethics and Friedrich von Hügel's spirituality. He believed that Christians of opposed theologies could achieve much by working together in the service of others. Nils Ehrenström was a disciple of his, and Dag Hammarskjöld grew up as his childhood neighbor.

41. William Temple (1881–1944), archbishop of Canterbury (1942–44), was the son of an earlier archbishop, an Oxford theologian, and a left-wing political social thinker. He was active in the SCM, in the Workers' Education Association, and in ecumenical affairs following his attendance at the Edinburgh conference in 1910.

42. World Council of Churches Library and Archives, Geneva, box XI.1.

43. Jacques Maritain (1882–1973) was born in Paris, studied under H. Bergson at the Sorbonne, and converted from Protestantism to Catholicism in 1906. He held chairs of philosophy in Paris (1914–33), Toronto (1933–35), and Princeton (1948–52). He was French ambassador to the Holy See (1945–48).

44. It is remarkable that Maritain's essay referred in a footnote to an article published by Fr. Pierre Teilhard de Chardin, S.J., in Beijing the previous year that foreshadowed his *Phenomenon of Man* (English trans., London and New York: Harper, 1959), with a preface by Julian Huxley, the first director of UNESCO.

45. The two Vatican II popes were among the twentieth century's most influential advocates of human rights even before their accession to the throne of Saint Peter; Paul VI, in the period when he served as sostituto in the Curia, and John XXIII, when he was papal nuncio in Paris. Sean MacBride, in his article "The Universal Declaration—30 Years After" (in *Understanding Human Rights*, ed. Alan Falconer [Dublin: Irish School of Economics, 1980], 9), speaks of Monsignor Roncalli's playing "an important part in the formulation of the draft Universal Declaration of Human Rights," and notes René Cassin's "eloquent tribute to the assistance which [he] gave to the French delegation." See Philippe de la Chapelle, *La Declaration Universelle des Droits de l'Homme et le Catholicisme* (Paris: Librairie Générale de Droit et de Jurisprudence, 1967).

46. It is seldom recognized how central to the modern ecumenical movement have been contributions on ecumenism and on the environment by the ecumenical patriarch of Constantinople, notably his encyclical letter to "All the Churches of Christ" in 1920 for "closer intercourse and mutual cooperation."

47. See appendix G, section VII (4).

CHAPTER 2

◆

The Man: Fred Nolde

To UNDERSTAND HOW the ecumenical movement's campaign for human rights developed once it had come center stage in international affairs between 1943 and 1948 requires that we know something of Otto Frederick Nolde, who was born in Philadelphia in 1899. The campaign was to be waged in the first instance in the United States, however "universal" the prize was to become. As in any conflict, there were judges, advocates and juries, strategists and commissariats, scholars and propagandists—in this case from many cultures—and a good deal of luck or (as many of those involved would have said) providence involved. However, Nolde was the particular "hero" of this struggle, the man whose temperament and capabilities were peculiarly fitted to lead nongovernmental organizations (NGOs) at a critical moment, and whose contribution was a condition of success. Yet he is now virtually unremembered in either the UN or the World Council of Churches.

Nolde's achievement was a victory in the first instance for two American Protestant bodies; the Federal Council of Churches (FCC) and the Foreign Missions Conference of North America. But it was of course forged in alliance with other forces in the United States and in many other countries, whose concerns overlapped to a greater or lesser extent. It is necessary to stress Nolde's contribution as a matter of justice to him and to his colleagues. The "history of human rights," as it emerged in the 1960s and subsequently, has found it difficult to fit their roles into its preferred story; that is, a story of a pure fruit of the anticlerical (rather than evangelical) stream of the Enlightenment, brought by "progress" to ripe plucking by the Jewish experience of the Holocaust. A point of view that looked to particular religious traditions was not compatible with this narrative. Nor were later United Nations circles anxious to attribute any considerable contribution to NGOs.[1]

This was not the case at the time, however, or the judgment of those who worked with Nolde in these years. There is convincing evidence that Nolde's work was valued at the highest level. Roswell Barnes of the FCC reported that, after tough talks on U.S. policy that he and Nolde (a lifelong Republican voter) had had with Dulles as secretary of state, Dulles said to Nolde, "It's too bad I'm not in a position where I can share my reasons with you. But any time you want a job as assistant secretary of state, it's yours."[2] At an anniversary celebration in 1955 held at San Francisco to mark the making of the UN Charter, Nolde was the speaker chosen by the body of

28

pioneer "consultants" (or NGOs) to represent them. Oscar Schachter of Columbia University, a senior figure on the staff of the UN in New York in the 1950s, judges that Nolde was generally recognized as the most influential NGO representative there in those years.[3]

Nolde's tenure as director of the Churches' Commission on International Affairs (CCIA), then based in New York and focused on the UN, lasted twenty-two years. The retirement dinner given for Nolde by the U.S. Conference for the World Council of Churches at its traditional meeting place in the Buck Hill Falls conference center in Pennsylvania on April 24, 1969, was an opportunity for old friends and colleagues to offer their tributes. If we are to follow the old maxim and weigh votes rather than count them, there are some heavyweight judgments among letters from those who could not be present.[4] For instance, John Humphrey, a secularist left-wing lawyer who had been the officer of the UN Secretariat responsible for servicing the Commission on Human Rights, wrote: "It isn't generally known that the human rights articles in the Charter are largely the result of a campaign carried on by a few individuals representing voluntary organizations at the San Francisco Conference, but this is the historical fact; and one of those individuals was Fred Nolde. He thus contributed to the launching of a great work which has had tremendously important consequences for everybody." Joseph Proskauer, the New York attorney whose eloquence (representing the American Jewish Committee) at the hinge point of the San Francisco conference helped convert Secretary of State Stettinius to including a Commission on Human Rights in the U.S. delegation's proposal, said, "At the age of ninety-one, one of my happiest recollections is my work with you and Dr Shotwell at the United Nations Conference in 1945. I think we three constituted an excellent team and that between us we put the human rights provisions into the Charter."

President Nathan Pusey of Harvard complimented Nolde on his ability to find words "to express the depth of Christian concern" that "would lead toward constructive solutions. That you found such words revealed not only concern and understanding, but also a kind of genius." Others wrote of Nolde's being regarded by diplomats as "the articulate and informed voice of conscience," and "I was always a thorough reader of your many policy statements and in particular your policy positions [the famous 'blue papers'] on the numerous issues coming before each session of the General Assembly."

These were mostly voices from the male diplomatic, academic, legal, and international affairs establishments—often faithful Christian laymen—whose lives were led in Washington and New York, and in frequent conferences in the world's capital cities. Those who knew Fred Nolde best, however, were his colleagues of over forty years on the faculty of the Lutheran Theological Seminary at Philadelphia. They joined in "celebrating not only Fred Nolde's achievements but also his sharp and analytical mind, his warm and sympathetic heart, his tenacious and complete commitment, and his convivial and contagious spirit." But they could hardly forbear pointing to the extent to which the seminary had carried—largely with good grace—the absence of its dean of graduate studies on seconded duties far away.

Whenever a plane passed overhead, the seminary students would say, "There goes Prof Nolde." There were also, of course, advantages. There was hardly another Christian seminary in the world that routinely had world leaders visit as course lecturers.

Nolde retired in 1969 to Wyndmoor, a mile away from the seminary, to the house that his father-in-law had built for him and his first wife at their marriage. She had died in 1961 not long after the death of their younger son.[5] In 1966, Nolde married again, this time a young member of the World Council of Church's (WCC's) communications team at Geneva, Nancy Lawrence, another Philadelphian, who is still active and living in their old home. He died suddenly in 1972. Therefore, he was not able to read of the events of the 1980s that ended the cold war, and in whose preparation he had played no small part. Even in the dark days, he had regularly pressed Dulles to keep open doors that could facilitate a Russian-American rapprochement when the opportunity came.

What, however, was extremely painful to Nolde from the mid-1960s on was the growing lack of esteem within the WCC for the UN-focused form of the CCIA that Nolde had created and staffed. The sophisticated structures he had built for engagement with the UN began to be seen as a misuse of available resources, and irrelevant to the churches' new style of campaigning in public on "issues." The Fourth Assembly of the WCC at Uppsala, immediately before Nolde's retirement, was a festival of the themes of that summer of 1968—race, women's rights, and the like. A student delegate came back talking of what Jesus had been able to achieve, "with his twelve guerrillas." These were important concerns, but guerrilla warfare was not Nolde's style, or his team's, or that of the various national CCIA commissions of academics, public servants, and diplomats. The CCIA was attacked (quite mistakenly) for being too close to the U.S. State Department,[6] as well as (undeniably) for not being female or teetotaling or young. It was also thought too Anglo-American. It did not help its situation that the Student Christian Movement ceased to be a force in university circles in the 1960s. The dominant theological positions in Protestant circles either posited an unbridgeable gulf between church and world or embraced short-lived variants of "secular Christianity." Neither did it help that Visser 't Hooft was no longer the WCC's general secretary. His family had served in the Dutch diplomatic corps, and the notion of a diplomatic role for world Protestantism was congenial. During the Visser 't Hooft years, the CCIA section was always given pride of place in the WCC's Reports.

Moreover, the circumstances of the CCIA's foundation in 1946 as an agency of two not-yet-united bodies, the WCC and the International Missionary Council, had helped establish its claim to a quasi-autonomous, substantive role. A useful apartness (until 1966, the CCIA home bases were its New York and London offices, not Geneva) had, however, its penalty once Visser 't Hooft retired. One of Nolde's achievements was his leadership, together with Sir Kenneth Grubb, of a close-knit team of four gifted and strong-minded players: Alan Booth, Richard Fagley, Dominique Micheli, and Elfan Rees. They clearly enjoyed each other's company as they flew off around the world on missions that brought photo opportunities with world leaders. Their principal daily associations were not with clergy. They rarely wore clerical collars. They were driven to distraction by the churches' reluctance to make the internal changes necessary for any successful input into secular public decision making at the right level and in the right week. It is not surprising that some of those who were deskbound in Geneva allowed themselves to be jealous or suspicious of these apparently not-very-"religious" colleagues whom they so rarely saw at work.

There has been little institutional interest therefore, either within the WCC of the last generation of the twentieth century or in the growing human rights professions, to celebrate Nolde's work.

THE BEGINNING

Protestants from Hesse had been settling in Philadelphia from its beginning—the Pennsylvania Dutch. Both Nolde's parents were within that long-standing tradition, originating from outside Darmstadt. His father Anton came to Philadelphia at the age of seven years in 1871 and became a U.S. citizen in 1885. They found many relatives across the river in New Jersey, mostly craftspeople and shopkeepers. It is thought that Anton worked in the carpet industry, but he appears to have had some nervous illness around 1908 that made subsequent employment only occasional. He and his wife had four children, of whom Fred (born in June 1899) was the third, and the only boy. In 1901, the family moved across from Philadelphia to Riverside, New Jersey, for a few years. The language at home was German, as was church, and grace was always said before meals. It was also deemed important that Fred, as a boy, should have an education. So his older sister was required (at the price of some lifelong resentment) to leave school and get a job so that Fred could attend high school in Palmyra, New Jersey. He proved to be a sufficiently talented student to get a scholarship to Muhlenberg College in Allentown, Pennsylvania. He was a good athlete and he had raised the possibility of ordination in the Lutheran Church, both of which were factors in his favor there. Several of those who worked with him in the 1940s commented that he came across as very "German." Fluency in the language came to be useful to him, however, in his international work. It is said that Fred and his family experienced anti-German hostility in the streets and at school during World War I; this may have contributed to his taking so wholeheartedly in later life to combating discrimination. His close friend and colleague on the seminary faculty, Ted Tappert, had a shocking story of similar violence against his family in Canada.

Nolde's time at Muhlenberg was interrupted by a few brief months when he was called up for service in the army in North Carolina as World War I ended, a period notable chiefly for his determination to become a speed typist—which he did. It was also his first absence from his immediate neighborhood. To a quite extraordinary extent, Nolde succeeded in living his whole life from a Philadelphia base, even when he was crisscrossing the world after being appointed director of the CCIA.[7]

At Muhlenberg, Nolde emerged as a very gifted games player and "gained his letter in football." He had so much energy to burn off that he did what was strictly against the rules and regularly played league basketball (under the back-to-front name of "Derf Edlon") the day after the college football games. It is central to understanding Nolde, whether in the context of "church" or "media" or "international politics," to give weight to the aura of leadership and human "good-fellowship" that his sporting achievements gave him. Physically, he had star quality. What his students at the seminary, even in the 1930s, remarked on was his enviable savoir-faire, his poise and innate social competence, and the way he wore his clothes. His passion for tennis, which he continued to play practically until his death, stamps his remembered image. After a period of work in New York, he would take the train home on a Friday afternoon, and he was at once on the seminary court. A colleague on the faculty was his regular opponent. One year, in a New Jersey tournament, Nolde, aged fifty, won both the men's and seniors' opens. He had a successful partnership with E. Digby Baltzell[8] in the doubles, too. His was a serious talent.[9]

THE SEMINARY STUDENT

After graduating with a B.A. from Muhlenberg in 1920, Nolde entered the Lutheran Theological Seminary at Philadelphia (LTSP) to study for his B.D. Unlike the high proportion of LTSP students who were sons of clergy, he was the first in his family to have gotten a degree, let alone to seek ordination. That year a number of the seniors were ex-servicemen. Of the twenty freshmen, thirteen had come from Muhlenberg. At the reception for new students in the president's home he was, it appears, a natural choice to be responsible for "impromptu musical numbers"; he had a fine voice and throughout his life much enjoyed playing hymns. One of the seminary societies, named for "Father" Heyer (a retired Lutheran missionary to India who served as LTSP's foundation house father), was the vehicle for missionary concerns. Nolde became its secretary in his first term, and the following year the seminary *Bulletin*[10] referred to "unusual interest" among the students. In his second year, he was elected secretary of the student body.

In retrospect, it is remarkable that two first-order leaders of the WCC—both notably ambitious personalities—were trained for the ministry at LTSP in these years. Franklin Clark Fry was a year younger than Nolde. He became president of the United Lutheran Church in 1944, and vice chair and then chair of the WCC's Central and Executive Committees from 1948 (when Nolde became associate general secretary of the WCC), until his death in 1968 in the months before Nolde retired.[11]

The LTSP had at this time an identity founded on two propositions that would not be thought favorable to such careers. The Lutheranism of the pre-1820 German immigrants to Pennsylvania—principally from Hesse—had become absorbed into American popular piety. The new surge of German immigrants after 1840 (with closer links to Prussia) was more self-confident and determined to retain a living

German language and a purer Lutheranism, which would reassert the central importance of doctrine, specifically that of the seventeenth-century Augsburg Confession. The LTSP was founded in inner-city Philadelphia in 1864 to assert these principles as against the seminary already established at Gettysburg. In 1889 it moved out from the "temptations" and noise of the busy city to its present site at Mount Airy outside Germantown. There it was serious and respected, but ethnically defined, and distanced in every sense from contemporary university life. Members of the faculty were expected to marry and to live in the houses provided on campus. It was considered a virtue that the sign on Germantown Avenue was small and made no claim on the attention of passersby.

In spite of the changes that began in the year before Nolde arrived, when German-language teaching was dropped, there is a consensus that the dominant tone of LTSP's identity was deeply introverted until the closing year of World War II. There was, of course, controversy about this between faculty members. But it was only the pressure built up in the early 1940s from outside—"surely LTSP ought to be seen to be *doing* something in this time of crisis?"—that broke the dam. Freeing Nolde for work in international affairs was LTSP's response.

For Nolde, however—who was something of an outsider in his notoriously status-conscious city of origin (and also as "only" a religious education specialist in his traditional theological faculty)—it is clear that his membership on the eight-strong LTSP faculty for forty years was intensely precious and liberating. It was a family to which he belonged, and to which he could always return. Its very insularity was protective. In order to remain in a position to describe himself in the world of diplomacy as "dean of the Graduate School of the LTSP seconded for part-time service to the WCC as director of the CCIA," he put his own daily life and family under heavy pressure and trespassed on the continued willingness of his colleagues to cover for him. It was an arrangement that, he believed, made him more personally authentic to those he encountered in government.

In 1919, a new curriculum was introduced. The LTSP faculty was being enlarged and the old guard replaced. Especially important for Nolde was Emil Fischer. He was the senior faculty member in the 1920s concerned with some of the same issues on which Nolde was working; and in 1927 he published *Social Problems and the Christian Solution*. Importantly for Nolde, by the early 1940s Fischer had for over a decade been the representative of the Lutheran Board of Foreign Missions on the ecumenical Foreign Missions Conference. This connection was to prove decisive for Nolde's later career, when the Joint Committee on Religious Liberty was looking in 1943 for an executive secretary. Fischer had at that point been elected president of the Ministerium (a Lutheran bishop-equivalent) of Pennsylvania, and he was well positioned to propose Nolde and to help negotiate the deal with LTSP that enabled him to take up the post.

EARLY WORK IN EDUCATION

The big new idea in the churches' mind in the early 1920s that LTSP felt it had to accommodate was "education." There was a sudden increase in the number of freshmen with a college major in education and psychology: In 1921 there were none, but between 1923 and 1926, an average of 20 percent. Previous provision at LTSP for teaching religious education had been academically weak and peripheral within the curriculum. It was decided to establish a post, and to raise a candidate from within the seminary. The one chosen was Fred Nolde.

The great names in education (e.g., John Dewey) in a discipline centered in America since the turn of the century had a world-renowned institution, Teachers' College of Columbia University in New York,[12] to disseminate their influence well outside school systems. Many of these guru-like figures emerged from close involvement in local churches. Their concerns were not easily separable from religion, even when, as in Dewey's case,[13] they came to reject its validity. Practicing Protestants on the faculty of Teachers' College were prominent in discussing subjects such as what should be the substance of the Christian gospel and of quality religious experience, as well as effective techniques of church-sponsored religious education. They spoke to an internationally organized and comparatively well-funded audience. The World Sunday School Association had been founded after a convention held in 1889. It grew from strength to strength and in 1971 became part of the WCC. It is hard to overemphasize the salience of Sunday Schools in anglophone Protestant church life in the century before World War I. With a clearly limited goal, to instill familiarity with the literal text of the Old and New Testaments in as many children as possible, it was a generally present institution in all the churches. From early days, Sunday Schools were a prime field for leadership by lay educated women in American society. Their goal was experienced, understood, and universally supported both within the congregations and more widely in the community as a whole.[14] This omnipresent network (with the YMCA and the YWCA) was to become the constituency for the mobilization of mass support from Protestant voters for the FCC's campaign for a postwar "global order."

This all-pervasive biblicism, based in the Sunday School movement, was to be greatly affected by controversies at more rarefied educational levels. The 1920s saw the birth of "fundamentalism." North American seminaries were rocked by a deeply felt conflict about the nature of biblical revelation and the freedom of interpretation to be enjoyed by ordained (and educated) ministers in their teaching authority. One of the most dramatic struggles took place at (the Presbyterian) Princeton Theological Seminary, which under President John Mackay became a principal pillar of the world ecumenical movement. The animus against "theological liberals-ecumenists-internationalists-socialists" among those Presbyterians (notably Carl McIntyre) who lost out has been vigorous and influential, and has lasted to the present.[15] Because LTSP was rather old-fashioned in its teaching (its professor of Old Testament in the 1920s, for instance, would have nothing to do with critical scholarship),[16] the violence of these storms largely passed it by. There is no record of faculty or students setting the seminary on fire with the theology of Karl Barth (with its insistence on the total human unknowability of God apart from his revelation in Christ),[17] as was the case in continental Europe throughout the interwar period. However, what was happening at Princeton, physically so close to Philadelphia (and with Einstein in residence!), and whose seminary had a national leadership role in Presbyterianism, inevitably affected LTSP, as it continued to attract more students and play a more prominent role in the structures of Lutheranism in the northeastern states.

The seminary's increase in prestige was accompanied by two developments of which Nolde was one of the first beneficiaries. In 1916 LTSP inaugurated a graduate fellowship, whereby a recent graduate could be ordained for tutoring work and further study. And in 1921 the University of Pennsylvania invited the seminary faculty to nominate up to ten students for scholarships with free tuition in its graduate school of arts and sciences. After receiving his B.D. in 1923, and ordination, Nolde held one of these fellowships and scholarships. He began to study for a university Ph.D. in education (awarded in 1929). His research was heavily practical: "The Department of Christian Education in the Theological Seminary: A Type Study of the Lutheran Theological Seminary at Philadelphia." When his fellowship ended in 1925, LTSP gave him the title of instructor in religious pedagogy, held with the pastorate of Grace Church, Wyndmoor (a suburb a mile from the seminary). The university made him an instructor at the same time. From the ages of twenty-six to forty-two years—through the Depression, the New Deal, and the coming of World War II—Nolde lived a professional life divided equally between teaching in an Ivy League university and in a leading denominational seminary in his native city. There is no evidence of any particular interest in politics or international affairs or speculative theology throughout that time.

Responsibility for a congregation for three years was an opportunity to put into practice an education program, and Wyndmoor was to continue to be a test bed for his pioneer attempts to fit a released-time religious education curriculum into the community grade school. It was just outside the city limits, which made it possible to get voter support for an experiment, as a high proportion of the then residents were respectable Lutherans.

Wyndmoor was also an area with some prosperous citizens and large homes. Walter Hahn Jarden lived in one of these, and in 1927 Nolde married his daughter Ellen. Ellen and Fred soon had four children. Walter's father had made money in bricks, and there were interests in publishing and in the Pennsylvania Railroad. Walter built the newly married couple a fine house on family land as a wedding present. Before long there was a tennis court at the end of the yard. In the basement, a complex rail network took shape that was a major attraction when students from the seminary came over and played crashes. The Jarden family had a summer home on the New Jersey shore at Mantoloking, and the Noldes soon had one there, too. In fact, Nolde was elected to its office of borough clerk and, as might be expected, was prominent in its tennis tournaments for a generation. He preached in the church there for VJ (Victory over Japan) Day.

Nolde's affable character and his reputation as a "good college man" and an effective teacher (he had a formidable reputation for training feats of memory via mnemonic tricks) cannot conceal that his pattern of life after 1928 had broken the LTSP tradition. To have a dual appointment with one foot in a university social science department was one thing (his elder daughter used to tell her school friends that her father "taught in the university"). But what was unprecedented was that the Noldes were never to live on campus; after all, Walter had built a new house for them as a wedding present. The Jardens were Presbyterians—a cut above Lutherans on the social ladder—and it is doubtful that Ellen would have agreed to live on campus even if her father had not provided an alternative. Ellen was a well-regarded teacher of English with progressive ideas, and for much of her career was on the staff of the Germantown Friends School, with very little interest in the seminary. She did, however, have a lifelong interest in international affairs. Therefore, when the opportunity came in 1942 for her husband to begin to stretch his wings on the national stage, she encouraged this more interesting and glamorous element in both their lives, and was open to persuasion to help fund the additional living expenses (books, travel, and accommodation in New York) that would be involved. Nolde and John Foster Dulles became the engines of what the churches were able to achieve in international affairs. Without the security of Jarden money behind Nolde in the early years and the Rockefeller millions accessible to Dulles, it might have been a very different story.

THE SEMINARY

There was a certain intellectual distance between Nolde and the generality of the LTSP faculty. From whatever source (perhaps it was through reading Troeltsch as a graduate student in social sciences), he admired the liberal theologian Albrecht Ritschl (1822–89).[18] For most continental European Protestants in the 1930s, such "liberalism" was tantamount to self-excommunication. The picture was less black-and-white in Britain and North America. But those faculty who saw religious education as a technical skill rather than a properly theological academic discipline were uneasy with Nolde's later prominence in the public perception of the seminary. Also, specialized professional attention to academic pedagogy gave Nolde an unusual formation among his peers. The pervasive consequences of this had not been foreseen when he had been pointed in that direction. Sociopsychological method helped measure achievement, and the social conditioning of such achievement, toward specifiable objective goals. But growth in religion could no longer be defined as memorizing more biblical texts. It was the child in his or her individuality who was in the driving-seat and had to be helped to learn. Loving solidarity and fair social relationships both in the classroom and in the community were critical factors. A "good society" from this point of view was one where openness—protected personal space and access to accurate information—led on to a formed identity's adult encounter with God in the conscience.[19] The availability of such patterns of thought for Nolde's picture of a universal system of human rights is clear.

Nolde's students agree that he was particularly proud of the way he had succeeded in re-presenting Luther's *Shorter Catechism* for use in the parishes, by changing the order of its contents. Few things could be as central as this catechetical task to the identity of any Lutheran pastor. Nolde believed that he had been able, in doing this, to take account of educational theory in understanding necessary process, the growth of a child into religion, without being unfaithful to Luther's intentions.[20] In the 1930s the general life of LTSP became much more open to issues of the moment and to students' questioning. C. M. Jacobs, the faculty's church historian, became its leading intellectual figure, and the so-called Baltimore Report that he and a colleague produced in 1938, *Declaration on the Word of God and the Scriptures*, played an important role in moving wider Lutheran discussion away from fundamentalism.

For such an apparently public person, it is surprising that Nolde took care to leave little personal material such as correspondence. From some of those who knew him, there is the impression that he was unwilling to put anything of himself on display. Where he came to excel—his diplomatic "genius"—was in listening carefully to disagreements between others, to what they said and where as persons they "came from," and finding a proposal on whose wording all those present could wholeheartedly agree. What could be a better training ground for this skill than for fifteen formative years to be the sole person who was a comember of two collegiate faculties—in a Lutheran seminary and in a university social sciences department? There is no evidence that his academic relationships within both faculties were other than affirming.

One of the few widely told anecdotes about Nolde, however, illustrates the danger of talking frankly in the wrong place. In the tension preceding Jacobs's Baltimore *Declaration*, accusations of inadequate orthodoxy were being bandied about among clergy. Word got around that Nolde had been saying the dogma of the Virgin Birth added nothing to Christian belief. A panel was established by the Ministerium to summon Nolde to defend himself. Using his phenomenal memory, he spouted long extracts in their original Latin from the Lutheran fathers of the seventeenth century—whether relevant or not, the panel was unable to guess. Unwilling, therefore, to enter a public debate with him, they let him off with a caution.[21] Nolde's own teaching responsibilities at LTSP were primarily to be in charge of the religious education department but also included "English Bible" and (from his notes) a conventionally Whiggish survey course on modern church history. Unlike that of his colleagues, his departmental work took him out routinely to parishes in the vicinity to supervise students on practical placement.

This outward-facing ministry was shared by Paul Hoh, who was seen by students as Nolde's closest colleague. Hoh had gone into parish ministry from LTSP, was also for a time (on behalf of LTSP) editor of the *Lutheran Church Review*, and then became an editor of religious education textbooks for the United Lutheran Church Board. He and Nolde shared authorship of a series of practical texts for "the church worker" (1934–36), and he published Nolde's best-selling manual *Yesterday, Today, and Tomorrow: A Course of Study for Pre-Confirmation Classes* (1936). Hoh joined the faculty in 1937 as professor of practical theology, and in 1945 he became the seminary's president until his death—hastened by overwork—in 1952. His support was hugely important to Nolde. What had been a notoriously introverted institution became (initially under their stimulus) exceptionally open to involvement in public issues at home and abroad, and in the 1990s took the lead in proposing that the Lutheran Church redefine its constituency as a representative slice of every ethnic community in America.[22] No more Germanitas.

THE UNIVERSITY

The records of the University of Pennsylvania show Nolde as first an instructor in the Graduate School of Education (1925–30), then an assistant professor (1930–32), and subsequently lecturer in religious education (1932–41). The history of the school describes a fascinating development under the leadership (1921–48) of Dean John H. Minnick during those years,[23] from a small and not very academic handful of teachers at the end of World War I to a major institution as the United States entered World War II, with a library "second only to that of Teachers' College." At his first appointment, Nolde was identified as a specialist in religious and "character" education (the latter became a fashion at the onset of the Depression). In those early years, the possibility remained open that there could be a future for religious education by which authorized instructors from the churches came into the public schools. Nolde's "Wyndmoor School of Christian Education" was designed as a model for more general use, both by LTSP and the university. A state decision reflecting the national movement of opinion toward a wholly secular education system finally closed off all such possibilities. It became clear that there was no longer a specialty for Nolde to teach part time in the university after a full-time appointment was made in 1939 to a newly created Educational Service Bureau to take over and develop extramural work with the profession.[24]

Nolde's dissertation for his doctorate in education had little to do with religious or pastoral questions. It is long on statistics and tables. There is stress on the reliability of outcome that a scientific program will bring. His doctoral supervisor was A. D. Yocum, whose interests are indicated by the courses he introduced titled "School Discipline as a Means to Moral Training" and "The Teaching of Democracy." The phrase that recurs in Nolde's work is "control of outcome," which presumably had its relevance to his course on "character-education." He was always the keen chess player, looking ahead to practical consequences. His interest in public affairs appears to have originated not from a conviction about abstract freedom but from concern for an optimum structure for managing the (Christian) potential of human "character."

In 1931 LTSP took the step of establishing a chair of religious education with Nolde as its first holder. His inaugural address, "Christian Education in the Theological Seminary," had virtually the same title as his dissertation. But its aim was to locate the new discipline (which he preferred to call "Christian education" rather than "religious education") within the institution. The educational role of ministers, he claimed, has now become more prominent for four reasons: Jesus himself is now seen as a teacher's model;[25] increasingly the church and not society has to take sole responsibility for teaching religion; "education" is taking the place of "conversion" as the normal path to Christian maturity; and the educational level of church members has risen markedly. Teaching within the life of the church had only recently been studied in an organized way as a process, whose principles "in so far as they have been discovered, constitute the science of Christian education." It was not "a pure science." Being concerned "with the human soul," it was "also intuitive." But "as a science [it] is concerned with the understanding of individuals, ways of controlling conduct, selection of objectives of Christian development, methods and materials for attaining desired results, and measurement." There was need for supervised practice by students in a parish context, and for more research.[26] As the 1930s ended, Nolde began offering a course on "research method" in the seminary.

The other contribution that membership on the university's education faculty made to Nolde's subsequent career was to give him daily contact with new kinds of people, and with world conflicts. When that half of his life was taken away in 1941, looking to a future of twenty-five more years confined to running religious education at LTSP must have been dismaying, both repetitive and claustrophobic.

His primary question, before agreeing to take his first major step into the churches' concern with international affairs in January 1942, was, "Is it a serious outfit?" He was looking for a substantial enterprise in which his active participation would be welcome, and one that would make a measurable difference to the world outside the seminary while retaining a base inside it. With what at first was the mild and general encouragement of his seminary colleagues, he agreed to attend the Delaware conference in 1942. It can scarcely be imagined that he (or they) foresaw even a small part of what that enterprise was to become.

There were people at the university, however, whose ideas may have influenced him. When Nolde first joined the education faculty, its dean stood out against the xenophobia, racism, and antisocialist paranoia that were being imposed on school systems by government, supported by assertions from "scientific" tests about "brain-power."[27] The influence of Teachers' College began to flow strongly at the University of Pennsylvania, and that influence was both politically radical and internationalist.

Closer to home was Thomas Woody, the education faculty's star, a local Philadelphia Quaker. He served as secretary of the International Committee of the YMCA, and had directed postwar relief work in Russia. He went back there in 1929 on a Guggenheim Fellowship before writing *New Minds: New Men? The Emergence of the Soviet Citizen* (1932). This was, after all, not so far from Nolde's central concern for "controlled outcomes." From 1930 on there was a growing program of "comparative education" that entailed frequent travel overseas by students and faculty. Whereas at the Lutheran Seminary there is little to indicate any interest in what Hitler was doing (in contrast to, for instance, Union Seminary in New York), the Penn education faculty set up a remarkable event, the "Cultural Olympics," in 1936 that attracted audiences of over 100,000. There were festival events and conferences in music, drama, dance, literature—all in reaction against the German government's using the Berlin Olympics to promote a "totalitarian political ideology." This became an annual occasion. Its historian says the aim in 1936–41 was "to develop among men, women, and children of the Philadelphia area a sense of personal worth" and to give "them an opportunity in such creative artistic activities as would stimulate self-realization." In 1948 its theme was pluralistic folk culture, under the banner: "People are more alike than different."[28] That is a human rights atmosphere. It is worth noting, too, that Kwame Nkrumah of Ghana, a leading figure among the first presidents of independent African states, claimed to have been formed by his time as a politically active student in education (M.S., 1942) at the University of Pennsylvania.

With regard to the churches, the scene was not so exciting, although in the summer of 1940 the FCC held the first of its National Study Conferences on International Affairs in Philadelphia, at which John Foster Dulles was a platform speaker. All that can be said is that Fred or Ellen Nolde might well have been involved in it or present at some of the meetings. What had certainly influenced LTSP was the experience of Ted Tappert, the professor of church history, who had been caught up in the chaos of the first days of war in Nazi Germany as he and his family tried to return from study leave. Tappert became a member of the FCC's international affairs panel. We must suppose that by 1941 Nolde had begun to be interested in postwar global order. He published a popular introductory survey in 1942.[29]

The ecumenical movement as such does not figure in the LTSP *Bulletin*. The United Lutheran Church was not a member of the FCC until some years later. Professor Luther D. Reed (who became president in 1939) and his wife were touring Europe in 1937, pursuing his interests in liturgy and church architecture, and he simply reported to the seminary that they had been invited to tea at Lambeth while the Oxford conference was going on and had met some of the delegates to the Edinburgh conference. But he showed no interest in the Confessing Church or alarm over Hitler's "German Christians." The most positive ecumenical or international entry in the *Bulletin* in 1939 was Dr. Rajah Manikam's visit to the seminary. He was personally known to many on campus as an alumnus of LTSP (1927). He had become secretary of the National Christian Conference of India, Burma, and Ceylon (whose creation a decade before had been a decisive moment in the indigenization of the Western Protestant missionary movement) in time to be a key figure in the preparation of the International Missionary Council's Madras conference in December 1938, about which he spoke. It was recalled with approval in the next issue that during his address Manikam had put rather crisply the Indian impatience with Western denominations: "Get religion like a Baptist, pay for it like a Presbyterian, hold to its doctrines like a Lutheran, preach it like a Methodist, govern it like a Congregationalist, dignify it like an Episcopalian, and enjoy it like a Negro." But there had been rather more to the ecumenism of the Madras conference than that.

There was, too, considerably more to the contemporary approach to international affairs by FCC church leaders in New York than was evidenced in the commencement address given at LTSP in 1940 by the editor of *The Lutheran*, Dr. Nathan Melhorn of the class of 1897. His ideas were presumably thought mainstream by the

faculty that invited him. He directed his listeners' attention to what "our American-
ism involves for religion. [It is] a possession whose value is next to that which comes
to us from the Holy Spirit by the more direct means of grace which our Lord established in order that His Kingdom might everywhere be instituted." He sets the scene:
"It was in the United States and in parts of Canada that something comparable with
the apostolic opportunities was possible for the Christian Church. . . . In one respect
the situation in the New World was more favourable to the spread of the Gospel
than existed in the days of the apostles. There were no persecutions by government
authority and therefore no reason to worship in secret and confess the faith in the
Triune God by mysterious symbols. The church was brother to business. It was recognized by the state by being duly chartered to carry on the worship of the almighty
God. In response the institutions of the state were cherished and supported by an
active, conscientious citizenry." The dagger to the heart of the gospel idyll that was
early America is seen by Melhorn as two-edged: On the one hand there is pressure
from secularists to force Christian churches from public influence, and on the other
a loss of theological nerve by the churches in exerting such influence.[30]

It is surely relevant to Nolde's initial self-imaging of his work on behalf of a just
and durable peace that his professional expertise was in the field of controlling educational outcomes and, for his colleagues on the faculty, that such powerful rhetoric
was coming from the leadership of their Lutheran Church to connect American
constitutionalism with optimum conditions for "the spread of the Gospel" (and
vice versa), and then to commend urgent entry by clergy into the public issues of
the day.

AFTER 1942

At the age of forty-two, Fred Nolde began a career lasting twenty-six years that,
while ostensibly a development of what had gone before, was dramatically different
and took him into a stratosphere of public exposure. It seemed natural by 1954 at
the Second Assembly of the WCC in Evanston, Illinois, that a press photo should
place him in the company of the archbishop of Canterbury and the secretary general
of the UN. What could always be said of him was that he had mastered his brief.[31]
It is hard to exaggerate his achievement, from a standing start, in reading up in
depth within two years the wide range of material relevant to where the American
Protestant churches sought to establish themselves with regard to international
affairs and the post–World War II world. He equipped himself to talk with authority
on every aspect—practical, philosophical, and theological—of religious liberty. In
an August 1949 letter from Gloucester, Massachusetts, to Eleanor Roosevelt, he
commented this was his first real holiday since the outbreak of war. He worked
ferociously, had a first-class retrieval system, and kept a meticulously well-organized
appointments diary.

His attendance at the Delaware, Ohio, National Study Conference on International Affairs in the spring of 1942 led to his being invited on to the FCC's Commis-

sion to Study the Bases of a Just and Durable Peace, and then to be the secretary of the Princeton Round Table in July 1943. This in turn led on to his appointment in early 1944 as executive secretary of the Joint Committee on Religious Liberty, set up two years previously by the FCC and the Foreign Missions Conference of North America. These two hectic years were critical for the future. There was clearly informal encouragement as well as official permission from his colleagues at LTSP to take up these opportunities. Even so, his teaching timetable had to be fulfilled. After having been one of the leaders of the LTSP Graduate School with Paul Hoh and Emil Fischer for some years, he became its dean from 1943 to 1962. This post was progressively allowed to become a general administrative responsibility for LTSP's continuing education program, and it was a sonorous title to use in the chanceries of the world.

The crunch came in December 1943 when LTSP was asked—and agreed—to free Nolde sufficiently to make it possible for him to take on the post at the Joint Committee on Religious Liberty. It was arranged that his teaching hours could be concentrated in half the week. The stresses of Nolde's rapidly more demanding attendance at the FCC office in New York, and then in San Francisco and at the UN, soon meant that an assistant in religious education had to be employed. It became normal for him to arrive for classes directly from the railroad station, and for him to talk mostly without notes about what the world leaders had said to him that morning. His courses (and therefore student exposure to these issues) changed their content radically. He continued to teach at least one Christian education course that—judging from his 1951 notes on "804 Christian Education and Community"—could be largely concerned with the ecumenical movement. Every year from 1942 ("The Role of the Church in Post-War Reconstruction") to 1959 ("The Work of the Congregation in Relation to World Order"), he offered a different course in this field to the Graduate School. But there was always time for tennis.

The seminary carried his entire stipend on its budget until 1953. He was deemed to be carrying a full teaching load. In that year the Commission of the Churches on International Affairs began to make a two-thirds contribution via LTSP, and then in 1961 paid the whole of it after Nolde resigned as dean of the Graduate School owing to health problems (continuing as "professor on leave of absence"). His pension contributions remained a charge to the seminary. It is worth repeating that without his seminary's willingness—corporately and individually—to make real sacrifices (at a time of staff shortage and financial stringency) to free Nolde to operate extramurally on the WCC's behalf, his remarkable achievements would have been unthinkable. The Mount Airy Lutheran Seminary at Philadelphia should be honored as a necessary (though hardly a sufficient!) cause of the inclusion of a mandatory Commission on Human Rights in the UN Charter.[32]

The folk history of Nolde, wherever he worked, included comment on his extraordinary capacity—by mastering the paperwork, getting inside people's minds, thinking ahead tactically, sheer charm—to persuade others. He and Ellen Nolde came to believe that working for a new postwar "global order" was a more than ordinary vocation. The challenge to the world's churches and to America was urgent, and Fred had the self-confidence he could meet it. And he was normally able to convince his colleagues, too—for a beginning, those at LTSP.

NOTES

1. This judgment was confirmed to me as valid until at least the late 1970s by the then-representative of the Churches' Commission on International Affairs at the UN in New York in 1998.

2. Personal communication, Mrs. N. Nolde.

3. In 1966, the *Journal de Genève* referred to the likely nomination of the CCIA (and therefore its director) for the Nobel Peace Prize. There is a Nolde family tradition that it was instead given to René Cassin on the ground that Cassin was then in bad health, and there would be another chance later for Nolde. A group of prominent Swedish politicians made a further nomination of the WCC in the spring of 1968. They referred to the global nature of the WCC's work, especially that of the CCIA in support of human rights. In the event, Nolde died in 1972, before Cassin.

4. These letters are now in the Lutheran Archives Center at Philadelphia, Nolde Papers.

5. It is evidence of Nolde's close relationship with Dulles that the latter took time from the State Department (when he himself was ill) to visit Nolde's son, who was dying in the hospital.

6. Demonstrators chanting "CCIA is CIA" at the WCC Study Department's Geneva conference on church and society in 1966 had already indicated a change of climate. Eugene Carson Blake (WCC general secretary, 1966–72) advised Nolde that he should limit his post-retirement visits to the WCC office in Geneva. Blake's experience of his own predecessor Visser 't Hooft continuing to hold court in a retained office is likely to have been relevant.

7. There is no evidence that he traveled, except to the New Jersey seashore on holiday and on seminary business in the northeast before his climactic attendance at the FCC's National Study Conference on International Affairs in Delaware, Ohio, in 1942.

8. This friendship is interesting. Baltzell (1915–96) was a leading professor (of sociology) at the University of Pennsylvania and a lay Episcopalian. He invented the acronym "WASP" for "white Anglo-Saxon Protestant." His principal work (1979) was a comparative study of the consequences of a Puritan (Boston) with a Quaker (Philadelphia) culture—to the latter's disadvantage. He also wrote an exhaustive study of tennis, *Sporting Gentlemen: Men's Tennis from the Age of Honor to the Cult of the Superstar* (New York and London: Free Press, 1995).

9. Though this takes us to much later in Nolde's career, it is relevant to mention a contribution made by his well-maintained athletic physique to the WCC. When the Russian Orthodox Church authorities (and therefore the Kremlin) invited a first delegation from the WCC to visit Moscow, it was clearly CCIA territory. Nolde was the only American included. He was the only one among this group of churchmen who had any hope of matching the Russians, while remaining coherent, in proposing toasts. Following this visit, the Russian Orthodox Church was received into the WCC at the New Delhi Assembly in 1961.

10. The *Philadelphia Seminary Bulletin*, published five times a year since 1916, is a house journal to keep alumni and their churches in touch with the seminary's life and future plans.

11. A generation later, William Lazareth was another LTSP student and then (1956–76) faculty member who became a leading figure in the WCC as director of its Faith and Order work in Geneva. His recollection of Nolde is first as a celebrity "mensch" on the LTSP campus and then as the one person able to keep an increasingly neoorthodox WCC coupled to the UN for twenty years.

12. For a fuller discussion of the importance of Teachers College, see chapter 5 of the present volume.

13. Dewey (1859–1952) grew up in a New England Congregational church and preached regularly as a young academic in Chicago. One of his continuing anxieties as a philosopher of public life (and a world celebrity) was the consequence for political life should his own death of religious commitment become general. High art might serve at a personal level, but it could not fill that gap. See Alan Ryan, *John Dewey and the High Tide of Liberalism* (New York and London: W. W. Norton, 1995).

14. See W. R. Kennedy, *The Shaping of Protestant Education* (New York: Association Press, 1966).

15. McIntyre pursued Nolde with extraordinary persistence and venom in his *Christian Beacon*. Nolde quipped that the only publication that could be relied on to print his speeches (though with marginal comments!) was the *Beacon*.

16. Theodore G. Tappert, *History of the Lutheran Theological Seminary at Philadelphia 1864–1964* (Philadelphia: Lutheran Theological Seminary, 1964), 101: "His [C. Theodore Benze's] view of the Scriptures had more kinship with the seventeenth than the twentieth century."

17. A student at Princeton Seminary in the late 1950s recalls Barth's final visit there. At the end of his lecture, he was asked if he could put his theology into a nutshell. He replied, "Jesus loves me / this I know / 'cos the Bible / tells me so." The Sunday School movement claimed this "best-known hymn throughout the Christian world" as "their song."

18. Ritschl taught at Göttingen. There is only a brief (and characteristically unsympathetic) entry under "Liberalism" in the *Oxford Dictionary of the Christian Church*, ed. F. L Cross (3rd edition, ed. E. A. Livingston) (Oxford: Oxford University Press, 1997). Liberal Protestantism is asserted to have "developed into an anti-dogmatic and humanitarian reconstruction of the Christian faith."

19. This is the position to which the English Catholic historian, Lord Acton, was drawn. Famously, he considered 200 definitions of liberty and chose "the reign of conscience." In his judgment, the constitutional politics of such a "good society" necessarily had to go hand in hand with general access to scientific historians and pastoral clergy. See J. S. Nurser, *The Reign of Conscience: Individual, Church, and State in Lord Acton's History of Liberty* (New York: Garland Press, 1987).

20. The effect of Nolde's revision was to delete "original sin" from the catechism. William Lazareth (his student at LTSP) tells the story that Nolde had baptized only one of his two infant sons "to see if there was any difference between them when they grew up." Nolde began the material for eight-year-olds for his day-release school at Wyndmoor with "experience of an Inner Voice."

21. Mrs. Nancy Nolde recounts that he told her his position was not in fact that the Virgin Birth added nothing, but that Christian dogmatics would be "enhanced" without it—a judgment he learned best kept within a private box.

22. The then-dean of LTSP, Dr. Faith Burgess (Rohrbough), contributed an essay "The Public Face of Mount Airy" to *Philadelphia Vision: Mt Airy Tradition* (Philadelphia: Lutheran Theological Seminary, 1991), a collection to celebrate the 125th anniversary of the seminary. She reinterprets the LTSP tradition, as against Tappert's 1964 history, in favor of this public engagement (though we should note that Lutherans were thought in the 1930s to be preeminent among Protestant denominations in social outreach). She concludes "whenever you hear anyone . . . speaking about human rights, remember that in some small way this is Mt. Airy's gift to the world. O. Frederick Nolde's name is not a household word even around his Alma Mater. But it ought to be."

23. William W. Brickman, *Pedagogy, Professionalism, and Policy: History of the Graduate School of Education at the University of Pennsylvania* (Philadelphia: Graduate School of Education, University of Pennsylvania, 1986).

24. Brickman, *Pedagogy*, 106. Nolde is given as coauthor with Dr. George Hill of the bureau's first publication, a booklet, *Religious Education and the Public Schools* (Philadelphia:

Graduate School of Education, University of Pennsylvania, 1941). Curiously, Nolde never included this in his list of publications.

25. Brickman, *Pedagogy*, 47. Citing Jesus as a model of teaching practice had been characteristic of F. P. Graves, dean of the School of Education from 1914 to 1921. His *What Did Jesus Teach?* (New York: Macmillan, 1919) was dedicated to Provost Edgar Fahs Smith "whose administration has been marked by a deep interest in religious education."

26. Nolde's Inaugural Lecture was summarized in *Philadelphia Seminary Bulletin*, October 1931, 9–12.

27. Brickman, *Pedagogy*, 54–56.

28. Brickman, *Pedagogy*, 90–93. The apparently natural fit between Nolde's work at LTSP on behalf of religious liberty and human rights and the establishment Quakerism of Philadelphia seems in the event, to an outsider, to have been surprisingly little used. For instance, William Draper Lewis of the American Law Institute, who was responsible for the *Essential Human Rights* project, appears to have communicated with Nolde only through his New York colleague Professor John R. Ellingston. Nolde is reported (by his wife, Mrs. Nancy Nolde) as often lamenting the gap between local Quaker rhetoric and the support it offered to the Commission to Study the Bases of a Just and Durable Peace and the CCIA.

29. O. Frederick Nolde, *Christian World Action: The Christian Citizen Builds for Tomorrow* (Philadelphia: Muhlenberg Press, 1942).

30. *Philadelphia Seminary Bulletin*, June 1940, 4–5.

31. "Fred liked and often used the term 'anticipatory familiarity' to describe the way in which he oriented himself to a new situation, say an important speech. He would imagine the room, the position of the lectern, etc. If possible he would visit the site beforehand" (personal communication from Mrs. Nancy Nolde).

32. This information was kindly given to me by John A. Kaufmann, who until his retirement was registrar of LTSP. He was also personally involved in making it possible for Nolde to delegate some of his administrative responsibilities.

$\mathcal{P}$ART II

CHAPTER 3

◆

To Write a Just and Durable Peace

THIS AND THE NEXT chapters marshal themes into a narrative. Its beginning is the establishment in 1938 of the World Council of Churches–in–formation (WCC) that had been resolved at the ecumenical conferences at Oxford and Edinburgh the previous summer. The particular aspect of the life of the WCC that this story follows is international affairs or, as it was more commonly called, global order. It ends on December 10, 1948, with the passage of the Universal Declaration of Human Rights (without any contrary votes) by the General Assembly of the United Nations. Rather like a Shakespeare history play, this drama is only a part I; but it nonetheless has a unity.

It has to be set in the context of unprecedentedly ideological conflicts—on a far wider world stage than in 1914–19—that caused suffering on a scale that it took virtually the whole war for many to believe.[1] In 1938 there was already Kristallnacht, Guernica, the rape of Nanking, Stalin's purges, and the gassing of Ethiopian villagers. By 1948 there had been three years of victory over some of the perpetrators of these "crimes against humanity." The romantic nationalisms of the 1930s had for the moment gone away, leaving two quasi-universal political systems to compete. The Berlin airlift was in everyone's mind as a clear signal of even greater dangers to come. Global harmony and well-being seemed as far distant as ever.

For ecumenical churchmen, as well as for the Allied cause, the entry of the United States into the war in December 1941 marked a decisive change. It stamped Allied war aims with an American mindset, more particularly with Franklin Roosevelt's. It gave a secure and less distracted base for meeting and reflection. And, because their leaders were now in a more or less coherent international grouping, it was easier to envision the postwar world as a common responsibility. The result was that John Mackay,[2] a leading Scottish-American figure at the Oxford conference, could in 1942, as president of Princeton Theological Seminary, voice the widely held conviction that Christians should organize "to write the peace." This time it had to be "just and durable"—not like the Versailles/Trianon settlement in 1919. The importance of this undertaking within the new WCC's work was in the minds of its leaders from the opening of its office in Geneva in 1938.

The intervention of war so soon after the WCC–in–formation was founded meant that its first constituting assembly had to be deferred for seven years, to 1948.

49

Until then, its letterhead had to carry a provisional title. It had no constitution to cite or clear-cut channels of authority for action. Its principal channel for contact with the "younger churches" of its overtly world constituency had to remain largely via another organization, the International Missionary Council (IMC), whose London secretary, William Paton,[3] served as associate secretary of the WCC. This meant that it became an unusually conciliar movement.[4] Appeal had to be made to the succession of "messages" from the international conferences so characteristic of twentieth-century Protestantism and Anglicanism.[5] Before 1938 the assemblies that formed the canon were associated with mission outside "Christendom"[6] (Edinburgh 1910 and Jerusalem 1928), with Faith and Order (Lausanne 1927 and Edinburgh 1937), with Life and Work (Stockholm 1925 and Oxford 1937), and with those of the YMCA, the YWCA, and the World Student Christian Federation. In March 1938 the conference at Utrecht was limited to the business of setting up the WCC.

Then came two very different meetings, the IMC conference in December 1938 held in Madras Christian College at Tambaram outside Madras (now Chennai) and the small consultation of international affairs specialists convened by the WCC in Geneva in July. These were the only meetings (apart from a major WCC youth event in Amsterdam that summer) before the outbreak of general war in Europe in September 1939 made international travel problematic. Consequently the WCC's officers in Geneva only had limited formal authority to act and speak in international affairs.

After the outbreak of war in Europe, there were a few national gatherings, particularly in Britain and Switzerland. One meeting that was noted widely across the world (more than its authority justified) was the Malvern conference convened by William Temple, the archbishop of Canterbury, in January 1941.

But it was in North America that the process was initiated that led to such influence being exerted by the ecumenical churches upon the shaping of postwar global order. From the Federal Council of Churches' (FCC) decision at its Biennial Assembly in December 1940 to set up a Commission to Study the Bases of a Just and Durable Peace (CJDP) flows the acceptance by John Foster Dulles of its chairmanship, and the mobilization of what he liked to call "Christian forces." In March 1942, the CJDP held its National Study Conference on International Affairs at the Ohio Wesleyan University in Delaware, Ohio. This was a major milestone. Following on from this, the CJDP convened a roundtable in Princeton, New Jersey, in July 1943 to involve—so far as possible—representatives of other parts of the world in agreeing on the direction its thinking had taken. And this introduced what became a remarkable attempt to mobilize local churchgoing opinion in favor of active support of what the CJDP called its "Six Pillars of Peace."[7] By the end of 1943, with the relief of Stalingrad, there was a general sense in America that the tide of war had turned, and it was time to get practical about the peace. That was the moment when Nolde was invited to take a national leadership role.

THE WORLD COUNCIL OF CHURCHES–IN–FORMATION

From its beginnings, the WCC was directed at unity; but variously interpreted and weighted. Faith and Order's conferences at Lausanne (1927) and Edinburgh (1937) had as their distant goal that moment when the motley flotilla of Protestant denominations would transfer their crews and passengers to a single vessel, the ship that came to appear as the (apparently unseaworthy) logo of the whole ecumenical movement. Life and Work was much more here-and-now in its orientation, at Stockholm (1925) and Oxford (1937) looking to find what practical vocations the Protestant churches could presently unite in pursuing. The unquestionable urgency of questions of international order and world economic depression in 1937 gave the Life and Work strand salience in pressing for the setting up of a World Council. This was enhanced by the appointment of Willem Visser 't Hooft as its first general secretary, for he was not only a YMCA man—his "dialectical" theology stressed engagement with current crises and competing ideologies. The fact that the IMC could reasonably count Edinburgh (1910) as its own battle honor gave it a certain seniority in ecumenical circles. That, however much many in the IMC's constituent mission societies wanted to keep the home "sending committees" in charge, led inescapably to the conclusion that the unity of the ecumenical movement must be built on every race and every nation, as well as every denomination, having its own voice.

The ground on which the family of Protestant organizations was built was the international conference, using reliable mail, telegraph, and public transport services.[8] A hundred or so of the same names keep recurring on the attendance lists of each succeeding conference, whatever the organization. The consequent personal friendships tended to increase the global and associational character of these movements at the expense of the European "folk-church" idea, which (though the circumstances of the German church in the 1930s made it suspect) remained a powerful tradition, particularly where Church of England bishops were prominent—as in the WCC.

The two second-line international conferences in the summer of 1939 set important pointers. First, there was a World Christian Youth Conference (prefiguring the WCC's Youth Department) in Amsterdam in the summer that took as its theme "Christus Victor,"[9] which was the last occasion most could meet again before 1945. It demonstrated that to be young you did not have to be fascist or communist, and that there were young Christians from across the world who could still show joy and hope.

Second, the small consultation of "experts" that was convened in Geneva in July 1939 was the first attempt by the WCC to sketch out how it was to work in an area such as "The Churches and the International Crisis," and what were to be its preoccupations. All those there knew that they would be lucky to complete their discussions before the second intra-European war of their lifetime broke out. This was a last chance to get together. It was carefully prepared, and can be seen as the condition for so much of what—across a variety of wartime groups—later appeared surprisingly creative. Most, outside the United States, would now have to work in conditions of hardship and isolation. It was therefore important that the Americans (Roswell Barnes[10] and John Foster Dulles[11] in particular) were able to carry away clear indications of the directions in which the body of participants wished to move.[12]

Why were international affairs so salient in the very first months of the WCC–in–formation? Admittedly only a sect unnaturally fixed on its apartness from "the world" would have been untroubled by the news that summer. But it seems an odd direction for very limited resources, and had not been an evident preoccupation of the institutional Protestant, Anglican, and (very few) Orthodox churches that had become founding members of the WCC. It is relevant, as personal backgrounds normally are, that both Visser 't Hooft and Dulles had had close family connections in professional diplomacy that nourished their lifelong passion for "global order." It is evident from the reports written by Visser 't Hooft how large this area of work loomed in his picture of the WCC's role and activity; and after the Churches' Commission on International Affairs (CCIA) was formed in 1946 it enjoyed first place among the WCC's associated instrumentalities.[13] The autobiography of Sir Kenneth Grubb, the longtime chairman of the CCIA's council (1946–68), provides a vivid picture of the envy and irritation its favored status provoked among the more ecclesiastical departments at their desks in Geneva, and of the dire consequences for the CCIA of the retirement of Visser 't Hooft in 1966.[14]

It is impressive how quickly and effectively executive action was taken to create a number of tools—think tanks, networks, commissions—that proved to be of great importance when the peace did in fact come to be written. The farsightedness of the bodies that set up these projects was matched by the quality of those who agreed to take part in their work. The consequence was that they came to exercise a practical influence that—at the beginning of hostilities—would have seemed disproportionate.

The British churches made individual contributions but were not organized enough to be capable of such projects at a time when London was on the front line of the military battle (and their loss of William Paton in 1943[15] and of Archbishop Temple in 1944 were body blows). The relative tailing off of British leadership[16] was principally due to an institutional fact that Dulles noted on his visit in 1942: The Church of England had scarcely any bureaucratic structure. Everything depended on the enthusiasm of a few overcommitted individuals such as George Bell,[17] who happened to hold endowed personal appointments—which, when prestigious (e.g., as were bishops, cathedral deans, and university heads of houses), could be the base for influence and power.

This left three major centers. Besides London, there was the WCC's Study Department in Geneva with correspondents throughout the world. It should be mentioned here that Robert Mackie set up a wartime office for the World Student Christian Federation in Toronto, to which the leadership of the WCC could have fallen back in the event of Geneva being abandoned. And in New York the Commission to Study the Organization of the Peace (CSOP)—with encouragement from the State Department—was set up under Professor James T. Shotwell by the Carnegie Endowment for International Peace and the American Association for the League of Nations. Also based in New York was the CJDP, set up by the Federal Council of Churches. A more informal international and interfaith network was set up by William Draper Lewis[18] at the American Law Institute in Philadelphia to work on "essential human rights," and this produced an especially useful first draft for the UN Commission to work on later.

Connections between these three centers remained close. The fortunes of war led to their conversations being held almost exclusively in English.

The early interest of the WCC in international questions had in the first instance to be determined by what its office inherited when it was located in Geneva. First, Geneva was still the seat of an active League of Nations organization, with a resident diplomatic corps, the coming and going of delegations, and brand-new buildings too full of peace symbolism for confidence. The league had there a number of highly effective associated organizations dealing at the world level with questions of, for instance, labor, health, and intellectual property. And of course other world organizations had centered their work there; throughout the war years, the leaders of the WCC, the Red Cross, the YMCA, and the YWCA met together regularly.

Second, however, a research group had been established there in 1931, whose Life and Work staff members, Nils Ehrenström[19]—a protégé of Archbishop Nathan Söderblom of Sweden—and Hans Schönfeld, were incorporated into the WCC in 1938. It had been a joint enterprise of Life and Work (founded by Söderblom at his 1925 Stockholm conference) and of the World Alliance (founded the day following the outbreak of World War I in 1914).[20] This group became the WCC's Study Department. Professor Henry Pitt Van Dusen of Union Theological Seminary, New York (then in its glory days), was appointed its chair. The principal initial project was "the ethical reality and function of the church." This was pursued steadily, but with the outbreak of war in Europe this was soon supplemented by "the responsibility of the church for the international order," the project that was to dominate the war years. Visser 't Hooft wrote: "We must make desperate efforts to carry out one piece of study, namely that which has to do with the international settlement at the end of the war."[21]

As Switzerland was gradually surrounded by Nazi-occupied Europe, it became more difficult (and impossible, when Vichy France also was occupied) for the churches outside Europe to make physical contact with the WCC's Geneva office. Scarcely anyone was permitted to travel to neutral Sweden, though Bishop Bell was able to meet Dietrich Bonhoeffer and Hans Schönfeld there in May 1942.[22] Ehrenström—as a Swedish citizen—was even able to hold the directorship of the Nordic Ecumenical Institute at Sigtuna (1940–42) in tandem with his post in Geneva. Later on, Visser 't Hooft had to play cat-and-mouse games with German agents in Geneva to prevent their intercepting WCC radio messages. His contact with church leaders inside Europe became intermittent and increasingly had to be via underground couriers, which was dangerous and time consuming, though surprisingly effective. Gradually more of the Geneva Study Department's time was taken up with this contact work, and by the growing demand (as the war drew to its chaotic end) for preparatory work to be undertaken so that strategic plans would exist in time to respond to the needs of the starving and bombed out, the endless columns of refugees, and of course the provisional reconstruction of church life.

Nonetheless, particularly up to the end of the Vichy government in 1943, the staff members in Geneva were conscious of themselves as manning a world head office, into which reports, and copies of papers, came in from "the regions." After that date they had, however unwillingly, to recognize that leadership in ecumenical post-war policy had for the time being passed to North America. A last substantial overview of the international affairs scene, however, was produced by Geneva in January 1943, "The Church and International Reconstruction," which was described as primarily an analysis of church disagreements about "the creation of a just and durable peace."[23] Ehrenström notes "the present consensus is as yet lacking both in theological substance and concrete content." His survey is intellectually powerful and salutary. It is unclear how much impact it had.

They foresaw that the next WCC event of substance would be a major ecumenical conference on international affairs to be held as soon as possible after hostilities, to bracket with the miniconference on these matters of July 1939. When the opportunity came, this first conference was indeed on international affairs, at Cambridge in 1946, to set up the Commission of the Churches on International Affairs. This conference, however, came to be organized not by the Geneva office but by the CJDP in New York.

PROGRESSIVE FORCES: CHRISTIAN FORCES

The words "force" and "youth" were prominent in all the European languages between the wars. Radical discontinuity into "modern" life experience was common, whether of Chinese or Indian students at Western-style universities, or Russian collective-farm workers, or of ordinary Anglo-Saxon citizens growing up into a world of cars, radios, and jazz. Some kind of social revolution had become normal for "youth," so why not a thought-out Christian one? Admittedly, to establish a "new age" or "world order" within the Christian tradition required something of a repudiation of its familiar past, but it was no different in principle from moving on to the next of the "stages" proposed in the analysis of historical process practiced by Marxist ideologues.

Both Christians and Marxists drew their templates from the same source in the Hebrew Bible. The "end of history," when it came, would validate its vanguard; and would be bad news indeed for those "forces" that had opposed it. Or even if there was no "end"—that it was all a matter of ongoing social Darwinism—those who had fought and won would at least be there (while those who lost would not). If the Christian Church was to lose out, that would be a global-scale disaster. In that case, either amoral laissez-faire competition or state-socialist morality would become the only alternatives. Visser 't Hooft, at the WCC's Amsterdam Assembly in 1948, was fiercely determined that the churches should not be co-opted into either one of these camps. The truths embraced by both positions needed to find their place in a human rights, or personalist, order. The ecumenical leaders asserted that the narrative of a trinitarian God in creation, redemption, and salvation—being worked out in communities' lives in histories everywhere—offered an explanation of those definingly human experiences that escaped secularist ideologies.

A time of such crisis required Christians to produce a philosophy of history[24] that suggested a recognizable path to the future, of a quality that would persuade and attract men and women of goodwill in every nation to own it. Particularly in North America, many of those who made up the committees of ecumenical bodies and projects held chairs in philosophy of history or of religion in universities and Protestant seminaries. As Lord Acton had asked, rather anxiously, a half-century before: "If there is no progress, what does God do?"

Many books were published on this subject, which meant that there was a lay public for them. Arnold Toynbee's Olympian ten-volume *A Study of History*[25] was the most distinguished. But the most influential of all the interwar philosophies of history in the English-speaking world made no claim to anything outside the grasp of "everyman." This was H. G. Wells's *The Outline of History*,[26] published in 1920 and continually revised and reprinted until 1941. His humanist metanarrative (by no means unsympathetic to Christianity itself) was hardly pluralist—and was probably not so far from the opinions held by most lay baptized members of the Church of England. Wells was a convinced internationalist and became one of the most persistent public advocates of human rights.

There had been no shortage of pious sentiments and theological analyses of world peace issues from Protestant church assemblies since 1900. They had made no practical difference. Well-disposed churchgoing lay diplomats were not prepared to give time even to read them.[27] Not least, any "message from the churches" tended to appear at a politically inopportune moment, to be innocent of background knowledge, to be irrelevant to those decisions currently under discussion, and to be posted into a letter box in the sky rather than to particular persons. So it is representative of a wider feeling that the two key players in this story, John Foster Dulles and Fred Nolde, should both have required assurances that it was "serious" before committing themselves to the Federal Council of Churches' CJDP.

In this competition of futures, Christians had to produce the most compelling manifesto. But like any group with practical objectives, they had to become an effective organization, with appropriate political, educational, and administrative structures. The "order" that would follow war would necessarily be global. It might well be chaos. Unless "Christian forces" exerted themselves, it could be assumed that any order would be unjust (and therefore short-lived), and hostile to church—and especially missionary—interests. To "write the peace," in Mackay's sense, would be critical for the future of the church.

THE MADRAS CONFERENCE

The bundle of themes that became characteristic of the ecumenical movement in the 1940s first became fixed and evident in December 1938 at the IMC's conference at Madras Christian College in India. Its leading figure was William Paton, the London secretary of the IMC and the associate general secretary of the WCC. The IMC was bipolar, with the New York office responsible for coordinating member-societies' mission work in Latin America and in East Asia, and the London office that in the rest of the world. The consequently very different field experience of the two staffs had wide resonance.

The thrust of Madras was that the ecumenical movement had become interracial, called to play a part in every continent. The conference was overshadowed by the sharp sense of imminent war. Visser 't Hooft,[28] appointed earlier that year as the first general secretary of the WCC, saw the WCC's creation in direct counterpoint with impending chaos, when world Protestantism might fulfill its universal potential.[29] An older and less Barthian delegate, the bishop of Winchester, began his report: "This Conference's . . . inter-racial character was a miniature of that world Christian unity that would make war impossible."[30] Many remarked on the quite new level of mutual trust that had come from so many senior delegates (including those from "younger churches") having spent four weeks in each other's company at the Oxford and Edinburgh conferences of the previous summer.[31] It was decided that a group of those from the "younger churches" who had distinguished themselves at the conference should go on to tour the "older churches," preaching and lecturing. This team of leaders formed a cadre of postwar WCC leaders who were often critical of its founding (white) fathers.

The important memories for the coming war years, however, were of older and younger Protestant communities sharing mission in a new way. The Chinese delegates, coming from the immediate experience of a brutal conflict, were impressive. Key debates were between Indian Christians. It became almost a minor issue that European denominationalism had necessarily to be left behind.

In Paton's own substantial paper, "A British Point of View on Madras,"[32] he ticks off issues that were to remain active. The British delegates had been too clerical, and therefore lacked the practical ability to contribute to many of the "pragmatic" topics raised. Not enough women were invited. No Orthodox or Anglo-Catholics had been present. The social and economic issues raised in the book commissioned from Merle Davis had not been given sufficient attention. The worship was relatively pedestrian. The race question (not least among mission-staffs) remained a problem. But on the other hand, there was so much to encourage hope for the future. Within a "peculiar intensity of feeling for unity," the Chinese and Japanese delegates met, and it was the only place on earth where they then could. The British and those "from the West were put to the test of forbearance and humility in receiving criticism" from Indians. The body of the worldwide church itself, it had become clear, was an integral part of the Gospel. The "revolutionary consequences of the existence and strength and claim to independence of these [younger] churches" have altered the status of the missionary and, not least, of the "sending" churches. As well as "the need for redemption and a radical change of heart," "the Church must either make its impact on the secular world of today and win it for Christ, or the secular world will increasingly encroach upon the spiritual life of the Church, blunting its witness and dimming its vision."

There were scarcely any Germans present. This allowed a new self-confidence to develop among other theologians, especially the Americans. Certainly, Van Dusen of Union Theological Seminary consolidated his position as a leader of world Protestantism. Theologically, a Barthian tone should have been set by the book *The Christian Message in a Non-Christian World*, which the IMC had commissioned Hendrik Kraemer[33] to write for study at the conference. But many Indians were not prepared to deny a revelation of God to those of other faiths; and the Americans and British were more stimulated by Barth than convinced by him. Because the most fundamentalist mission societies were rarely members of the IMC, many painful intermissionary society disputes in the field did not arise at Madras.

THE COMMISSION ON A JUST AND DURABLE PEACE

Late in life, Nolde remarked that without John Foster Dulles and Walter Van Kirk there would have been no effective impact by the Protestant churches in the United States on international affairs.[34] It was their pressure (and also that of Roswell P. Barnes) that led to the Federal Council of Churches of Christ resolving at its biennial meeting in December 1940 to set up a Commission to Study the Bases of a Just and Durable Peace. Barnes (who had been a minister at the Manhattan church of which Dulles was an elder) and Van Kirk paid a visit to Dulles to invite him to serve as the CJDP's chairman. Van Kirk was to be secretary. This was the entry point to what Dulles later called "the happiest period of my life, working with the churches" in what rapidly came to be called the Dulles Commission.[35]

Alongside the Dulles Commission was the Commission to Study the Organization of the Peace,[36] also based in New York and soon known as the Shotwell Commission. This enjoyed substantial backing from the Carnegie Endowment for International Peace, in which both Shotwell[37] and Dulles (and later Nolde) were leading figures.[38] Both the Roman Catholic Church and the American Jewish Committee also set up groups. New York was the nerve center, full of émigrés from wartime Europe and China, where leading players wore hats (or merely circulated) in a bewildering number of organizations, associations (including churches), and clubs.

Dulles and Van Kirk were complementary. Dulles brought the connections of his firm of Wall Street corporation lawyers, the prestige of two earlier secretaries of state in his family history, personal involvement in State Department business in Europe in 1907 and 1919, and continuing prominence in the Republican Party's discussion of the world situation. He had been a platform speaker on international affairs at the Oxford conference in 1937, praising its dynamism (following his postgraduate study of Henri Bergson, always a favorite word) to the disadvantage of the League of Nations meeting he had attended in Paris immediately beforehand. On shipboard home, he began to write *War, Peace, and Change*, which was published in New York in 1939.

Van Kirk[39] made a less Olympian impression. He was a personally warm Methodist minister from a midwestern university of the second rank. It was only slowly that he modified his disposition to see disarmament as the crux of a Christian contribution to world peace. His particular skill was with the media; he managed communication with the press, and for many years broadcast a weekly radio program of news from the churches. In sharp contrast with the situation in Britain, he had available to him the resources of an established national office, with a secretary and files. He was the FCC's international face. In that capacity he was of course present at conferences and committees almost beyond human endurance, and thus known to many.

After the war, a meeting was held on March 11, 1948, in the National Cathedral in Washington to support the Marshall Plan, the European Recovery Program, at which Dulles gave the address. He asserted: "It was the Christian churches of America that in 1941 took the initiative in demanding that, after this war, there should be a world organization in which the United States would participate. That peace aim had been omitted from the Atlantic Charter because President Roosevelt and Prime Minister Churchill feared that the prevalent American mood was still that which twenty years before had rejected the League of Nations. Whether or not they were right at the moment, they were not right for long. The churches saw to that. They conducted intensively throughout this land national missions and study groups on world order with the result that our political leaders knew they were following the popular will when, two years after the Atlantic Charter, they made world organization an added peace objective."[40]

The CJDP took as its starting point the papers from the WCC's Geneva conference of July 1939 (at which Dulles and Barnes had been present). In the American context, it chose to inherit the first National Study Conference, held under the joint aegis of the FCC and the Foreign Missions Conference (FMC) on "The Churches and the International Situation" in Philadelphia in February 1940.[41] The success of the Philadelphia exercise in alerting influential church members to world affairs was the immediate background to the FCC's decision in December to set up the CJDP as a study commission. The FCC's Executive Committee of January 17, 1941, spelled out what were to be its goals: clarifying the "foundations of an enduring peace," preparing "the people of our churches and of our nation" to assume responsibility for such a peace, maintaining contact with the WCC's Study Department, and considering a post-armistice gathering of lay and clerical international Christian leaders.

The FMC agenda, including reports of the sufferings of the church in China, had been prominent at the Philadelphia conference, and a paper was circulated whose final section, "Missions and the Future," included a paragraph whose every word illuminates where CJDP thinking began. It ran: "Twenty years' experience with institutions—World Court, League of Nations, treaties, mandates, pacts—show us that it is not enough merely to strengthen these. We must bring into existence the common spirit without which such institutions will be ineffective. Toward this common spirit Christianity has a vital contribution, for, through Christian witness, men in every land are led to believe in a purposeful God who governs the world in a brotherhood of man under their Father God. Christianity claims that it is universal, that its Gospel is true for all men. The implications of these fundamental convictions for world government should be made explicit, if missions are to make their contribution to the problems of world organization in our day."[42] So began the phrasing that a global order would require a global ethos.

Dulles and Van Kirk put together an introductory publication in April 1941, *A Just and Durable Peace—Data Material and Discussion Questions*. It set out the CJDP's formation and membership to preface a selection of excerpts from relevant documents, which it proposed to use. As elsewhere in the world, perhaps rashly,[43] it took very seriously the report (largely written by William Temple from his immediate recollections of the conference) of the informal Malvern conference in Britain of January 1941.[44] Also considered was the rather more sober Report of the Church of Scotland Committee on Church and Nation of May 1941, with its contention that "the nations which believe in free institutions and which are willing to accept a charter of human rights must have in their hands an acknowledged preponderance of force." The WCC convened a North American Ecumenical Conference in Toronto (where Robert Mackie had established the World Student Christian Federation's wartime office) in the summer of 1941. This approved the CJDP's work program. Visser 't Hooft was able to cross the Atlantic to attend, and he gave a paper.

During the CJDP's first year, the United States was officially neutral. Dulles held to the opinion that the president should so far as possible be held back from drawing America in—however desperate Britain's case had become (though leading figures on the CJDP, such as Van Dusen, the Niebuhrs, and Mackay, were actively campaigning for America to join the struggle against fascism before it was too late). His emphatic ruling was that the commission's first task should be to establish what were the objective principles by which to take any positions in international affairs as "Christian."

No difficulty was found in getting together a large body of church leaders as participants[45] (including representatives of the missions constituency) in the committees of the CJDP. Work began directly. Attendance at meetings was good. For the whole of 1941, there was little attempt to exert public influence—in sharp contrast to the following stages. Some papers were given limited circulation, in particular *Long Range Peace Objectives* by Dulles in September. This was a response to the Atlantic Charter, the statement of Roosevelt and Churchill of the previous month. The documents of the pre–World War II conferences (especially Oxford in 1937, Madras in 1938, and Geneva in 1939) were taken as its foundation texts. Also noted were the Christmas radio messages of Pope Pius XII. Alongside this ecumenical tradition, great (and increasing) energy was attached to making a normative tradition of allied war aims out of President Roosevelt's short "Four Freedoms" radio address of January 6, 1941, with its reference to human rights, and the Churchill–Roosevelt "Atlantic Charter" of August 1941. This latter "tradition" of cords with which to bind the commitment of the United States—even before its entry as a combatant—(and later of all the Allied states) to a forward postwar policy was insubstantial, but it is a tribute to both the CJDP and CSOP that their recurrent glosses upon it and their combined efforts to give it public weight became so effective.

By the autumn of 1941 the CJDP felt ready to spread its wings. It decided to hold a National Study Conference on International Affairs in Delaware, Ohio, in March 1942. This was an opportunity to co-opt substantial figures, mostly clergy and academics, into preparation of materials based on the commission's provisional conclusions, and to use conference members' involvement of their local constituencies (and their criticisms) to promote the view that the report had the authority of the FCC and of its associated bodies, such as the YMCA/YWCA and the Foreign Missions Conference of North America.

Regional committees based in New York, Chicago, Boston, and Philadelphia[46] were appointed, each to prepare a conference paper on a different aspect of "a just and durable peace." Philadelphia was given "the relation of the church" to it, and the other committees its "political bases," its "economic bases," and its "social bases." They worked hard, meeting every fortnight, and produced serious papers for delegates to consider. Whether significantly or not, the batting order was switched before the conference met to give first place in the program to the Philadelphia committee's section chaired by John Mackay, the president of Princeton Theological Seminary, which included Nolde.[47]

Coming as it did—however fortuitously—so soon after America entered the war, and being the first public presentation from the CJDP (known to be heavily backed by church leaders, but regarded as "eminent" and up to that point rather mysterious), the Delaware conference made a deep impression both on the large numbers of delegates present and on the secular press. It was well prepared, well organized, and well publicized. Delegates also came from Canada, and a few from overseas. Dulles himself gave the keynote Merrick-McDowell Lecture, "Toward World Order." Leo Pasvolsky of the White House staff (charged by the president with oversight of peace-aims policy) and William Paton from London were among those who gave addresses.

On the evening before the conference, the CJDP agreed on its "Statement of Guiding Principles," the culmination of its first year's work. These were set out in thirteen credal formulas.[48] The tenth, a hard-hitting review of America's role, ended with, "If the future is to be other than a repetition of the past, the United States must accept the responsibility for constructive action commensurate with its power and opportunity."

The program eventually set out in the conference Message, *The Churches and a Just and Durable Peace*, was comprehensive and coordinated.[49] There could be no doubt of the position that the churches had established on Christian responsibility for world affairs, on economic justice, and on racial equality. This Message was communicated to the State Department in Washington (where it was well received)[50] and to ecumenical and mission leaders around the world. From this point on, the CJDP was recognized as the world churches' center for work on postwar world order. Dulles's reputation in America as a leading public figure in international affairs was boosted by this achievement—rightly regarded as largely his. He became secretary of state in waiting for two unsuccessful Republican presidential election campaigns. And Van Kirk had the cooperation of denominational leaders in giving this National Study Conference prominent coverage in their newsletters and publications, urging their clergy to commend it to congregations across North America.

Delaware was the springboard for the subsequent history of mainline American Protestant commitment to "global order" matters. At one level, this emphasis involved networking from a newly public FCC position with the substantial number of organizations such as the CSOP (and the State Department)[51] working in this field. At another level, the way was opened to educating and mobilizing ordinary congregations with an energy and professionalism without precedent.

The leadership agreed that Dulles and Van Kirk would visit Britain in July (and it was a testimony to William Temple's influence as well as Dulles's reputation how many members of the British war cabinet gave them an interview); that Samuel Cavert[52] would visit Geneva; and that in November lay and ordained church leaders should embark on a "Christian Mission on World Order." They set out two by two to speak at large public meetings organized by councils of churches in the major cities across America. In the days of rail, and in wartime, it was a punishing schedule for busy and often elderly churchmen to undertake. Nolde and Dulles were the team in Mobile, Alabama, which was the beginning of a personal friendship of considerable importance through to Dulles's death in office.[53]

The British political leaders whom Dulles and Van Kirk interviewed in London in July shared (with the exception of Sir Stafford Cripps)[54] Churchill's decided view that this was not the time to switch attention from actually winning the war. The real work of the visit by Dulles and Van Kirk to Britain was done at an extended meeting at Balliol College, Oxford, convened by its master, A. D. Lindsay, and chaired by Temple, now archbishop of Canterbury. The "strictly confidential" nineteen-page record of this, "Notes of Meeting on 'Peace Aims,'" is a remarkable document.[55] It began with Dulles and Van Kirk introducing the current American scene, and in particular the work of the CJDP. It was an elite group in every sense.[56] Cavert's time in Geneva—though less stellar—was equally useful, and it established the personal relationship with staff there that made his attachment at the end of the war mutually acceptable. He spent some months working to organize immediate relief aid.

The CJDP set about producing publications. Nolde gave time in the autumn of 1942 to mastering world documents on postwar reconstruction, and he published a list of the available literature in the FCC's *Information Service* of January 16, 1943. Overwhelmingly the most useful was the "Six Pillars of Peace," which aimed to be a popular digest of the Dulles Commission's policy recommendations.[57] Van Kirk sent copies to 60,000 ministers. Methodist churches and YMCAs ordered it in bulk. The president received a delegation to present it, and there was a major launch ceremony at which Dulles spoke in March 1943. Other publications were prepared for congregational use, and sales were good, so there was no need for a subsidy. A real popular concern on these issues was taking hold.

If the Delaware conference had succeeded in gaining the attention (and the acceptance) of the FCC churches, of their associated academics, and to some extent of North American political leaders also, then, thought the CJDP's leaders, it would be useful to get some international validation. The decision was made to host a "Round Table on International Affairs"—in the light of wartime travel difficulties not an "ecumenical conference"—in Princeton in July 1943. The Methodist bishop G. Bromley Oxnam was its chairman, and Nolde took his first major step into the CJDP limelight when he was appointed its secretary. The event was organized very competently, with voluminous carefully assembled preparatory papers. A surprisingly substantial representation of non-American delegates was secured from various refugee scholars and from the offices in New York of governments-in-exile and overseas bodies (the Chinese were agreed to have made a specially valuable contribution). Three British delegates crossed the Atlantic, and three Australasians the Pacific (courtesy of General Douglas MacArthur's provision of transport on a military aircraft). The Americans and Canadians (the cosponsors) nevertheless heavily outnumbered the rest. After a rather starchy atmosphere on the first day, the meeting took off and fizzed. Its "Christian Message on World Order" was put together by a committee of the continents and was widely circulated.[58] Van Kirk led a small delegation of Craig, Macaulay, and Warren[59] to present this report to Secretary of State Cordell Hull.

Another cooperative project of related significance a few months later, in October 1943, was the "Interfaith Declaration on World Peace" (more widely known as "Patterns for Peace"), which was not a CJDP document (though Nolde was actively involved) but, from the Protestant side centered on Richard Fagley, the education director of the Church Peace Union and of its associated World Alliance. It was a joint declaration following discussion by a group of Catholics, Protestants, and Jews.[60] Father Edward Conway, S.J., from Colorado, who was to be a valued colleague of Nolde's at San Francisco in 1945, played an active part in this.

By the end of 1943, with President Roosevelt again confirmed in office in the White House and giving indication of his personal support for CJDP thinking,[61] the way ahead had been clarified. There seemed reason to hope—in the event not wholly justified—that this perspective was acceptable to WCC opinion outside North America. Observers remarked on the new sense of a nation mobilized for both the war and the peace to follow. The CJDP's work had drawn on leading prophetic minds, such as Reinhold Niebuhr and Paul Tillich. People were confident that it would only be a short time before the Allies won the war.

NOTES

1. An emissary from the Polish government in exile came to Washington in 1943 with photographic evidence to acquaint the U.S. government with what had happened to Jews in the Warsaw ghetto. He called on Supreme Court justice Felix Frankfurter, himself the son of an immigrant Jew from Vienna, who told him that he did not and could not believe what he was being told (U.K. Channel 4 television, August 5, 2002).

2. John Alexander Mackay (1889–1983) was born in Inverness, Scotland. He was educated at Aberdeen University and went on to further studies at Princeton Theological Seminary, to

study under Benjamin Warfield. He was awarded a traveling studentship, which he used to study at Madrid, where he was much influenced by Miguel Unamuno, preparatory to mission work in Latin America. As a missionary of the Presbyterian Church (United States), he founded a Protestant school in Lima and gained his doctorate at the university there. From 1926 to 1932, he was religious work secretary of the YMCA in Montevideo and then in Mexico, before being called back by R. L. Speer to the Presbyterian Board of Foreign Missions in New York. As the newly appointed president of Princeton Theological Seminary and chair of the Commission on "the Universal Church and the World of Nations," Mackay was a leading figure at the 1937 Oxford conference. He prided himself on being the pioneer teacher in America of "ecumenics" as a seminary discipline. He was a member of the provisional committee of the WCC from 1946 to 1948, chair of the IMC from 1947 to 1957, and a member of the joint WCC–IMC committee from 1948 to 1954. His background had been tribally anti-Catholic, and this was reinforced by what he experienced of Roman Catholic Church authorities in Latin America. He became more reconciled to Catholic patterns of discipleship—he was a mystic with a lifelong devotion to Saint Teresa (whose portrait in rapture hung in his study).

3. William Paton (1886–1943) was one of the small group of English Presbyterians. He had a mission strategist's mind and inspired personal confidence. At the thanksgiving service for his life at Saint Paul's in London, Archbishop William Temple spoke of his "surety of judgment" and that "men not only in the churches, but responsible men serving this and other nations, looked to him in a way which was with hardly a parallel." Like so many of the WCC pioneers, Paton had staff experience both with the YMCA and the World Student Christian Federation, and he became the first secretary of the Indian National Christian Council before his appointment as secretary of the IMC in 1927. His understanding of Christianity was not as a denial of other faiths, but as "their crown."

4. When the Church of England broke from its Roman obedience in the sixteenth century, it chose to put the councils of the early church, alongside Scripture, as its dogmatic authorities. The conciliar movement had been very much to the fore as a counter to papalism in the fifteenth century.

5. The straightforward identification (by others) of the Church of England as "Protestant" became an unresolved problem for world Anglicans within the ecumenical movement. They were not prepared to abandon the claim to be also Catholic and Apostolic.

6. One of the controversies at the 1910 Edinburgh conference was about the status of Protestant missions in "Christian lands" that were traditionally Catholic, Orthodox, or Syrian. The Anglican (Episcopalian) delegates were adamantly opposed. It was eventually resolved, against substantial opposition from American Presbyterians, that it was out of bounds to conduct mission work in such territories (e.g., Latin America, except in the tribal areas). This was never fully accepted.

7. See appendix D.

8. I am indebted to Professor G. Stanton of Armidale, New South Wales, Australia, for pointing me to the early history of the Evangelical Alliance, which "arose out of several preliminary meeting which culminated in 216 'Brethren' from twenty denominations of Protestants meeting in Liverpool on 1–3 October 1845"—directly after the introduction of rail transport and a postal system.

9. The Swedish theologian Gustav Aulén's well-known treatment of the atonement, *Christus Victor*, had been published in English in 1931.

10. Roswell P. Barnes (1901–98) did graduate work at Union Seminary, New York, and became associate minister of Park Avenue Presbyterian Church, New York. He attended the 1937 Oxford conference and began his work on the FCC staff as Van Kirk's associate secretary. He was active in calling the WCC conference on international affairs in 1939 and was its American secretary. In January 1940, he was sent by the FCC on a special mission to Europe to maintain contact, and he became associate general secretary (under Samuel Cavert) of the

FCC. Throughout the war, his special concerns were relations with the WCC and the U.S. government.

11. John Foster Dulles (1888–1959), the son of a professor of dogmatics at Auburn Presbyterian Seminary in Watertown, New York, graduated from Princeton in 1908, was at the Sorbonne 1908–9, and was admitted to the New York Bar in 1911. He was strongly influenced by Woodrow Wilson and was a junior member of his legal staff at Versailles in 1919. He became senior partner of Sullivan and Cromwell, a leading Wall Street law firm, and an elder in his Fifth Avenue church. He gave a paper on international affairs at the Oxford conference in 1937 and was prominent as a foreign affairs expert in the Republican Party before becoming President Dwight Eisenhower's secretary of state in 1952.

12. See appendix A.

13. See W. Visser 't Hooft, ed., *The Ten Formative Years 1938–48* (Geneva: World Council of Churches, 1948), a report prepared for the Amsterdam Assembly of the WCC, and its successor *The First Six Years 1948–54* (Geneva: World Council of Churches, 1948), prepared for the Evanston Assembly of 1954.

14. Sir Kenneth Grubb, *Crypts of Power* (London: Hodder and Stoughton, 1971); his chapter on the CCIA is on pages 163–200. Bishop Patrick Rodger, who was on the staff of the WCC in Geneva (1961–66), commented how the resident staff saw the CCIA as no doubt doing good work, but very rarely in Geneva (personal communication).

15. As late as the meeting in London of the WCC's Provisional Committee in April 1945, there are constant references to the unfilled gap caused by Paton's death; School of Oriental and African Studies (SOAS), University of London, Conference of British Missionary Societies Collection (CBMS), folder 547.

16. The effect was felt of Churchill's unwillingness to allow space in wartime government for discussion of the postwar situation before that war was won.

17. G. H. K. Bell (1883–1958) lived at the center of Anglicanism from 1914, first as chaplain to the archbishop of Canterbury, then as dean of Canterbury, and from 1929 as bishop of Chichester. He was a founder of Christian Aid, a patron of art and drama, and almost alone in his care for the "non-Aryan Christians" expelled by Hitler but rejected by the Jewish relief agencies. He was especially close to Dietrich Bonhoeffer. As the international chair of Life and Work in the 1930s, he encouraged the "Kingdom" stance of its Oxford 1937 report, and he was invited to preach at the official service held during the UN's San Francisco conference in 1945. He was the first moderator of the Central Committee of the WCC and its honorary president until his death. His *Christianity and World Order* (Harmondsworth: Penguin Books, 1941) was a Penguin Special.

18. William Draper Lewis (1867–1949), born and educated in Philadelphia, was professor of law at the University of Pennsylvania (1896–1924) and the founder and director of the American Law Institute (1923–47). An Episcopalian, he married Caroline Cope, daughter of one of the great Quaker families, and he lived on the Awbury estate in Germantown, known locally as the "Quaker Kremlin."

19. Nils Ehrenström (1903–84) was the son of a pastor in the Visby diocese in Sweden, where he himself later served. He studied at Uppsala and was sent by Archbishop Nathan Söderblom to Geneva as an early staff member of Life and Work, where he remained until 1955 (from 1938 in the WCC Study Department). In addition, he was the founding director (1940–42) of the Nordic Ecumenic Institute at Sigtuna. He was professor of ecumenics (1955–69) at Boston University. On retirement, he returned to Sweden, where he was active in interconfessional negotiations.

20. The World Alliance for Promoting International Friendship through the Churches grew out of peace discussions between German, British, and American Protestants before World War I. Andrew Carnegie endowed its affiliate, the Church Peace Union. It decided not to become part of the WCC and lost its significance (and its Carnegie income) at the end of World War II.

21. Visser 't Hooft to Roswell Barnes, Geneva, September 22, 1939; World Council of Churches Library and Archives, Geneva, box XI.1.

22. Schönfeld, representing the WCC, accompanied Bonhoeffer, who had been empowered by church-related groups in the German armed forces to discuss in secret the possibility of a negotiated peace, should they launch an attack on Hitler. Bell conveyed this message to the British government, but it was rejected. In all such approaches, the Soviet government was to make clear its commitment to unconditional surrender.

23. WCC Archives, box XIII.

24. Two central figures of the U.S. ecumenical movement commented in *Christendom* (vol. 4, no. 3, 1939): "The most vital area of human thought today [is] the philosophy of history" (H. P. Van Dusen, p. 590), and "what we most need—what the citizens of all nations most need—is a frame of reference in terms of a philosophy of history" (Roswell Barnes, p. 623).

25. London: Oxford University Press, 1934, 1939, 1954. Toynbee (1889–1975), the director of studies of the Royal Institute of International Affairs (1925–55), was one of "the best minds" invited into ecumenical projects by J. H. Oldham, and he became a member of the Churches' Commission on International Affairs. The essay "Religion: What I Believe, and What I Disbelieve" in his collection *Experiences* (London: Oxford University Press, 1969) expresses very clearly his "inability to pass the tests of religious [Christian] orthodoxy" and yet his deeply "religious" view of history.

26. Wells (1866–1946) was—with George Bernard Shaw and G. K. Chesterton—preeminent in British public debate between the 1890s and his death. His writings often took science and the future as themes. He was active in the socialist Fabian Society.

27. It was J. Foster Dulles's experience of ineffective "Christian" input to the Versailles treaty negotiations in 1919 as a member of President Wilson's staff that started him on his work with the FCC (q.v. appendix I). It is evident from the Roosevelt Papers (though he subscribed $10 a year to the FCC throughout his presidency) how little time the president had for FCC delegations or their memoranda advocating disarmament and "peace" in the 1930s (folders labeled "Federal Council of Churches," Franklin D. Roosevelt Library, OF 213 and PPF 1628). The climate began to be more welcoming as war drew near. In letters to Pope Pius XII, to Dr. George Buttrick (FCC), and to Rabbi Cyrus Adler (Jewish Theological Seminary, New York), dated December 23, 1939, Roosevelt announced his appointment of Myron B. Taylor as his "personal representative" to the Vatican. This caused passionate opposition among Protestant church leaders, and it remained a grievance for many years. It was perceived as a threat to the principles of the American Constitution. Recognizing this likely concern, the president's letters to Buttrick and Adler included an invitation: "I would therefore suggest that it would give me great satisfaction if you would, from time to time, come to Washington to discuss the problems which all of us have on our mind" (Roosevelt Library, PPF 1628). These opportunities for communication were taken up more frequently and carried more important traffic throughout the subsequent FDR years. This significant development was helped by the congenial Bishop Henry St. G. Tucker's (a fellow Episcopalian) tenure as president of the FCC.

28. Willem A. Visser 't Hooft (1900–85) came from a well-known professional family in the Netherlands. He became a Student Christian Movement leader and was active in war relief work while at university. He began his life of international conferences with the YMCA (attending the Life and Work conference at Stockholm in 1925 and serving as personal assistant to John R. Mott at the World YMCA's conference in 1926). This led him to a doctoral dissertation on the Social Gospel movement in America from a neoorthodox perspective. In 1932 he became general secretary of the World Student Christian Federation and, from 1938, general secretary of the WCC "in formation" and then after Amsterdam (1948) of the WCC until his retirement in 1966.

29. Visser 't Hooft's "An Impression of the World Missionary Conference" (International Christian Press and Information Service, January 1939).

30. *Church of England Newspaper*, July 21, 1939, quoting from his article on Tambaram in *East–West Review*.

31. *Christendom* (Journal for the American Committee of Life and Work and then of the World Council of Churches, 1935–48, New York), vol. 2 (1937): 549–52. Pastor Marc Boegner (1881–1970) made this comment, pointing out how delegates from Europe, the United States, the Orthodox churches, and the Younger Churches came together. Boegner was president of the Protestant Federation of France from 1928 to 1961.

32. Tabled for Standing Committee of CBMS, December 1938 (SOAS, CBMS S.1).

33. Hendrik Kraemer (1888–1965) was a Dutch layman. After training with the Dutch Bible Society, he worked as a missionary in the Dutch East Indies (Indonesia) from 1922 to 1937. Starting from a strong Barthian theology, he recast the missionary's role as a "guide to maturity." On his return from Java, the University of Leiden appointed him to a chair in the sociology of religion, and he played a leading role there during the German occupation. He became the first director (1948–55) of the WCC's study center, the Ecumenical Institute, in Bossey outside Geneva. He wrote *Theology of the Laity* (London: Lutterworth Press, 1958).

34. Personal communication from Mrs. Nancy Nolde.

35. There is a revealing passage in the address Dulles gave on Sunday August 28, 1949, from his father's pulpit in the First Presbyterian Church at Watertown, New York. He began from his memory of the Oxford conference of 1937, where "we dealt with each other as brothers irrespective of national or racial differences. . . . Then I began to understand the profound significance of the spiritual values that my father and mother had taught, and by which they had lived, here at Watertown. From then on I began to work closely with religious groups— Protestant, Catholic, and Jewish—for I had come to believe, of all groups, they could make the greatest contribution to world order. Most of all, I worked with the Commission on a Just and Durable Peace of the Federal Council of the Churches of Christ in America. During these same years I helped organize the United Nations and attended its meetings and those of the Council of Foreign Ministers. Serving at the same time in both religious and political groups made ever clearer the relationship between the two. I saw that there could be no just and durable peace except as men held in common certain simple and elementary religious beliefs; belief that there is a God, that He is the author of a moral law which they can know, and that He imparts to each human being a spiritual dignity and worth which all others should respect. Wherever these elementary truths are widely rejected, there is both spiritual and social disorder." Library of Congress, Washington, D.C., G. Bromley Oxnam Papers, box 65.

36. The CSOP was an initiative in spring 1940 of the Carnegie Endowment for International Peace (CEIP) in association with the Association for the League of Nations in the United States. Its center of gravity was at Columbia University in New York, where Shotwell, its chair, was a long-serving professor. The CSOP had many committees, a specially important one was that on human rights, and together with the CEIP it was active in educational programs on international affairs in New York city and state. The CSOP was the center for communication among the various groups working in this area, including the committee on postwar policy set up in the State Department.

37. James T. Shotwell (1874–1965) came from Ontario to Columbia University as a research student in history. He taught modern history there, much influenced by Lord Acton (q.v. his *The Long Road to Freedom* [New York: Bobbs-Merrill, 1960]), and latterly held the Bryce Chair in International Relations. In the interwar period, he was particularly active in International Labor Organization and League of Nations affairs. He edited a history of the economic consequences of World War I in twenty-six volumes and was prominent in the successful work of the league in the field of intellectual property.

38. Shotwell, Dulles, and Nolde each held high office in the CEIP. Shotwell was on its board (1925–51) and was president (1948–50). Dulles was a trustee (1944–52) and chair (1946–52). Nolde was a trustee and member of the Executive Committee (1951–70) and vice chair-

man of the board (1959–69). It is worth noting in the CEIP context how important it was for the postwar development of the CCIA that Dulles, from its base, was able to rely on John D. Rockefeller's financial support for a succession of projects.

39. Walter W. Van Kirk (1891–1956) was born in Cleveland and attended Ohio Wesleyan University before Boston University Theological School. He was ordained in the Methodist Episcopal Church in 1919. After pastorates in Massachusetts, he joined the Department of International Justice and Goodwill of the FCC in 1925, where he served till his death, the day before he was due to fly to Europe to celebrate the tenth anniversary of the CCIA.

40. LC, Oxnam, box 34.

41. Emil Fischer, Nolde's patron on the faculty of Lutheran Theological Seminary at Philadelphia and the Lutheran representative on national mission committees, led the conference worship at the evening meeting addressed by Dulles. The Committee on International Relations of the Philadelphia Federation of Churches was active in the hosting arrangements.

42. Swarthmore College, Peace Collection, Group 48, Series 1, box 3, National Study Conference, "Paper for Discussion at the Seminar on Mission on the World Crisis."

43. Dulles sent (July 30, 1942) a draft report of his English visit to Vice President Henry Wallace, with whom he frequently discussed world problems—"There is, perhaps, a certain lack of democracy within the established church and a rather small group seems to be depended on to maintain contacts of the type I represented. We have, I think, somewhat exaggerated here the influence, in England, of 'Malvern,' etc"; Roosevelt Library, box 20.

44. The report's ideas are expressed by Temple also in his *Christianity and the Social Order* (Harmondsworth: Penguin Special, 1942).

45. Nolde's LTSP colleague Emil Fischer was one of these who had been active in Lutheran mission organizations and in concern for social questions.

46. The areas of the United States away from these metropolitan centers were scarcely involved.

47. The Philadelphia section had ten members, including Fischer and Nolde. The tradition of the Lutheran Theological Seminary at Philadelphia is that Nolde only became involved in international questions after receiving a phone call on New Year's Day 1942 that his colleague Ted Tappert, who had been going to Delaware, wished to withdraw. He was asked to replace him, which he agreed to do. This is also the account given by Nolde in his draft autobiography written in his final years. However, it is clear from minutes of Mackay's Philadelphia group preparing the section for Delaware (January 9, 1942) that Nolde had been a member before the end of 1941. It would also have been odd for Nolde to have been entrusted with leading intercessions at the conference service if he was an entirely unknown person.

48. See appendix B.

49. This booklet is in the archives of the Presbyterian Church (USA): National Council of Churches Records, Federal Council of Churches Records, Presbyterian Historical Society, Philadelphia (hereafter PHS [FCC]), RG 18, box 28, folder 9.

50. Dulles reported to the CJDP after Delaware that "in the 35 years in which he had had fairly close contacts with the responsible officials of foreign affairs, he had never known a time when such officials were as responsive to the view of the Christian community as they were today" [and he] "believed there is an important governmental element that wants the same thing that we want."

51. The State Department circulated a paper at Delaware which is of great interest. It sets out the history of arrangements for postwar planning from the time (1939) of the National Resources Planning Board, which was a "standing advisory agency" to the President in his Executive Office. Notable elements in this fifty-two-page document are the inclusion of the so-called "social" human rights (p. 9) in the demand for "a new declaration of rights." It is "assumed [that] the international behavior of American private interests" will conform to the requirements of "peace and the elevation of human dignity everywhere" (p. 51). Finally, "the Secretary of State has designated a Special Assistant to supervise the Department's inter-

ests in future international relations" (p. 52). Easton Rothwell acted in close collaboration with Archibald MacLeish, the president's personal assistant. PHS (FCC), RG 18, box 28, folder 9.

52. Dr. Samuel McCrea Cavert (1888–1976) was a Presbyterian minister, general secretary of the FCC, and a founding father of the ecumenical movement. The question of his being granted a passage across the Atlantic went all the way to the president's desk, and he gave permission on May 19, 1942, for Cavert to be given a priority Clipper booking and a passport to go; Roosevelt Library, box 213.

53. Both Dulles and Nolde needed a glass of whiskey at the end of a long day, and Nolde was deputed to bring necessary supplies to postwar Cambridge 1946. Their friendship in so many campaigns enabled Nolde to continue to have personal access in the 1950s, and to make criticisms of the State Department's cold war policy (however painful disagreement might be).

54. Sir Stafford Cripps (1899–1952) exerted a charismatic influence, like H. V. Evatt in Australia, within public opinion in wartime. He was seen as a puritanical figure from the middle-class "socialist" wing of the Labour Party. Like Dulles, he was a theologically literate politician. On his appointment to the British War Cabinet in 1942, George Orwell wrote, "that such a man, without any party machine behind him, can be put in the government in direct response to the wishes of the common people is a testimony to the strength of British democracy." See Peter Clarke, *The Cripps Version* (London: Allen Lane, 2002).

55. See also "Confidential Memorandum Prepared by Dulles and Van Kirk on their Recent Visit to England," 14-page typescript, WCC Archives, box XIII.

56. A. D. K. Owen (b. 1904) represented Cripps at this meeting as his personal assistant. He had worked on social policy in various universities and think tanks. He was in the U.K. delegation to the UN Conference on International Organization in 1945 and had a distinguished career at the UN from 1945. Owen had been active in the Student Christian Movement and was reported to Nolde as believing that the CCIA should relate primarily to UNESCO.

57. See appendix D.

58. The editorial committee consisted of Yi-Fang Wu (China), Leonard Hodgson (Britain), and Alwyn Warren (New Zealand), with Nolde and Dulles as secretary and chairman. The Message text can be found in PHS (FCC), RG 18, box 28, folder 20. The two Australians, Bishop Moyes and Wilson Macaulay, wrote vivid accounts of their experiences for their home churches, and for the Australian Student Christian Movement. Princeton was for them a window into a new world–dimension of church life.

59. Van Kirk chose these three to accompany him as carrying global credentials, having actually traveled to Princeton from the United Kingdom, Australia, and New Zealand. Alwyn Warren, Anglican dean of Christchurch (and later its bishop), was active in WCC leadership after the Princeton meeting for many years. He brought an original contribution to the roundtable, circulating a report there on the ecumenical "Campaign for Christian Order" that had made a big impression on public life in New Zealand over the previous year. This was taken as a model by the FCC in the United States for its own campaign of popular education and is an important indication of the diffusion of leadership within the WCC. The campaign was explicitly recognized by its organizers as a response to Oldham's *Resurrection of Christendom* (London: Sheldon Press, 1940). See Colin Brown, *Forty Years On: a History of the National Council of Churches of New Zealand 1941–1981* (Christchurch: National Council of Churches, 1981).

60. FCC *Information Service*, October 9, 1943. This declaration was signed by 144 Protestant, Catholic, and Jewish leaders and was given separate preambles by the three faiths. Seven points were made, very similar to those of the Six Pillars. The bodies responsible were the FCC, the Synagogue Council of America, and the Social Action Department of the National Catholic Welfare Conference.

61. See T. Hoopes and D. Brinkley, *FDR and the Creation of the UN* (New Haven, Conn.: Yale University Press, 1997).

CHAPTER 4

◆

Mobilizing Christian Forces

THE PROTESTANT CHURCHES

THE DECISION BY THE Federal Council of Churches (FCC) to set up the Commission to Study the Bases of a Just and Durable Peace (CJDP) was amply justified. There had, however, been significant differences in commitment among the denominations. Although Fischer and Ted Tappert of the Lutheran Theological Seminary at Philadelphia faculty had shown early interest in international questions (from before the FCC's Philadelphia conference in 1940), the Lutherans, as institutional churches, had not yet joined the FCC. Similarly the Episcopalians, as a church, only entered the FCC in these years, though Ashton Oldham, the bishop of Albany, New York, had been a principal figure in the World Alliance, and of course both Franklin and Eleanor Roosevelt were active lay members. The Northern Baptists had one of the strongest denominational programs of international commitment by 1945 but, though in close touch, they were not members of the FCC. Cooperation with the Catholic hierarchy remained considerably less warm than with members of religious orders, in particular the Jesuits.

It was the Presbyterians and Methodists in the United States who were the mainstays of the whole CJDP project. This was not only due to their leaders; it was also that they were specially able to conceive the place of Christianity in the world order in ways congenial to their theological traditions, spiritual temperaments, and social constituencies. Those who came from the Reformed tradition of Protestantism were undoubtedly the intellectual powerhouse of the World Council of Churches (WCC), but the special contribution of American Methodists deserves to be highlighted.

Perhaps having been so prominent in the organization that delivered prohibition to a less than grateful country, and its having failed, they were ready to use their campaigning talents for a better world in a less personally intrusive cause.[1] Van Kirk was a Methodist through and through, even when he was not acting to represent "international justice and goodwill" among the Protestant churches. He and his colleagues were not generally convinced by any dogmatic claim that "gospel" is utterly alien to "world." Whenever in the CJDP there was financial anxiety, the generosity of the Methodist churches could be relied on. It was the Methodist feeling of responsibility to help fellow human beings that gave the necessary warmth and persuasive power to the mobilization of general lay Protestant opinion. Local Methodists were especially likely to be also members of Rotary and YMCA and other community organizations.

One of the most influential voices in molding Protestant opinion in favor of committing America to make a new and better world organization was *The Methodist Woman*[2] (whose first issue of September 1940 flew the flag of opposition to Hitler as a faith commitment). One of the most substantial figures in mid-twentieth-century Protestantism, Bishop G. Bromley Oxnam,[3] gave the keynote address in July 1941 to a Methodist World Peace Commission conference, and he is reported as sounding the chords of subsequent CJDP policy: "economic foundations of a just and enduring peace," "status of colonial peoples," "that unlimited national sovereignty as now practiced is outmoded was taken for granted," "local federations such as the United States of Europe . . . nevertheless subject to the all-inclusive world body." In November it is stated that "persisting in the nation-state complex means . . . more devastating wars. The change cannot be accomplished unless public opinion is aroused"; and a contributor declares "the Church of Christ should see through the morning mists of rank nationalism and racial pride."

That American churches themselves had a race problem was an accusation that *The Methodist Woman* was to continue to hammer home—with some courage, granted the number of segregated Methodist congregations. Thelma Stevens, herself from the South, was an outstanding advocate of this cause in her regular column as executive secretary of the Department of Christian Social Relations and Local Church Activities. Lists of "timely books" on world affairs abound. By November 1943, the phrase "the price of peace" had entered the Methodist bloodstream, and Florence Gordon was writing on its "racial price" and on "something women can do today."

The December 1943 issue of *The Methodist Woman* marked the launch of the remarkable "Crusade for a New World Order" led by the Methodist Council of Bishops. This was serious mobilization—declared somewhat disingenuously to be nonfinancial, nonpolitical, and nonprogrammatic. It began with an account of the week in February that the council had spent in Washington. It had met not only the president but also Madame Chiang Kai-shek (a heroine at this time for *The Methodist Woman*) and other "important leaders." The council's agenda was to "discover what the religious forces of the country might do to secure a peace that would endure and insure a Christian social order throughout the world." The bishops found Washington full of conflicting notions; our "leaders are gravely concerned, and the situation will be determined by public opinion." So the bishops appointed a commission to draft the plans that became the "Crusade." A few weeks later, Roosevelt wrote to Oxnam: "I like the sentence in your letter in which you say 'We are resolved to translate these ethical ideals into the realities of world order, economic justice and racial brotherhood.'"[4]

The crusade got to parts in the body politic not often reached by churches. It involved sending out printed materials by January 1, 1944, to the executive team in every parish that would be responsible: "The president of the Women's Society of

Christian Service and the charge lay leader in co-operation with the pastor." In the latter half of the month, there were to be "inspirational meetings" in major centers. These would feature special music, "pictures of the Crusade painting 'The Coming Peace and the Prince of Peace' by the famous artist Howard Chandler Christy" and personal cards sent from them to local men and women on active service. On Sunday, January 30, "every Methodist minister will be requested to preach on 'The Crusade for a New World Order.'" From that afternoon, and during the week following, lay men and women were "to go out two by two to call upon the membership of the church." It is not surprising that Bromley Oxnam's vivid description of this event and his consequent estimation of the potential place of global matters in ordinary Christian discipleship should, he believed, have turned opinion at the WCC's Girton Conference of August 1946 in favor of establishing the Commission of the Churches on International Affairs.

TEACHERS' COLLEGE

Union Theological Seminary, Columbia University (including its Teachers' College), and Rockefeller's great ecumenical Riverside Church complex are almost "Oxbridge" in their neighborliness on uptown Broadway in New York. And the national offices of churches, associations, and mission bodies (and of Dulles's law firm) are easily accessible downtown in Manhattan. The epicenter of ecumenical thinking about the postwar world in the war years was here.[5] Its leaders were a small group.

Teachers' College had a specially influential role. In the interwar period, it enjoyed a status in this academic grouping that was quite unlike education faculties elsewhere. The names of John Dewey, W. H. Kilpatrick, George Counts,[6] and George Coe[7] were known around the world, and were reinforced in the 1930s by education-oriented social scientists fleeing from Germany. There were close personal links with Protestant practice, even when that practice had been rejected.

It is evident that the great tide of progressive education, an academic field in which North Americans were leading players from the beginning of the twentieth century, was likely to favor Roosevelt's definition of war aims as Four Freedoms. Such principles as: the definition of education as centered on students' needs; the respect for what potential could be nurtured in each individual; the coeducation of boys and girls through to professional formation; the excitement of self-motivated and self-paced discovery of truths through experience; and, not least, the recognition that the quality of relationships both inside the school and outside with its community is crucial to the education of whole persons—all of these marked a post–World War I revolution.

If twentieth-century human rights is a doctrine that rests on protecting (in Maritain's word) the "blossoming" of human potential, it emerged in the 1940s from these new educational theories. Rousseau's *Emile* similarly had had political consequences for 1789. They were self-consciously scientific as well as philosophical. Educational journals became filled with statistics. As a science, pedagogic findings were applicable universally in every discipline and culture.

Religions that stressed particular revelations found this development required difficult adjustments of their practice. Top-down rote learning of biblical texts under untrained teachers had been the common experience of Protestant children; and no text was more faithfully practiced in the home than "Spare the rod and spoil the child." Because Sunday Schools had been and remained the principal institution of American Protestantism, their future was necessarily a prime concern for church leaders, and a source of controversy. Teaching about sin (whether original or sexual) began to divide congregations and lose popular conviction as sub-Freudian vocabulary entered everyday life in the 1930s.

Tackling modernization of the Sunday School meant changing lay understandings of the interpretation of Scripture in revelation and of the place of conversion experience in normal religious growth, so that a well-regarded parish education program became in the 1950s "all-age." George Coe, Dewey's colleague, did not (like him) give up church membership, but with others on the faculty saw his own Christian ministry as transforming the understanding of education. In 1903, he was a founder of the Religious Education Association, which brought the tension between old and new into the open.[8] More pressure for change came during World War II, when chaplains to the armed forces complained at the puerile inadequacy of the religious education troops had been given as children. Contemporary church "Kingdom of God" talk irritated Coe. He was for substituting the "Democracy of God." Democracy was to be interpreted to become a central plank in the Christian gospel for the world.

Paul Limbert of the YMCA became the Teachers' College specialist in "character education" (which was the topic of Nolde's lecture course at the University of Pennsylvania) in 1931, when it was already ceasing to be fashionable. He saw his studies under Coe as having prepared him for the task: "Our schools exist," he said, "not only to transmit facts and figures but to communicate and instill values, to 'educate for democracy.'" This required a holistic approach, especially in the YMCA's education programs for young adults. He saw his "central goal" as forming "respect for personality" and "creative good will," and "making it possible to predict how an individual will react" in "growth toward accepted goals."[9] Such conative "goals talk" has echoes in Nolde, who saw the social and pedagogic sciences as primarily tools for attaining the goal of religious development—"the highest standard of relationship to self, to man, to God, to the universe."

The idea of model institutions as globalizing "mission" was commonplace in the nineteenth century. The most effective way of changing traditional hygiene practices and local religions was by planting accessible exemplars of best practice as widely as possible. The practice might be either technical (as in model farms) or communitarian (as in Robert Owen's New Harmony, Ind., or in Benedictine monasteries—"colonies of heaven" they were called). Mission stations in Africa shared both ambitions. The Christian notion of a proleptic group—now here and few, tomorrow everywhere and everybody—had been taken up by Marxists as the "vanguard of the proletariat," and given a historic mission. There was an element of this among Teachers' College educators, with "demonstration schools." It had been a strong tradition in English "established church" religion. Rugby School had been shaped by Thomas Arnold as a tool of national mission. The colleges of Oxford and Cambridge in the 1890s were pictured as examples of Christian community and workshops for changing the world through elites.[10] A school is the principal model a local community has available to it for social change.

A representative Teachers' College man, F. Ernest Johnson,[11] was a central and long-term member of the FCC staff. He served in the Research and Education Department of the FCC from 1918, and from 1924 (the year before Van Kirk joined as international secretary) as its executive secretary and as editor of the FCC *Information Service*, until retirement in 1952. He and Warnshuis[12] (New York secretary of the International Missionary Council, or IMC) were the two initiators and continuing pillars of the Joint Committee on Religious Liberty (JCRL), which became under Nolde the instrument of church pressure for human rights. Like Van Kirk, Johnson was a Midwestern Methodist. And to complete the pattern, he had directed an international survey on behalf of the YMCA and YWCA in 1929–31 and attended the Oxford conference in 1937. He was professor of education on the faculty of Teachers' College, principally teaching philosophy, from 1929 to 1950, and president of the Religious Education Association from 1944 to 1946. It is clear that in the late 1920s, like so many on the faculty, he was not so much attracted politically to communism as concerned to follow the progress of the Russian experiment to use education to make a "new Soviet man" with thoroughly communitarian values. His writings had a strong "social gospel" thrust, and it is no surprise that he was invited to give the Rauschenbusch Lectures in 1939.

Comparable sympathies were commonplace among 1930s ecumenical leaders with regard to the building of a Christianly acceptable "good society." The faculty colleague of Limbert's at Teachers' College who captured his imagination was George S. Counts, and in particular Counts's manifesto, *Dare the School Build a New Social Order?* (1932). This split the Progressive Education Association. Counts had become critical of the political pressures on city schools in America, and what he saw as teachers taking refuge in the safety of methodology and scientism, when civilization was breaking down. He proposed a "socially oriented" rather than a "child-centered" school, for the latter worked "from a misleading conception of the nature of human freedom." Culture required a taught tradition, and "without such a tradition, the condition of freedom was that of mediocrity, incompetence, and aimlessness."[13] His call to the America of the Depression was to substitute "human rights for property rights." His "new social order" is a working out in practice of the Deuteronomic divine injunction to "choose good," but (he wrote), "there can be no good individual apart from some conception of the character of the good society; and the good society is not something that is given by nature: it must be fashioned by the hand and brain of man."[14]

The social engineering aspect of the churches proposing the goal of "writing the peace" was patently there. It cannot be ignored. However, its main thrust was not a religiously self-deluded Pollyanna optimism or one based on "blank slate" psychology. It was (like so much in the first decades of the WCC) an open-eyed assumption of responsibility by Christian churches for action in the world as it is. There was considerable respect both for the findings of the social sciences and for the wisdom of those with practical experience of the measures and structures required to guard against ever-to-be-anticipated human imperfections.

THE LAY ASSOCIATIONS

Pride of place in moving opinion forward in a purposeful way has to be given to the three great lay associations of global Protestantism: the YMCA, the YWCA, and the World Student Christian Federation (WSCF). In the United States (unlike national Student Christian Movements, or SCMs, in Great Britain, Australia, and New Zealand), there was scarcely an organizational distinction between these affiliations. For instance, the *Inter-Collegian* student journal had strong links to the YMCA.

These three associations had become indigenized in many different cultures, and their leadership cadres were thoroughly internationally minded by the 1930s. Because they were locally led, and engaged in clearly welcome provision for young people, the YMCA in particular was accepted in a way missions generally were not. The 1932 *Laymen's Report* on mission—notorious in the eyes of many theologians— was to a substantial degree inspired by YMCA and YWCA ideas. John Mott, the world's "Mr. YMCA" and "Mr. WSCF" for two generations, was the assurance of apostolic continuity on the platforms of all ecumenical conferences up to and including Amsterdam in 1948.

But it was the robust good-citizenship ideals of the YMCA—Jesus as the model of a living discipleship, care for healthy bodies, learning teamwork, service to the community, education for civic responsibility, a sense of the inclusive brotherhood of all peoples—that undergirded so much of the early wartime Protestant commitment to a better postwar world. And as Paul Limbert remarked,[15] their network of local associations across the world had a special contribution to make in any attempt by the churches to form opinion; for their strength was where church attendance constituencies were normally weakest, among young males of the skilled working class.

The leaders of the Committee on Public Affairs of the National Board of American YMCAs were from two age cohorts.[16] Its chair at the outbreak of war, Archie E. McCrea, was editor of the *Muskegon* [Mich.] *Chronicle* and had been a member of the National Council since 1926. As early as 1940, McCrea and the committee's secretary (J. Edward Sproul of Ridgewood, N.J.) sent all YMCA program committees a four-page memorandum headed "Urgent." It asked what they were "doing to help young people in your Association and your community to think clearly and objectively about the meaning of the European War and its meaning for America." They gave hints on how to organize groups, recommended magazine articles (including

WCC material), and encouraged associations to invite speakers. Above all, they were anxious that members in every locality get facts on current world affairs and be trained to see through propaganda. The YMCA was perhaps the first nationwide institution to embark on such a program.

Limbert and Wesley F. Rennie were leaders in a younger cohort, who took Mott's internationalist concerns aboard in a more sophisticated way. Limbert (1897–1998), born in rural Pennsylvania, was ordained as a minister in the Reformed Church. His career was in community education. At the age of 101, he was still serving as an active president of his local UN Association branch in North Carolina. Remarkably, in a generation of Protestants profoundly influenced by Kierkegaard's individual existentialism, Limbert took Bishop N. F. S. Grundtvig more seriously. Grundtvig[17] had been in the opposing corner from the "gloomy Dane." His inspiration of "folk high schools" to educate citizens "for life" had been the origin of the familiar community institutions of twentieth-century Scandinavian social democracy.

Limbert had studied at Teachers' College and been influenced by Coe, who was prominent in YMCA and SCM literature in the late 1930s. Coe's "marks of a well-educated man" were often quoted. Their final thrust was: "This is and ought to be a rapidly changing world, and the prime function of educated men and women is to make appropriate social changes." In the later years of Limbert's time as professor of education (1939–43) at the YMCA's national Springfield College in Massachusetts, he was seconded to work half time, and then full time, in program services at the national office mobilizing opinion. From 1946 to 1952, he returned to Springfield as president, and then went to Geneva as general secretary of the World's Alliance of YMCAs.

Rennie (1893–1974) was by contrast a professional YMCA organizer. He came from the Midwest, but his base was Seattle, which in the war years exploded into a high-technology manufacturing center. A contemporary account describes him presiding over a YMCA of extraordinary reach and vigor, a model association that would, a writer in the *Toledo Blade* declared, "make a beehive look like a lot in a cemetery." He was a man whom everybody knew, the leader of a group of a dozen men in the city known as "Rennie's Lambs," who met in one of their homes monthly "deciding what is good for Seattle, for the state, for the nation, and, I judge, for the world." Rennie began there in 1916 as Boys Work Secretary and in 1933 became its general secretary.[18] Presumably his own interest in international affairs (as well as support from his local committee) led to the first of many visits overseas in 1930—to Europe—preparatory to the 1931 World's Conference of YMCAs in Cleveland.

In 1936–37 he traveled the world on his way to the YMCA World's Conference at Mysore. A remarkable letter from John Mott spells out the "front-line importance" of the "real life-work" to which Rennie was already being seen as called.[19] His Seattle colleagues could hardly not release him for it. He went on to represent the YMCA at the turning-point meetings (e.g., San Francisco, 1945; Girton, 1946; Amsterdam, 1948—where he had no hesitation in attacking Karl Barth's address) and to become a member of the Commission of the Churches on International Affairs and the

YMCA's accredited consultant to the UN. He had extended study periods in Europe in 1946 on "The YMCA and International Affairs." At home he was president of the Seattle Rotary Club, vice president of the Seattle Council of Churches, and chair of the N.W. Region's Commission to Study the Organization of Peace (nationally, the Shotwell Commission) and its successor, the Association for the UN. His word carried democratic weight.

Another name of consequence rooted in the YMCA was Harper Sibley (1886–1959), who with his wife traveled the world as members of the *Laymen's Report* commission on mission, after attending the IMC conference at Jerusalem 1928. It is hard to conceive a more "establishment" (and useful) life, built on financial foundations laid by his grandfather, a founder of the Western Union Telegraph Company. His home was in Rochester, New York, where he was a member of the YMCA's Board of Directors. Among a multitude of offices held, he was treasurer of the FCC, a trustee of the Carnegie Endowment, president of the U.S. Chamber of Commerce (which he represented as a nongovernmental organization consultant at San Francisco in 1945), and president of Church World Service. There was scarcely a national YMCA office he did not hold, from president down, and he was chair of its International Committee (1917–50).

A figure more open to controversy was Kirtley Mather (1888–1978), who in 1946–48 was president of the YMCA National Council—after having served as chair of its Committee on Public Affairs. Mather was professor of geology at Harvard from 1927, and active in adult education in his community of Newton, Massachusetts. Echoing Coe, he had written *Adult Education: A Dynamic for Democracy.* In 1949, however, he was branded in *Life* as member of a "Communist front," and these McCarthyite attacks continued on him until 1953. Defending him was an unfamiliar—and, for the local YMCAs' middle-class lay committees, disturbing—obligation, but one of considerable consequence.[20] Red baiting clearly went against both the faith basis of the YMCA and its prized "open platform."

As America entered World War II in December 1941, Limbert, working from the national office, sent out a discussion paper—"The YMCA and Public Affairs." Scarcely more than half the local associations did anything at all in this field, though interest was said to be growing. He defined the field as "designed to fit men and boys as Christians for civic-economic-political responsibility." He saw the YMCA's special potential as going "beyond talk about citizenship and democracy to demonstrating the true character of group life under Christian auspices and giving its members experience in democracy" and "in the difficult techniques of bringing about social change." In October, the program executive had published Limbert's handbook *Educating for Civic Responsibility* as a product of his recent attachment to the national office.[21] Within a month it was sold out, followed by a second edition. The reading list at the end of the booklet was quite radical, including Norman Thomas, H. J. Laski, and Mohandas Gandhi.

Limbert stressed the educational brief of the YMCA, as a citizen's ministry of reconciliation and of reconstruction, to bring about "those fundamental changes in communities and nations that alone will make for social justice and lasting peace."

A sentence prophetic of the movement of Christian opinion inaugurated by the YMCA (and central to Nolde's achievement) ran: "We need to do more than state goals and ideals; we need to learn to understand and participate in the democratic process if we as Christians are to affect the world." This attitude led directly to victory in San Francisco in 1945.

The membership publications of the YMCA (led by *Citizenship and Public Affairs*, the newsletter of the Public Affairs Committee, edited by Limbert), pushed for consideration of the postwar settlement from late 1940. The April 1941 issue was largely devoted to "Christian citizenship and a new world order." It started from the seminar on "The Churches and the International Situation" held in tandem with the biennial meeting of the FCC in December 1940, which set up the Dulles Commission (i.e., the CJDP). In the following month, Dulles addressed the YMCA National Board on "The Christian Forces [a trademark Dulles phrase] and a Stable Peace." President Roosevelt's message of January 6, 1941, to Congress setting out his vision of "a world founded upon four essential human freedoms" and concluding that "freedom means the supremacy of human rights everywhere" was not only given editorial prominence, but associations were also encouraged to send for colored posters to set out on display—at $1.50 for 100 copies.

"Where does religion come in?" was an obvious question. A cartoon answered it. A youngish man, named "religion," sits before a window where aircraft can be seen in the sky outside on their way to bomb a city glimpsed on the horizon. He is writing "Principles of a new social brotherhood of brotherhood and justice." The title below runs, "His job in the crisis." The box opposite quotes from the FCC, disclaiming any identification of "the Kingdom of God" with "some imperfect structure of society," but claiming that "the churches can and should create the underlying conditions indispensable to the attainment of a better international order." Substantial quotations are given from the Malvern conference and from men such as Paton and Oldham. It is pointed out that opposition to Hitler's race laws is right, but then "re-examining our Oriental Exclusion Act and our Jim Crow laws and practices" has to follow. A shrewd point is made that any good businessman has to look ahead to the market in "five or ten years from today," so those responsible for YMCA programs "must take constantly into account the probable 'shape of things to come.'" Groups should be set up to meet and reflect—"call your group a Commission on the Post-War World if you like."

Rennie contributed an article, "The United States and a Durable Peace," to *Association Forum* in May 1941. From the failure of the League of Nations, he develops a depressing argument, both about any illusions that America could remain on an island of security in a world gobbled up by fascism, and about the quality and energy of current thinking about international affairs. To talk of peace issues among ordinary people is to invite active disinterest—"very little is heard regarding revival or reaffirmation of the society of nations or of any permanently satisfactory order of things." He aims to reverse this, in YMCA circles to begin with, and starts by asserting the "surprising" fact that "the man in the street" grants that the United States "should have been in the League [of Nations]."

He therefore proposes "the true solution of the problem of a permanent peace." He foresees an international police force strong enough to make disarmament "feasible and logical"; an economic role as essential for a new League of Nations; the United States "as a member and participating wholeheartedly as a responsible party to world order"; a path to independence for colonial peoples; and a new emphasis on regional groupings (including a federated Europe). Such developments would in truth be in the national interest of the United States as well as of the world. The practical "task becomes one of enlightening public opinion on this mutuality." The church, he concludes, "should press upon its people and the community at large the claims which arise out of the fatherhood of God and the brotherhood of man. These doctrines provide mankind the only sure platform for durable peace. They can hardly be espoused without a recognition of their logical international implications."

The CJDP's international affairs conference at Delaware, Ohio, in March 1942 included high-level YMCA and YWCA representatives, who made sure its conclusions were given publicity. The April issue of *Citizenship and Public Affairs* asserted that YMCA "interest in post-war problems is spreading rapidly." Limbert proposed this topic as a "current program emphasis with almost unlimited possibilities," and offered a package to help overworked leaders with resources and practical suggestions. A traveling field officer in this area had been assigned full time for the first half of the year to giving full-time advice and addressing conferences. From that point to VJ (Victory over Japan) Day 1945, when a sharp falling-off was noted, this program direction received a committed response.

With John Mott as its global-mission icon for the past half-century, and Visser 't Hooft having graduated from a career in the YMCA/WSCF to become the WCC's first general secretary, it is fair to claim salience for the lay-focused tradition of the YMCA/YWCA in this narrative. It could influence hundreds of thousands of voters in many countries. Many of them were not church attenders or, especially in Asia, Christian, or, especially in Latin America, Protestant. It was not only in itself remarkable, but politically important, that men such as Nolde and Rennie were to have such a wide international network of YMCA and SCM contacts and supporters to call on in their lobbying on behalf of a human rights–based "global order" in San Francisco.

Within the United States, the coordinated drive by lay and clerical leaders of the mainline Protestant "Christian forces" to produce an educated democratic majority for American commitment to a United Nations organization vision of global order in 1945 was an invaluable precondition for its political achievement. The membership constituencies from which they could draw ought not to be underestimated. It was the biggest organized family of voluntary associations in the country.

NOTES

1. A letter from G. Bromley Oxnam to the president, March 26, 1943, refers to this: "It was an unfortunate short-sightedness that prompted the Church to spend its full energy in a

single reform such as Prohibition; but to establish world law and order, to move towards economic justice, in a word to preserve our liberty, and to find the techniques to establish equality and thus move to fraternity, seem to us to be of greater importance, and we are eager to cooperate. This is not to say that we are turning aside from the results that are associated with the liquor traffic, not at all; but it is to suggest that the narrow interests of yesterday do not characterize the largest Protestant body in the nation." Library of Congress (LC), Oxnam Papers, box 36.

2. The campaign for Prohibition had given Methodist women experience of successful political action, and this is not a negligible factor in explaining their effectiveness in the campaign for a new world order. *The Methodist Woman* succeeded *Women's Missionary Friend, Women's Home Missions, Missionary Record,* and *Methodist Women's Association Bulletin.* It was the voice of the new Women's Division of Christian Service of the Methodist Board of Mission and Church Extension.

3. G. Bromley Oxnam (1891–1963) was born in Sonora, Calif., and after training at Boston University he was ordained as a Methodist minister. His academic interests were in social ethics and education, and throughout his life he maintained close links with the labor movement. He was Secretary of the Methodist World Peace Commission (1928–32) and was successively bishop of Omaha, Boston, New York, and Washington. He was president of the World Council of Churches from 1948 to 1954. His last years were marked by Senator Joseph McCarthy's vendetta against him and his associates.

4. FDR to Bromley Oxnam, March 9, 1943. LC, Oxnam Papers, box 36.

5. The leading figures in English ecumenical circles, e.g. Sir Walter Moberley and Archbishop William Temple, were active in discussions about education. Most had been formed in the English "public school" tradition with its commitment to the Greek and Latin classics as the foundation of a liberal education. The recasting of a national education system (which would include religious teaching) in the 1944 Butler Act was a remarkable preoccupation in wartime. The British Student Christian Movement's sustained high-level concern for education is one of the continuing themes in Marjorie Reeves's (ed.), *Christian Thinking and Social Order: Conviction Politics from the 1930s to the Present Day* (London: Cassell, 1999). See especially chapters 5 and 7.

6. George S. Counts (1889–1974) attended the University of Chicago. His first faculty appointment was teaching educational sociology. He had chairs in education at Yale and the University of Chicago and was professor of education at Teachers' College (1927–56) and associate director of its International Institute. He visited the Philippines and Russia in 1927 and Russia again in 1929. Gerald L. Gutek has written on Counts's contribution in, e.g., *George S. Counts and American Civilization: The Educator as Social Theorist* (Columbus: Ohio State University Press, 1984).

7. George A. Coe (1862–1951), the son of an upstate New York minister, trained at Boston University where he received his Ph.D. in 1891. He was professor of philosophy at Northwestern University (1891–1909), professor of religious education and psychology of religion at Union Seminary, New York City (1909–22), and professor of education at Teachers' College (1922–27). Coe was dismissive of the Oxford Conference of 1937 because he believed the Americans there had betrayed the cause of twentieth-century Christianity by accepting the dogma of human depravity. Coe to Edwin Aubrey, April 10, 1938; George A. Coe Papers, box 2, Yale Divinity School.

8. It was twenty years later than in America, in the 1950s, that British religious education began to take the pedagogic social sciences seriously. Edward Hoffman, the biographer of Abraham Maslow (1908–70), a central contributor to American humanistic psychology, chose as his title *The Right to Be Human* (Los Angeles: Tarcher, 1988).

9. Limbert, *Reliving a Century* (Asheville, N.C. : Biltmore Press, 1997), 79–80.

10. See Sheldon Rothblatt, *The Revolution of the Dons* (London: Faber, 1968).

11. F. Ernest Johnson (1884–1969) came to the United States from Ontario, Canada, in 1889 and studied in Michigan and at Union Seminary. He was ordained in 1908 and held pastor-

ates in Michigan and New York (1906–16). For three terms, he was on the American National Commission of UNESCO. His writings were principally in the 1940s and 1950s, beginning with *Economics and the Good Life* (New York: Association Press, 1934). In 1944 he edited *Religion and World Order* (New York and London: Institute for Religious Studies), and in 1945 *World Order: Its Intellectual and Cultural Foundations* (New York: Jewish Theological Seminary of America).

12. A. Livingston Warnshuis (1877–1958) was the son of a "severe" pastor in the Dutch Reformed Church of America, into which he was ordained in 1900. He grew up in small towns in the Midwest, and he spoke of his Iowa school classes in "universal [Whig] history" as important in his formation, and of how in his picture of Europe he thought not of Holland but of Wordsworth's Lake District. He was a lifelong Republican voter. He became a missionary in Amoy, China (1900–15), where he was much influenced by a visit from John Mott and Joe Oldham. He served as secretary of a national committee in Shanghai (1915–20). He was joint secretary of the IMC from 1921 to 1943 (from 1925 in New York), president of the FMC (1943–44), executive vice president of Church World Service (1946–48), member of the American Committee for the WCC, Executive Committee member for the Foreign Policy Association, and trustee of Nanking Theological Seminary.

13. Gerald L. Gutek, *The Educational Theory of George S. Counts* (Columbus: Ohio State University Press, 1970), 120.

14. Gutek, *Educational Theory*, 121.

15. Paul Limbert, "The YMCA and Public Affairs," December 1941, Kautz Family YMCA Archives, University of Minnesota, Minneapolis.

16. A representative grand old man of the YMCA was a Californian, Galen Fisher (1873–1955). He completed twenty-five years on the International Committee staff in 1922; went on to a serve for a substantial period with the YMCA in Japan, where he was concerned to "apply Christian principles to social problems"; returned to the United States as executive secretary of the Rockefeller Institute of Social and Religious Research, writing *Public Affairs and the YMCA*; and finally chaired the Board of the Pacific School of Religion at Berkeley, Calif. He was voted "Berkeley's most useful citizen" in 1954.

17. Bishop N. F. S. Grundtvig (1783–1872) and Kirkegaard have been the inspiration of the two opposing traditions in modern Danish Lutheranism.

18. Andrea Hinding, formerly YMCA national archivist, commented, in the context of the influence of educational theory on the FCC's international outlook in the 1940s, what a high proportion of YMCA initiatives had come from Boys' Work leaders.

19. Mott to Rennie, April 27, 1936, in John R. Mott Papers, box 74, Special Collections, Yale Divinity School Library. "In the light of this [Mott's recent attention to 'the program of the World Mission of Christianity'], I have no hesitation in saying that this coming meeting is to be without shadow of doubt the most important single opportunity which has come to our organization. God help us not only to see it, but to seize it! It is a tremendous responsibility . . . to shape the program for a period like the one before us for the youth and leaders of youth of all the nations."

20. See article for degree of the University of Minnesota, n.d., by Adele Cloutier, "Free to Disagree: YMCA Response to the Challenge of McCarthyism," YMCA National Archives.

21. This project was engineered by Sproul, McCrea, and Fisher and was funded by the Carnegie Corporation and the American Association for Adult Education.

CHAPTER 5

◆

The Joint Committee on Religious Liberty

THE FEDERAL COUNCIL of Churches (FCC) and the Foreign Missions Conference (FMC) decided in January 1942 to set up a Joint Committee on Religious Liberty (JCRL). This was a small but important group, often with its ex officio staff members from the parent bodies outnumbering voting members at its meetings. The two sponsoring bodies had come together with separate presenting problems in mind. The FCC's concerns were in the conflict of ideologies behind World War II—national fascisms in Germany, Italy, and Spain, and the consequences for religion of atheistic communism, exemplified in Soviet Russia but a rising threat everywhere. The missions agenda was more widely practical: On what basis could a position be advanced that would discountenance the legal obstacles to Protestant church life in Latin America and in the African colonies of Roman Catholic European powers (and by extension in the homelands of these powers via Vatican concordats)? And similarly, what might counter the inflexible public resistance to Christian presence in Islamic territories, and the gamut of community penalties for Christian conversions from Hinduism in an India still under the Raj, but clearly approaching independence?

There is little doubt that the missions impetus was the stronger, at least until 1944 when Nolde was invited to take over in a new beefed-up role as its executive secretary. A. L. Warnshuis, the New York secretary of the International Missionary Council (IMC), claimed later that it was his initiative.[1] Emil Fischer (of the Lutheran Theological Seminary at Philadelphia, or LTSP, and nominated by the missions group) was a regular attender. Its chair was John Mackay, whose whole background before becoming professor of ecumenical theology and president of Princeton Theological Seminary in 1936 had been shaped by his experience of missionary educational work in Hispanic America.[2] The Free Presbyterian tradition in which he had grown up in the north of Scotland was that of passionate rejection of Constantinian "establishment" and of Roman Catholic tradition. He had been a major figure at the 1937 Oxford conference.

F. Ernest Johnson of the FCC was its senior representative and faithfully attended meetings—even outside New York. The importance of his role in the JCRL was analogous to that of Van Kirk's in the Commission to Study the Bases of a Just and Durable Peace (CJDP). He was a lay political radical close to Reinhold Niebuhr.

81

Like others in the 1940s, he saw a "third way" open, Christianly validated, steering between the unacceptable faces of "global capitalism" and Stalinism on display in the 1930s. It is remarkable how enthusiastically, for instance, Shotwell spoke of the éclat with which the United Kingdom's Beveridge Report—the "welfare state"—had been received across the world in 1943.[3] For Johnson, religious liberty was always only part of a holistic social program.

It was this tension that was at the root of the JCRL's creative role in international politics. The personal backdrop to its work was, from the FCC side, the immense attraction for contemporary academics and labor leaders in Europe and North America of Marxist-Leninist analysis, and from the FMC side, the missionary experience of increasing cultural resistance to proclamation of the Christian gospel. The former ideology was claimed to be universally valid (so nothing "religious" could by definition exist), because it was "scientific." The indigenous societies, whether in Mackay's Peru or in Cairo or in Lucknow, were now concerned to resist any apparent attack on their culture—essentially that society's group identity. Concepts such as individual salvation or religious truth claims or modern social developments were being rejected as disruptive. No change affects a culture more than religious conversion. For Mackay, the work of the JCRL had even more to do with propagating truth claims that were universal than had the work of the commissars. God and eternity were always in his mind. It was the marriage of this sharp edge to a more generalized outline of what were the necessary features of any "good society" that produced the Protestant churches' political commitment to a definition of religious liberty that led them on to universal human rights.

THE PROBLEM OF "CATHOLIC POWER"

There is no point in pretending that the work of the JCRL—so far as Mackay influenced it—did not share in the strongly anti-Catholic disposition of leading American Protestants at that time. This was not without relevance to their readiness to promote human rights as the grounding of a universal world order (but ironically, their own anti-Catholicism also illustrated an internal American Protestant culture reacting against perceived alien aggression). There was something paranoid in the air in this respect among most of the older leaders of the FCC in the 1940s. Particularly was this so in their response to President Roosevelt's decision in December 1939 to send Myron B. Taylor as his personal representative to the Vatican,[4] ostensibly informally and for the duration of the war. The initial objection was that an overtly diplomatic state-to-state relationship was, in the case of the Vatican, a state-to-church relationship infringing on the founding constitutional principle of the United States. Throughout the 1940s, there was a rising Protestant fear of conspiracy by Roman Catholic clergy in general, and in certain cities and professions in particular, to establish whole territories of political dominance. This led to a secret committee being formed at the end of the war, which commissioned research on Catholic advances in, for example, control in city governments, and ultimately was responsible for the publication of Paul Blanshard's *American Freedom and Catholic Power*.[5]

Mackay himself was convinced that a growing Catholic presence among State Department officials had led to an unflagged change in policy toward Latin America (and the exclusion of Protestants such as himself from consultation). This new policy was, he thought, so far as possible to send Catholic U.S. diplomats to posts in Latin America, and to arrange for distinguished visitors to the United States from those countries to be hosted by Catholic institutions and given a misleading impression of the strength of Catholicism in American life. Mackay's anxiety was based on his fear that this would lead to these visitors being given a false picture of North American culture, and specifically of the determinative force of its Protestant tradition of free competition between churches, "the part that religion had played in the political, cultural, and philanthropic life of this country." Falsifying the picture in this way would undercut Protestant missionary work in Latin America.

Curiously, Mackay did not see the irony when, later in the same letter of March 1942, he referred to his continuing contacts with Peru, where the previous year members of the faculty of the Catholic University had asked that "no form of religious propaganda should be allowed in Peru except that of the Roman Catholic faith." This was grounded upon the contention that Peruvian life and culture and aspiration were bound up so inextricably with Roman Catholicism that the free propagation of other faiths tended toward the disintegration of Peruvian nationality and life.[6] This was also Mackay's contention, that Protestantism held the place of privilege in the United States, and in its history. But he wanted religious liberty for missionaries to demonstrate the contrasting consequences, and to ask individuals what they preferred. His experience of educated Peruvians was, he argued, that very few of them practiced that Catholic faith that was available to them.

Put bluntly, many of those in the JCRL who made arguments for a way forward through a "global ethos" to a "global order" were more than a little influenced by the generalized folk convictions of English-speaking peoples. They expected that a free field for religious advocacy would lead to the choice of their kind of Protestant Christian presence in society as the irreplaceable basis for any economic "progress" or "democracy." Many felt that they had more in common with secular socialists than they had with the Vatican. The Enlightenment tradition had, after all, only forked into Unitarianism, Benthamism, and secular socialism on the one hand and evangelicalism, biblical world-mission, and associationist models in church and state on the other.[7] Both strands shared genes claiming to own modernity and truths that were true for all humankind.

A SEMINAR ON RELIGIOUS LIBERTY

The American Anthropological Association made clear in 1945 its alarm at the concept of "universal human rights" in the UN Charter, which would be adopted in 1948.[8] Australian aboriginal cultures have had singularly painful experiences, both from invasion and from protection. If there is to be no common destination, should every way of life threatened by globalization be preserved from corruption in a kind of no-exit game reserve (sealed away from modern media) as part of a "bank of world cultures"? If so, can its members possibly own that decision? What is to happen when a whole tectonic plate of humanity, such as Islam, through no formal process disaffiliates from what has been deemed by representative "world leaders" to be universal?[9] The interwar leaders of Protestant mission who saw the conversion to Christianity of at least the greater part of the world's leadership cadres (if not their whole populations) as the prime condition of a human rights "global order" did have some logic on their side. If, of course, the conversion was to be to "scientific socialism" of the Soviet kind, then—as Mr. Andrei Vyshinsky was to show in his powerful contributions to the 1948 debates—there was again a real chance of global order, derived from a doctrine of humanity that could allow no other grounding than the state.

The JCRL was able in a few years to integrate these elements in its thinking and produce a more complex and nuanced set of proposals that were friendlier to other traditions, such as those being developed in contemporary Catholicism, that were equally fearful of a Soviet-style solution. Broadly speaking, the first year of the JCRL was a high-powered seminar, and the second was the resourcing of support for M. Searle Bates in producing the substantial book on religious liberty that it had commissioned him to write.[10] The third year saw the extraordinary activity generated by the appointment of Nolde as executive secretary. The fourth (after which it was felt the job had been done) was the year that the JCRL was selected by the FCC to send Nolde, as an assistant consultant, to the UN Conference on International Order in San Francisco in 1945 to promote human rights (and with them, religious liberty) in the UN Charter.

It is remarkable how salient the religious liberty question was to the leaders of American Protestantism in late 1941. For instance, S. A. Morrison—an able man who represented the Church Missionary Society in Cairo—continued to press the IMC, through Warnshuis, on behalf of the Near East Christian Council that attention be given to the intractable problems of working in Islamic societies. Could there, he had asked in 1940, be some agreed-on statement on religious liberty included in the postwar settlements?[11]

Warnshuis spoke with Ernest Johnson, who he found had been asked by the FCC to prepare a paper on this aspect of engagement with Russia. They were enthusiastic in deciding to recommend to their respective bodies that these projects should be brought together in a joint committee (which, of course, had to have as its partner from the missions world not the IMC but the Foreign Missions Conference). This was agreed.[12] Especially important, it was also agreed that Johnson's research assistant, Inez Cavert, could give time to this proposed committee's work. As a result of her attendance as minutes secretary, full shorthand records were taken of some lively discussions. For example, Johnson met Bates and Warnshuis in March 1942 to make an initial attempt to "define the study" they had set in train, and plan its process.[13] There is no doubt that they, with Mackay (who was appointed chair), Van

Dusen, and Roswell Barnes were a core group personally committed to working on this question, and that they were all (considering their major responsibilities) surprisingly regular in their attendance in the JCRL's first year.

The first meeting of the JCRL was held on May 6, 1942.[14] Preliminary statements were made on expectations, and it was agreed that the primary function of the JCRL was as "a Board of Strategy for the whole study of problems in religious liberty." The agenda of this first meeting was understandably a diffuse "tour d'horizon," and it indicates the JCRL's starting point

The JCRL's settlement on the constitutional-legal approach as the way forward set the tone for its work, and it is the origin of its decision to follow the human rights–UN Charter–universal declaration path for securing religious liberty. Reference to law recurred throughout the previous agenda items of this first meeting. Those there were close enough to centers of power to know that substantial work on the postwar world had already been set in train by the State Department, and that the Shotwell Commission was well into its task and "had asked the churches for their counsel." If, therefore, the FCC and the FMC wished to make any input toward agreement on a postwar international framework for religious practice along this chosen "constitutional-legal" route, the JCRL needed to act at once. Any such action would have to be in language that could stand up intellectually and be heard by a wide range of professionals in the "public square." Personal contacts needed to be made with the groups already engaged in the field.

Certainly, diverse strands were contributed to that day's discussion. Very early, in "the scope of the task" agenda item led by Bates, he observed that, although his own approach had been "highly empirical," it "was important to have in mind rather early the possible relation of these field problems to a general body of principles of religious liberty." He suggested that "an historical study would reveal the multiform character of the problem," specifically with regard to where nationalism "has taken the form of the rediscovery of the national soul" and makes it "hostile to everything foreign," as for example in contemporary Mexico. So it remained a question of "whether or not these countries will learn from the present war that they cannot be self-contained." Then, under the item "Attempt at Prescription," the question was raised: "What should be suggested to the negotiators of the postwar international order as basic principles to be recognized by all countries?" recognizing that a platonic ideal was one thing, but that the situations where the church had to carry on its work (where these principles, even in the United States, were "not granted or operative") were another. Fundamental questions were then raised. For example, the relevant decisions would be taken not by church leaders, but by politicians, so the "inwardness" of specifically theological assertions about Christian liberty—close to Mackay's concern—could only with difficulty be accommodated.[15] And should they work for a "Charter of Religious Liberty," recognizing that there was much less agreement in this field than over civil issues, or would it be preferable to include their concerns in a general package of human rights? And, fascinatingly, the thought was advanced that the religions of the world should themselves come together to agree on a position on religious liberty, and that the monitoring of this should be put into the hands of a world bureau, on the analogy of the International Labor Organization. Some telling criticisms were included in observations on the "Basis of 'Rights.' "[16]

Altogether, the impression lingers of not always conscious tension within members of the group between conviction that a universally valid frame for human religious liberty was available (if it could only be discovered) and professional familiarity with the variety of practical difficulties and philosophical uncertainties that governed any specific case known to them. It is perhaps at this point that it is appropriate to mention the wide-ranging influence of W. E. Hocking, head of the Philosophy Department at Harvard. His pamphlet on religious liberty was distributed before the JCRL's next meeting on June 29. The minutes of this meeting give insight into the range of issues and approaches that would be the frame of the committee's work. Mackay and Fischer (and Morrison from Cairo) continued to struggle with how the claim to revealed truth within the Protestant traditions, and space for the experience of grace, could find acceptable public expression; while Johnson (with Norman Padelford,[17] a lawyer, and John Badeau, a younger expert on the Islamic world on the faculty of the University of Pennsylvania) constantly sought to limit discussion to what could be presented to those formulating public policy.

The members of JCRL had well-argued papers circulated to them for discussion in meetings during late 1942 and early 1943. It became an intellectually exciting seminar. During this period, there was constant exchange with the WCC office in Geneva, and with William Paton's group, which was working on the same issues. These were the months of the latter's extraordinarily warm and open relations with a group of English lay Catholics in London known as the "Sword of the Spirit," which enjoyed the support of Arthur Cardinal Hinsley. After his and Paton's deaths in 1943, this rapidly lapsed. But, however brief, it did have an effect and was not forgotten. Though continuing to be alarmed at "papal aggression" in general and local Catholic interpretations of religious liberty in Latin America and the Portuguese and Belgian colonies in Africa in particular, the JCRL began to seek a conversation partner among American Catholics. This led to an Interfaith Conference on Religious Liberty in New York on April 18, 1943, between a JCRL group and four New York Catholic priests.[18] Mackay, Bates, and Father W. Eugene Shiels wrote single-sheet drafts of what might be proposed for inclusion in a postwar charter. At the same time, in October 1942, that this was being organized, the Dulles Commission was also planning conversations with Catholic collaborators.

The FCC's biennial meeting fell in December 1942, to which reports had to be made. Mackay's presentation on the JCRL was brief, and it played down the deeper issues of religious liberty that it had begun to explore. That meeting, however, could hardly have given a more central positioning to religious liberty and the postwar order. Van Kirk's department drafted its "Message to Christians of all Lands." The opening paragraph asserts: "We believe that to us and our comrades in Christ throughout the world an opportunity will be given to build a new civilization." Notice is given of the WCC's intention to convene "a representative conference" at the end of hostilities to support a "world order consonant with Christian principles." Catholics and Jews, as well as the WCC and its national councils across the world, are co-opted to a project of postwar reconstruction that will embody seven "principles," which are spelled out at length. They were all radical, none more so than the first: "We believe that the United States must not hereafter revert to policies of isolation but must join with other nations in the establishment and maintenance of some form of world government."[19]

RELIGIOUS FREEDOM: THE KEY TO ALL OTHERS

Dean Luther Weigle also chose to deliver his FCC presidential address on the topic "Religious Freedom." He began from the common pre–World War I prejudice that religion is necessarily the enemy of liberty, noting the radical change, and pointed to a recent manifesto by a group of European Catholics living in North America (including Jacques Maritain, "the outstanding Catholic philosopher of our time"), published in *Commonweal*, August 21, 1942, where it was declared the issue at stake in the war was "the very possibility of working toward a Christian civilization." A recent British account of religious freedom was cited.[20] Then he mentioned the setting up of the JCRL, how it was preparing the "desiderata for post-war international agreements." However, the JCRL had not been involved in what he was about to set out, "the rights that may be claimed in the name of religious freedom." He lists nine such individual rights, twelve church rights, and two citizen rights. In a concluding passage that pledges the FCC's dedication to Roosevelt's Four Freedoms (almost to his role as a "good king" of Christendom days!), Weigle declared: "The truth is that religious freedom is not a special privilege which the state accords to folk of peculiar temper. It is a right which has entered into the very making of the state. Historically, logically, and in practice, it undergirds and sustains human democracy. Without it, all other freedoms are in danger."[21] This would not be the heritage of most of the United Nations as they prepared to draft "reconstruction," nor even that of large sections of the American population. There was much education to do.

Intense engagement within the JCRL in early 1943 led over the following months to an original synthesis. A paper of Morrison's, born out of generations of apparently fruitless Christian mission within Islam, was rejected by the editor of *Christendom* for the issue he was preparing on religious liberty.[22] Badeau, before being co-opted—as was Padelford—into the State Department, rebutted Morrison in December 1942. He proposed, as himself an academic Islamist, that the only way forward was to encourage leaders in the major faiths (including the Christian ones) to meet together to begin to develop a common position on religious liberty. He hoped that each faith would then be able (and come, over time, to be eager) to find supportive material within its tradition. Two papers from Johnson, and one from Padelford on the one hand and from Mackay on the other, with one from Van Dusen as a bridge, made the April and May meetings particularly creative. The goals of the JCRL were narrowed down to enabling Bates to produce his book as soon as possible,[23] and to working on what should be contained in the form of words that would carry the religious liberty agenda into the postwar settlement. There was talk of "charters" in these months,[24] and many were trying their hand at drafting.

The JCRL's major decision was to give up any plan for a "religious" document or for any drafts governed by declarations of the one truth of the Christian gospel. Instead, while fully taking aboard the theologians' contention that any properly religious liberty derives from living within an absolute, and their reference to Saint Paul's "liberty of the Christian man," they distinguished that liberty from what could possibly be the concern of an international agreement. As Johnson said, anything they came up with would need to pass Soviet objections. It was agreed therefore that the way forward for the JCRL's agenda of religious liberty was to work for the proposed international charter of human rights, and to establish within that, after cooperation with as many national groups and faith communities as possible, a satisfactory place for the protection of religion and conscience. This was to be Nolde's job description, and it was a major step to have taken.

It is rather ironic that Morrison, whose request to the IMC in 1940 for action had contributed to the setting up of the JCRL, should find himself greeted with a policy far from what he had in mind. It remained the case, however, that the IMC was a powerful player, so mission concerns remained high on Nolde's agenda during the preparation of the Universal Declaration. Among these were the rights of minorities (sadly left as "too difficult" in 1948), the right of conversion out from a closed community and, most tendentious, the right of foreign missionaries to "persuade." There was a pleasant exchange within the JCRL when a member referred to the "absolute right" of an individual to follow his vocation to go out and preach the gospel, which was countered by his being told that the Indian National Council of Churches had declared the "absolute right" of the state to keep him out. The JCRL had something of a tortured conscience about undomesticated Protestant missionaries who made life impossible for the mainline missions, but who—presumably—were entitled to their "religious freedom." It is to the credit of the JCRL members that they recognized many areas of folk Protestantism in the American South as instances of closed community, and in the following generation their successors experienced the resistance of established communities there to outside "missionaries" offering them—uninvited—a "higher good."

In effect, the package Nolde was to be invited to promote as a human right inherited three intertwined passions. Warnshuis mediated not only a ruthless evangelical—indeed dominical—priority for the world mission task,[25] but also the newly realized Protestant experience—not theory—that there is a genuinely interracial family of Christian churches in a normatively one-world perspective. Johnson, at bottom the educationist social engineer, put his giving of space for a free response at the heart of Jesus' Galilean ministry, and chose to see the future of the state not as the traditional threat to the church but more as an ally, the coming "welfare state" (and what human being is possessed of greater welfare than—from a rights-based living-standard—to have been free to respond in reason and conscience to the church's offer of salvation?).[26] And Mackay burned with conviction of the utter primacy in anything human of individuals entering (or not) the life of the one God; so that if human rights had any relation to that, they were important.[27]

December 1943 saw intensive discussions. The JCRL meeting on December 1 resolved "to appoint an executive officer as soon as possible to give his whole time to problems of religious liberty at home and abroad." The five functions specified made oddly little reference to missions.[28] The impression they give is that Nolde was in mind from the beginning. In a memo to Miss Cavert on December 8, Mackay hoped that Nolde would accept, and be in post full time for some years. On December 9, a JCRL meeting of ex officio members considered the issue. A foundation was being approached whose particular requirement was a Pennsylvania base for any appointment it financed. Nolde had said "no" when Barnes and John Decker (who had succeeded Warnshuis on his retirement as cosecretary of the IMC) had proposed a year's full-time appointment to him. He was and remained deeply unprepared to sever his connection with LTSP, or with the CJDP, of which he had become assistant secretary under Van Kirk in connection with the roundtable at Princeton in July.[29] But he was always ambitious and was quite clearly keen to take on this major development of his new career path. He proposed that he rearrange his teaching program at LTSP so as to give three days a week to the JCRL, without cost to it (apart from expenses).

The meeting was hesitant, overtly as to whether the job could be done on that basis, and there was no meeting of minds as to where the office should be, with the FCC or with the FMC—"if the executive is not an expert on missionary matters, some people would fear that he might neglect that part of the problem." Could a half-time secretary in Philadelphia nourish contacts in the New York–based church institutions and engage in the necessary travel? There are no public records of LTSP faculty discussions, but the decision to allow Nolde to propose his part-time solution (even for a year) must have been a serious one. It is hard to suppose that Emil Fischer did not play a part in them. The financial and faculty-teaching consequences for LTSP were never negligible and over the years grew substantial.

Little progress had been made by the time the JCRL met again on December 28. The agenda was twofold: the choice of an executive secretary, and Bates's book. Apparently there were difficulties because JCRL's parent bodies had not been consulted about its wish to appoint an executive secretary, which was strange for two bureaucrats. This headlong zeal argues both their personal enthusiasm for the project and their need to reduce their own workload by shedding the time-consuming responsibilities in networking for the JCRL that they had come to take on. Their search for funding for a full-time appointment had got bogged down. Richard Fagley had been approached and had refused. Barnes and Decker's opening report of their further talk with Nolde had stressed his enthusiasm to build on his recent work as secretary of the roundtable, his readiness to continue to hold himself available at the level of commitment he had indicated, his intention to work intensively into the subject in the following month, and his willingness to accept on a provisional basis. This straightforward solution to the JCRL's problem commended itself as the meeting went on.

The strands had come together. A role was created that Nolde was able to shape (as a volunteer) to his own vision, and to build up within four years to what was widely perceived as an embassy of the WCC at the UN.[30] When it had become clear that his post on the university education faculty was to come to an end in 1942, he had thrown himself into mastering the field of a Protestant contribution to international affairs, apparently from scratch. It was his organized grasp of the whole range of printed resource materials and the sureness of his touch in establishing authority to speak on behalf of the diverse institutions and factions that were always in play in Protestant life (not only in North America) that convinced the churches—and later, diplomats—that he could be trusted.

NOTES

1. A. Livingston Warnshuis was cosecretary of the IMC, with William Paton in the London office. He was a member of the Commission to Study the Bases of a Just and Durable Peace and was at Princeton in 1943.

2. The missionary work of the American Presbyterian Church was for many years directed by R. L. Speer. Mackay was his protégé. One of the great issues at the Missionary Conference in Edinburgh 1910 was the validity of Protestant missions in traditionally Catholic and Orthodox territories. It was only with great difficulty that the Anglicans there persuaded the group led by Speer that they could not remain present if proselytism of Latin American Catholics was on the agenda of the conference. This led to an unfortunate inclusion of the word "Christendom" (in its territorial meaning) in the Edinburgh proceedings. I owe this point to Dr. Brian Stanley of the Henry Martyn Institute, University of Cambridge.

3. Shotwell wrote this of Beveridge in the context of presenting the Third Report of the Commission to Study the Organization of the Peace (February 1943) to the State Department. Franklin D. Roosevelt Library, box 192.

4. Roosevelt Library, PPF 1628.

5. Paul Blanshard (1892–1990), a Congregational minister who became a Unitarian, was active in left-wing movements for industrial democracy in New York City. Blanshard's book was published in Boston in 1949.

6. Mackay letter to Cavert ("Strictly Confidential"), March 12, 1942, National Council of Churches Records, Federal Council of Churches Records, Presbyterian Historical Society, Philadelphia (hereafter PHS [FCC]), RG 18, box 66, folder 23.

7. Cp. Linda Kirk's discussion of the transition to "happiness" as the goal of Christian life in catechetical texts of the Genevan church in the 1740s: "Eighteenth-Century Geneva and a Changing Calvinism," in Stuart Mews, ed., *Religion and National Identity* (Oxford: Basil Blackwell, 1982), pp. 367–80; also Dale Van Kley, *The Religious Origins of the French Revolution* (New Haven, Conn.: Yale University Press, 1996); W. R. Ward, *The Protestant Evangelical Awakening* (Cambridge: Cambridge University Press, 1992).

8. American Anthropological Association, "Statement on Human Rights," *American Anthropologist* 49 (1947): 539.

9. E.g., Sir Zafrullah Khan, foreign minister of Pakistan, famously spoke (at the request of Charles Malik) in favor of acceptance of the proposed Article 18 in the Universal Declaration on December 9, 1948, the eve of ratification by the UN General Assembly, arguing that as a missionary religion Islam necessarily envisaged the right of conversion. This has not been widely received by Muslims as their position.

10. M. Searle Bates (1897–1978) was from 1920 to 1950 "under appointment as Professor of History by the United Christian Missionary Society to the Faculty of the University of Nan-

king." He was consultant on the Far East for the IMC starting in 1939. From 1917 to 1918, he had served with the YMCA in Mesopotamia. He was professor of missions, Union Theological Seminary, New York, from 1950 to 1965. During 1943, when he was visiting lecturer at Yale Divinity School, he attended the Princeton Round Table. The JCRL book was *Religious Liberty: An Inquiry* (New York and London: International Missionary Council, 1945) .

11. Morrison circulated "A Charter of Freedom," April 8, 1940: "The experts of the IMC should begin now to work out in detail the contents of such a Charter, and visualize the machinery necessary for making it effective." PHS (FCC), RG 18, box 66, folder 24.

12. The history of the JCRL is summarized in a "Report" of December 31, 1943, that leaves its agenda subsumed in the completion of Bates's book (whose outline is attached). PHS (FCC), RG 18, box 66, folder 24.

13. Warnshuis wanted to bring in Professor Chamberlain, with whom he had already been in touch over the early stages of the American Law Institute's "Essential Human Rights" project. PHS (FCC), RG 18, box 66, folder 14.

14. Extracts from the minutes of this meeting can be found in appendix C.

15. Minutes of the JCRL, May 6, 1942, 6–7. PHS (FCC), RG 18, box 67, folder 2.

16. Minutes of the JCRL, May 6, 1942, 6–7. PHS (FCC), RG 18, box 67, folder 2.

17. Norman J. Padelford (d. 1982), a Congregationalist, was professor of International Law at the Fletcher School, Tufts University (1936–44) and of Political Science at the Massachusetts Institute of Technology from 1945. He was a consultant at the State Department (1942–46 and 1948–49), and a U.S. delegate to the Dumbarton Oaks Conference in 1944 and to the UN Conference on International Organization in 1945.

18. The two groups were, first, the Rev. George Ford (Roman Catholic chaplain, Columbia University), Fr. Gerald Walsh (editor of *Thought*, Fordham University), Fr. W. Eugene Shiels (editor of *America*), and Fr. E. Harold Smith (Corpus Christi Catholic Church, West 121st St., New York); and, second, from the JCRL, Barnes, Bates, Johnson, Mackay, and Warnshuis.

19. John A. Mackay Papers, box 15, Special Collections, Princeton Theological Seminary Libraries (PTS).

20. William Temple chaired the British Commission of the Churches for International Friendship and Social Responsibility, whose statement ran "religious freedom must include, both for individuals and for organized bodies, liberty to worship, preach and teach according to conviction, the right of public witness, and freedom to bring up children in the faith of their parents; and it should definitely include the right of individuals to enter or leave a religious community or to transfer from one to another, for a man has no true religious freedom if he is free only to remain in the religious community in which he was born." Weigle, "Religious Freedom," p. 2, Mackay Papers, box 40, PTS.

21. Weigle, "Religious Freedom," Mackay Papers, box 40, PTS.

22. In the spring issue of 1944, vol. 9, no. 2, pp. 180–94, there was a long article by Johnson titled "Religious Liberty."

23. Bates's book grew from private and short, as in his discussions with Johnson at the setting up of the JCRL, to a large and weighty publication in 1945 with a world distribution.

24. There are in the Mackay Papers drafts from this time, not only from Mackay, Bates, and Fr. Shiels but also from Padelford, Van Dusen, and Weigle. The one from the *Commonweal* journal article August 1942 is often referred to. When the JCRL was challenged for using Catholic drafts, the reply was that Maritain and Don Sturzo had best expressed the essence of religious liberty (though it was commented that while these Catholics were exemplary in their defense of democracy in politics, they failed the challenge of democracy in church life). Another list was that drawn up by Paton's group and the Catholic "Sword of the Spirit" group in London. In the JCRL meeting of September 1943, Decker, back from London, commented that he found that "no organized representations were being made in regard to religious liberty in Great Britain. Questions were dealt with on an ad hoc basis."

25. Minutes of JCRL, February 20, 1943, p.11. Mackay Papers, box 40, PTS. The minutes in the Mackay Papers are a fuller private version of what was said than the official minutes which are collected in the Presbyterian Historical Society archive.

26. Minutes of JCRL, February 20, 1943, p. 5. PHS (FCC), RG 18, box 67, folder 2.

27. A personal reference to Mackay is relevant here. Mystical unity in Christ was central to his faith. It is said that he was given a copy of Saint Paul's Letter to the Ephesians on his twelfth birthday, took it out on a lake in Scotland, and was so captivated he had to be called back urgently as his rowing boat drifted away. Ephesians is dominated by the idea of cosmic unity.

28. The proposed functions for an executive officer were revised six months later to mark the transition to the renewed mandate.

29. After Nolde's prominent role at the roundtable in July 1943, his first major task (and travel overseas) on behalf of the FCC nearly ended in his death. He had been invited to fly to Sweden in October for discussions with Ehrenström, but he had to pull out due to pressures at LTSP. His replacement, Theodore Hume, died when the plane was shot down. He remained very conscious of his escape (personal communication, Mrs. N. Nolde).

30. It is an insight into Fischer's mind that he set out his "two general thoughts" about the proposed joint committee in a letter to Mackay, February 17, 1942. These were: "The first, is the uncertainty with regard to the kind of world we shall have when this war is concluded. It is not at all improbable that conditions will appear which will require some statement on the part of the church which cannot now be anticipated. The second concerns means and methods of making the church's influence felt. We shall have to reckon with the Pope's plans for influencing the peace. Protestantism should have some strategy whereby it can assure itself of a hearing at the Peace Conference. This is a delicate matter to voice in public, but someone should be thinking about it." Mackay Papers, box titled "Correspondence," PTS.

CHAPTER 6

◆

Preparing for San Francisco

I⊤ HAS BEEN A rare luxury (or confidence that God, or "the historical process," is on their side) for states fighting seriously dangerous wars to spend time thinking about rearranging the world afterward. That was Churchill's feeling. But the Kremlin thought otherwise. So did the White House. So did Visser 't Hooft and his staff of five in the newly installed World Council of Churches (WCC) office in Geneva. The most doggedly maintained promise of the ecumenical movement was that its first act after hostilities would be to call a world conference on international affairs to take up what had been begun at the July 1939 conference outside Geneva. The Shotwell and the Dulles Commissions in New York were well into their work before the United States entered the war. They (and Roosevelt's State Department committee) were in touch with several weighty groups that had been committed to the same field. Christian churches (e.g., the Catholics and Presbyterians), Jewish associations (e.g., the American Jewish Committee), professional associations (e.g., the American Law Institute, or ALI), and university centers (e.g., the Princeton Group for the Study of Post-War International Problems)[1] all felt it necessary to establish their positions. This intense ideological preparation for the short postwar window of opportunity to remake the world makes the cold war even less surprising than it already was on "realpolitik" grounds. Without it, perhaps there would have been no cold war because U.S. voters would have quickly sunk back into isolationism.

Roosevelt began to take the thinking of the churches seriously during 1942. He remarked in the autumn of 1943 that there was a new sense of national mobilization. It happened to be the moment when the groups at work on the postwar world were publishing their findings and commending them to their constituencies. From the beginning of 1944, much energy went into mutual collaboration and mobilization of public opinion. When the moment of victory came, there could then be a widely agreed corpus of proposals to put before the U.S. government, and a body of voters convinced enough to press their democratic representatives to support them. On the latter point, there were no illusions as to the scale of the task. When Dulles later spoke of the central role played by "Christian forces" in securing the UN Charter, it is worth noting that their contribution was not only putting their own normally undisciplined divisions into the field. Their participation was also a key element

93

in raising other battalions whose common goals could express an extension of the American myth of constitutional history.

The decision of the Joint Committee on Religious Liberty (JCRL) to appoint Nolde—and Nolde's decision to accept—marks a moment in this political transition. When Mackay wrote to Nolde in February to wish him well in his appointment, his thoughts naturally ran along defensive lines. Nolde's reply was appreciative (and "somewhat appalled by the enormity and complexity inherent in the situation"), but robustly focused on getting a firm control on process. He wanted a list of what religious liberty memoranda had already been submitted to the State Department, with copies, as "the first step in the direction of co-ordinated effort."[2]

It soon became clearly understood in the JCRL, and therefore in the Federal Council of Churches (FCC) and Foreign Missions Conference (FMC), that the task for which it had been set up in its first term had been changed for its two-year extension.[3] M. Searle Bates's book, encapsulating unrivaled information from across the world together with stating the common position on religious liberty that the JCRL had so recently worked out, had still to be seen through to its publication in the spring of 1945.[4] But the effective brief from January 1944 was to use Nolde's time to the best advantage (also on behalf of the Commission to Study the Bases of a Just and Durable Peace, or CJDP) in contacts with the Shotwell Commission and similar groups such as the American Law Institute, with church leaders, and with representatives of government. Also, with the assistance of the FCC (which began to provide a half-time secretary and an office in New York), he was to collect a resource center of currently useful material—principally but not exclusively from North America—such as cuttings, offprints, journals, and reports, and of course stocking and distributing the educational study guides being produced.

The JCRL's will to do this continued to run ahead of its finances. Approaches for funding were continually being rebuffed. Without Nolde's volunteering his time, it could not have happened at all. He concentrated on the tasks he chose. He saw a clear need, from his CJDP experience, for someone to take a grip on coordinating Protestant church contacts with the State Department, and Van Dusen was emphatic that Protestantism needed to have an able man in Washington "to speak on its behalf." So even such issues as grievances from missionaries in the Congo and jealousies about Hollywood's consistently favorable picture of Catholic priests (which fed Protestant anti-Catholic anxieties) were relegated to the pending basket, not followed up. At the JCRL meeting on May 24, it was "agreed that Dr. Nolde should devote his time to contacts with the organizations devoted to human rights and with government, in preference to less crucial matters." That "human rights" had replaced "religious liberty" is a pointer to the way Nolde's mind was working.

In January 1944 the CJDP launched another of its contributions to public debate, a New Year message, *World Organization*, that introduced a new phrase, "curative and creative," in its subtitle and foresaw that the year ahead would have to turn "generalities about the peace" into "concrete decisions." On the basis of its "Six Pillars," it looked forward to a postwar international system that was not purely "repressive," to legitimize military actions by "great powers"—the dominant model for the Soviets at Dumbarton Oaks later that autumn. What was going to be needed would be just as much "curative and creative," and capable of flexible adaptation to a changing world in pursuit of such tasks.[5] Support of this emphasis was of course to be central to the churches' policymaking in San Francisco.

The president of the FCC, Bishop Henry St. G. Tucker (who was more personally congenial to Roosevelt than Dulles), wrote to President Roosevelt asking for a message of support in commending the FCC's Race Relations Sunday on February 13. He received a more than formal reply, in which Roosevelt laments the damage caused to the war effort and to the reputation of Christianity worldwide by acts of racist violence and bigotry in America. "Our hopes for lasting peace beyond victory must depend" on "the divine teachings that every day give emphasis to the spirit of brotherhood among men."[6] On February 2, Bishop Tucker wrote again, this time to ask if he, with the Methodist bishop Oxnam, Dulles, and the CJDP secretary, Luman Shafer, might call on the president to present him with the "Curative and Creative" statement. Roosevelt's memo to his staff was, "I would very much like to see Bishop Tucker and his colleagues," which he did on February 15. Dulles wrote to express the appreciation and encouragement felt by the CJDP.[7]

In the spring of 1944, the church bodies found their former situation reversed; it was they that were now being pressed for usable documentation by the State Department. The JCRL meeting of March 3–4 received Mackay's temporary resignation as chairman on health grounds. Warnshuis was elected, and reported that Emory Ross "had learned that developments in the State Department make it urgent to present a brief statement." The immediate trigger was current preparation of a treaty formula for use in relation to colonies and dependent areas. Nolde thought something could be put together for Ross to use on a visit to Washington in the following week, based on "the British Ten Points, Oxford–Madras, and the recent Inter-Faith Statement." Warnshuis, using Nolde and Bates, was empowered to draft. But then there arose the idea of a "brief statement of religious liberty," which was agreed on. The same subcommittee was to submit a draft to the FCC.

Nolde had clearly begun to get into his new post by the next JCRL meeting on March 31. His secretarial assistance was proving "very satisfactory." On March 10 he had accompanied Ross on the visit to the State Department about "dependent territories." They had spoken with Bunche, Gehrig, and Rothwell,[8] and Nolde had passed to them the religious liberty documents of the WCC corpus of tradition, and even a first draft of the proposed "brief statement," with illustrations of how it could be "translated into declarations." Avenues were starting to spring open. Miss Inez Cavert of the FCC had spoken with Dr. Levy of the Shotwell Commission and learned that its Committee on Human Rights was "not proposing to recommend any statements that might be included in peace treaties," but to call "an international conference to consider all these questions and some sort of continuing organization to work on them." Levy had wondered if the JCRL could "write a paper on religious liberty which they might distribute." He was not certain, but "he would like to suggest it to his group." In response to this, it was agreed that Nolde should "confer with Dr. Levy regarding the introduction of religious liberty into their study program." Not only that. Warnshuis had written to Judge Manley O. Hudson, commenting, "there was only slight reference to religious liberty in the report of his group on international law" and suggested that Nolde get in touch with a view to "the introduction of religious liberty into its program." Nolde needed no second invitation.

Nolde took responsibility for producing a statement, circulated drafts (including one to Mackay on March 15 on FCC note paper from the New York office), and put the resulting text to the FCC meeting on March 21.[9] This was passed on to the FMC meeting on April 12, and issued in both their names on April 22. There had been no indication at all, when the JCRL minuted that it should be produced, whether it deemed the statement important, or how it might be used. However, Nolde soon made the answer to such queries crystal clear. This *Statement on Religious Liberty* was the first major document for which he was responsible.[10] At the JCRL meeting of March 31, he reported how it had been shaped; first by Nolde and Barnes together, "then submitted to Dr Johnson, Dr. Van Dusen and three persons in the State Department," then revised and sent to all members of the JCRL. As a result, when Warnshuis submitted the text to the Executive Committee of the FCC, it was "approved without a question." The FMC seems to have had less say, but after an interval of uncertainty also approved it. By this time the JCRL had become fired with enthusiasm for what it had done. Barnes had sent a copy to the archbishop of Canterbury and the British Council of Churches, proposing that they get a British "weighty group" together to produce a parallel statement. The archbishop of York was to visit the United States and he should be involved in a conference on the issue. John Decker had sent a copy to Visser 't Hooft in Geneva.

Methodical deployment, once approved, was another demonstration of what were to be Nolde's trade marks. On the Saturday morning of its issue, a good time for weekend press coverage, Nolde accompanied Sam Cavert and Reed, the two top officials of the FCC and FMC, to Washington to present the *Statement*, with its definition of religious liberty, to Secretary of State Cordell Hull. At the JCRL meeting on May 24, Nolde reported that he had had a conference with Rothwell and seven State Department officials to discuss it, at which "it was evident they had studied it very carefully." Rothwell asked for clarifications, and how it might be applied in different countries. As a result, Nolde produced a draft "Memorandum on how the State Department might use the Statement," which was "discussed at length" in the meeting, and subsequently sent. The JCRL was very pleased with the progress now being made. Nolde felt there was now "a way definitely open for further consultation" with Rothwell's group and further meetings were being arranged. It was thought that this should be reported to London and Geneva. Plans were laid for waves of distribution of the statement: First, to members of the Senate. Then, to the "whole list of Ambassadors and Ministers in this country"—"with a letter putting the emphasis on the fact that this represents American Protestant public opinion." Then to members of the House of Representatives. And of course to the churches.

These approaches brought many encouraging responses. Senator Raymond E. Willis of Indiana had an address by Nolde inserted into the April *Congressional Record*. This had been given, "with the authority of the Dulles Commission," on "The Christian Movement toward World Order" to a Lutheran laymen's fellowship in Washington. Van Kirk was not idle. The first issue of a bimonthly *Post-War World*, an ambitious CJDP newsletter, was published in December 1943.[11] The FCC published an eighteen-page pamphlet about its work—"what it is and does" in April 1944, with a copy to the U.S. president.[12] With 140,000 local congregations and 25 million members of its constituent denominations, the FCC claimed to "hold a unique place in strengthening the spiritual foundations of our national life"— particularly so in the context of the dislocations at home and overseas due to war. Because it was a central agency, the FCC had been granted radio facilities over a national network. These programs provoked in response "an average of a thousand letters a day." The FCC had sent out the first religious program on television at Easter 1940. In publicizing the ways the FCC was answering the challenge of war, these programs gave the CJDP a prominent place—"a group of thoughtful leaders, both ministers and laymen of special competence in international affairs, are pursuing a continuous study of the kind of world organization for which Christians should strive."

At this time John Bennett[13] of Union Theological Seminary, who as by then chair of the WCC Study Department was well placed to speak, concluded a paper in *Christendom* by defining the post-Oxford 1937 direction of study characteristic of the ecumenical movement. There had been a "development of types of church teaching and leadership which lack full official authority but which can give guidance which has great intrinsic authority concerning concrete problems." He cites the Delaware conference of 1942 as an example. This became the model for much work to be done by Nolde, not least later on as director of the Commission of the Churches on International Affairs (CCIA). Reports from groups "appointed by the churches to study a problem and to formulate conclusions" have "great weight but that does not grow out of any external ecclesiastical authority but only out of the confidence that the churches have in the insight of those who formulate them. This kind of teaching on very specific and controversial issues should have an important part in moulding the minds of Christians. It may show us the way in which the church can take risks in helping Christians to make judgements concerning the very mixed problems which history presents, without identifying Christianity with their judgements."

For whatever reason, it was in the spring of 1944 that the JCRL became much less mission-driven. As Nolde was encouraged to swim in Washington's political waters with the Shotwell Commission and others, it became clear that the current on-the-ground church-based agenda of the mission societies would not fit easily with Nolde's sitting at table with humanists, Catholics, and Jews to plan a postwar world for humankind in general. At the April JCRL meeting, Ross made the points that the FMC would be unhappy for its links with the State Department to be confined to Nolde, and that the diffuse organizational character of the FMC made it a more difficult body than the FCC to represent. In the coming years, both the FMC and the International Missionary Council (IMC) were to remain yoked with the FCC and the WCC until their fusion in 1961, but there was a growing sense of grievance that the mission bodies were being taken for granted.

There are other signs of distancing. In the spring issue of *Christendom*, an article was published by Johnson titled "Religious Liberty."[14] He had after all been a core member of the JCRL since its formation. In the article, his whole thrust is to deny the missionary societies' position on any "rights" relating to missionary preaching and conversion. He sees the individualistic ethos of American Protestantism as profoundly inadequate as a starting point for serious discussion of religion. He requires contexts for any assessment of religious liberty, and he refers to the difficulty of disentangling a separate strand of "religion" from culture. In the end he comes down in favor of eventually putting religious liberty into the care of a world interfaith body. This approach was widely appreciated at the time in FCC circles, but not thought practical. At the July meeting of the JCRL, in final discussions of the text of his book, Bates himself "raised the question whether there was not too much stress on conscience" but "the general opinion of the committee was that this could not be avoided."[15]

Nonetheless, the distribution of the *Statement* proved helpful to the FMC. The "dependent territories" group in the State Department found it a good basis for discussion. It asked Ross to answer questions on which the confidential experience and opinion of the FMC would be valued. A fourteen-page report was produced. Circulating this within the FMC on May 5, Ross remarked how sections of the *Statement* were capable of being lifted into it verbatim.[16]

It was increasingly, however, the topics being worked on by the State Department committee on postwar international order that concerned Nolde. At the JCRL meeting at the end of May,[17] he reports that "there is a serious question how his time could be best used," and he refers to contacts in train with Dr. John R. Ellingston of the ALI, Manley Hudson's international law group, the International Education Association, the Shotwell Commission, and "a group of Negroes and Chinese whom Laurence Foster of Lincoln University is bringing together." The Canadians were invited to share in the JCRL's work. It was reported from Britain that a new committee on religious liberty was being set up, with Max Warren as secretary, with parentage similar to that of the JCRL.[18] This was active for two critically important years, before falling victim to the endemic problem of the British churches—financial impotence leading to urgent work being loaded onto (and accepted by) already busy individuals until they break.

June 1944 was a busy month, and not only for the troops landing on the beaches of Normandy. The State Department was having to prepare its plans for the four-power Dumbarton Oaks conference to begin in Washington on August 21, to draft proposals for the postwar world. Nolde began to be caught up into the heart of the debate. He wrote a piece titled "Religious Minorities in the Peace Settlement."[19] This ranged widely, and indicates Nolde's concern that an international court be set up with an appropriate police force. It asserts the necessity of planning an educational system for a cultural pluralism that was no threat to national cultures. Then, at the JCRL meeting on August 29, he reported on the publication of the ALI's *Essential Human Rights*[20]; that he had the previous week attended "an off-the-record meeting" of the American Civil Liberties Union human rights subcommittee; that 1,500 copies of the JCRL's *Statement* had been distributed; and that he had begun writing a course for high schools and a pamphlet on religious liberty for general distribution.

More important, perhaps, he had made contact with Dr. Levy of the Shotwell Commission and had rapidly found himself being asked to represent a churches' interest on its behalf. The commission's Fourth Report included a part III, "International Safeguard of Human Rights," published in May. This was followed by a meeting that Nolde was asked to attend, which proposed that the U.S. government be asked to convene a conference of the United Nations on human rights. Nolde was included in the delegation to present this to Secretary of State Hull. Nolde's involvement with the members of the human rights subcommittee of this commission from that point on became intense, and laid a foundation stone for his achievement in San Francisco a year later.

At the request of Rothwell's group, he had prepared the first of four memoranda on the *Statement*, on "ways in which [it] may be used by our government," for the meeting on May 26. He was asked there to give thought to any distinction between religious and civil liberties, and on June 12 he produced "Memorandum No. 2" in response. This is one of Nolde's most telling pieces.[21] It shows him grappling with the issues that had been debated in the JCRL in the previous year; but after his recent work with groups in law and government, he was particularly anxious to set the concerns of religious liberty in a frame that could make sense of them in a secular context. No absolute distinction between civil and religious rights was possible. But he wishes to make a practically important "relative" distinction. This identifies some civil rights (and not others) as capable of a special character when employed as the necessary bases for conative[22] behavior. Religion is by no means the sole field for such behavior; it can equally well be intellectual or political—wherever humanity has "objectives or areas of conviction." In these areas of human life, there is more at stake than in the "rights which have to do with the actions or functions of man in society." As could be expected, the rights to missionary presence and preaching in a foreign state pose a special problem, and stand somewhat apart. Nolde again seeks a ground that does not leave religion exposed; such a "freedom demands a broader base than can be offered by religion alone." He finds it in "the need and desirability for cultural exchange among the peoples of different countries," so he proposes "freedom of access and exposure to the cultures, ideas, and beliefs of other peoples."

Nolde's placing of the requirements of religious liberty in a conative or goals-oriented box of rights is interesting. That box enjoys qualitative priority. Something comes through here of Nolde as the university specialist in "character education." There is in it a real differentiation from the general "human potential" school of human rights thinking; neither is its emphasis quite the metaphor of "blossoming" used by Maritain. "Striving" may be more congenial—at least as a thought—to Protestants.

The position Nolde worked out in the summer of 1944 and the portfolio of interlocking roles in significant "postwar world" groups that he had accumulated were now a sufficient basis for his effectiveness at the UN Conference on International Organization (UNCIO) in San Francisco the following summer. He was confident that this position "in no sense minimizes the worth of Christianity," that it is advanced "on the basis of the inalienable rights of man," and that "Christianity can stand on its own merit and truth will ultimately prevail."[23] From this point on, there was no question but that religious liberty had become a cause wholly embedded in the struggle for a postwar order of international affairs in the key of human rights. The steps had already been taken to mutate the November 1943 Moscow conference's world of "peace-loving" states into an international organization that would be open to any state prepared to define its love of peace as recognition of spelled-out human rights.

What remained was to practice the management of persuasion, at which Nolde was naturally gifted (with relevant training and a capacity for hard work). He had become confident enough in handling his brief to operate freely at the highest levels in these far from straightforward fields, and to be trusted as their public representative by the Protestant churches.

THE CLEVELAND NATIONAL STUDY CONFERENCE

Two principal tasks occupied the winter of 1944–45: persuading the nation and persuading the government. One involved ratcheting up the programs already launched in church-related groups and through the public media. The other was crystallizing around the calling of another CJDP National Study Conference, in Cleveland in January 1945. This was to stiffen the resolve of the U.S. delegation to the UNCIO called for April 1945 in San Francisco in the belief that hostilities would soon be ended. The groups that Nolde had joined were anxious to make changes to the draft structure for international order decided by the four Allied Powers at Dumbarton Oaks (in Washington) and published in October 1944.

Van Kirk's department took the opportunity of "World Order Day" on November 12, 1944, to prepare a careful case that could be distributed via the denominational offices to members of all their congregations.[24] The first section asserts the purpose on which ministers in 150,000 pulpits will build their sermons: "to enlist the total strength of the churches behind an intelligent and concerted effort to achieve a world settlement consistent with Christian principles." The second lists six "spiritual" foundations followed by six "political and economic" foundations—essentially the "Six Pillars." The third directs attention to current issues to which Christians "must now be alert," largely the dangers of a lazy peace that would not be "curative and creative." The fourth points to nine "elements of promise," not least the quest for bipartisan support in the Senate for U.S. participation in postwar international institutions. The fifth suggests "what the churches can do," particularly in writing to their elected representatives. The sixth, headed "Church crusade for world order is already under way" recounts, impressively, what the various FCC member churches have done or are about to do, and also what was happening in other countries. Methodists had earned their place at the head of the march-past.[25] But as yet no Lutheran churches figure.[26] Nolde and others could only at this stage be "concerned individuals" in FCC projects.

Ammunition for the same campaign was being prepared by Nolde. He printed 50,000 copies of his fifteen-page pamphlet *Religious Liberty: Meaning and Significance for Our Day* with the notice on its cover: "Basic among the rights of man; Indispensable to world order and security; Helpful in the conduct of Christian work." Its final section was on what parishes can do, and what resources are available to them.

The Cleveland conference of January 16–19, 1945, was important. Wartime travel restrictions meant that only the personal intervention of the secretary of state made it possible at all.[27] The Dumbarton Oaks conference had ended on October 7. Its draft proposals for a "United Nations Organization" gave the first clear picture of a basis for discussion. The Cleveland conference provided a rare opportunity for a variety of groups wishing to mobilize U.S. government support for their revisions to meet and find a common position. That it was a Protestant church event hospitable to other interests may have contributed to the acceptance of Nolde's leadership in San Francisco in April. The month of November saw both the presidential election (during which Dulles as Republican secretary of state–designate faced unpleasant political accusations) and the Biennial Assembly of the FCC at Pittsburgh on November 29. This produced a statement, "Maintaining the Separation of Church and State," witnessing to the continuing semipublic alarm over Catholic intentions in the highest levels of the FCC; and a number of recommendations following enthusiastic receipt of the JCRL's report—for example, to distribute Bates's book and Nolde's pamphlet, and to urge the State Department to support an agency on human rights.

The CJDP organized its National Study Conference during September. It was to be in Cleveland because it was one of the few cities where there were no problems with color-bar hotels. A major innovation in current conference process was the "curtailing of speeches in the interest of group discussion." There would be prior discussion of the themes in local councils of churches. Two commissions were set up to produce a statement with recommendations; and this material would go to conference members in mid-December. William Hocking was to chair the "International Situation" Commission, drawn from the Northeast coast, and Walter Horton the "Peace Strategy of the Churches," drawn from the Midwest.

The JCRL meeting on October 20 sparked a Nolde initiative that outran its members' intentions. It arose from Nolde's report at the meeting that he had joined the Shotwell Commission delegation to Ambassador Edgar Wilson in the State Department on August 20 "to petition the government to recommend the calling of a UN conference on human rights" and that "they got the impression that the idea was cordially entertained." There was "extended discussion," and Nolde was asked to press "the State Department urging international action to safeguard human rights." Without more ado, Nolde drafted his Memorandum No. 3, circulated it to JCRL members for revision, and on October 30 saw "Mr Rothwell, Secretary of the Post-War Planning Committee" and submitted it to him under the heading, "Pertaining to Immediate Steps in the Promotion of Religious Liberty through International Negotiation."

Following his usual practice, Memorandum No. 3 begins with a listing of the relevant previous papers he is attaching.[28] It then expresses pleasure at what was public of the achievements at Dumbarton Oaks, and homes in on religious liberty "in its proper and inevitable relations to all other human rights." So Nolde presses the United States to put the "human rights and fundamental freedoms" acknowledged at Dumbarton Oaks firmly into the brief of the proposed Economic and Social Council as a specialized agency. He goes on to highlight the "moral and humanitarian implications," notably in adherence to human rights, of application for "membership in a world organization." This was followed by two suggestions: First, that the substance of the JCRL's *Statement* should be received into U.S. policy, for "our democratic tradition not only permits but compels our government to advance a position of this kind" in international negotiation. And second, that "international agencies and procedures" for implementation be specified in international agreements.

Nolde's report of what followed illuminates the chagrin he and others felt at UNCIO in the following May when they heard that the State Department had withdrawn its proposal for a Commission on Human Rights. In the aftermath of Dumbarton Oaks, he found his contacts eager to talk. Rothwell implied to him that the JCRL had had influence on the inclusion of "humanitarian purposes" and "human rights and fundamental freedoms," and that he himself favored the idea of a human rights commission under the proposed Economic and Social Council, which had in fact been defined flexibly enough to make this possible. Nolde was all for seeing Edward Stettinius, but Rothwell advised against, saying Edgar Wilson had been appointed special political adviser for this area by Cordell Hull. So Nolde left papers for Rothwell to give Stettinius, and to discuss them with him and Wilson. Surprisingly, Rothwell arranged a meeting the following day for Nolde with Wilson. Nolde told him the full JCRL story; at the end of which Wilson "seemed to concur in the feasibility of recommending a special UN Agency on Human Rights under the assembly," and urged the JCRL to submit "any criticism or suggestions"—both with respect to religious liberty and world organization.[29]

It was therefore with some government indication of policy support (and very practical help in warding off cancellation) that the organization of the Cleveland conference went forward. Van Kirk and the CJDP's secretary, Luman Shafer,[30] were active, but Nolde seems to have been given the major role in managing the preparation of documentation by the two appointed commissions. When the time came to prepare Cleveland's *Conference Message*, Bromley Oxnam chaired the committee, and Nolde was secretary. Nolde's hand is evident in the text.[31]

The CJDP's approach to Cleveland was based on the new practicality of its task. At Delaware it had set out "guiding principles," which had led to the "Six Pillars," and this in turn had been used to educate and mobilize opinion in favor of rejecting an isolationist future for America. After Dumbarton Oaks, there was something specific on the table to evaluate.

Subcommittees for one section of its report were appointed by both commissions in various locations (unusually, there was one in Nashville), and the results were edited to make two weighty essays, totaling fifty pages of typescript. Nolde prepared the section titled "Human Rights and Religious Liberty" (the priority of human rights is worth noting) and an evaluation of Dumbarton Oaks as against the "Six Pillars"; he concluded that they had been reasonably well provided for, with the exception of "autonomy for subject peoples" and "religious and intellectual liberty."

Also in the mail that Christmas came papers from three leadership figures, the one by Reinhold Niebuhr being particularly valuable. His assessment of Dumbarton Oaks had something of the school-report chestnut: "Pleasing progress, but should try harder." In the light of its development in San Francisco, it is significant that he could only see the proposed Economic and Social Council as a lightweight "enlargement" of the International Labor Office. He sees the proposals as "obviously a stopgap solution with no real security against either war or injustice in it. . . . It is an effort to transfer the balance of power policy from one which had its fulcrum in Europe to one which manages the forces of the whole world and which is manipulated by three rather than one nation." He concludes, however, "When it is considered that the nationalist and isolationist elements in America are sharpening their weapons against not the vices but the virtues of this agreement, it must prompt more responsible critics to caution. We must not allow our desire for an ideal constitutional system to play into the hands of those who want no international commitments at all. Yet we cannot accept the agreement as it stands. There are not enough constitutional guarantees of justice in it."[32]

The conference materials available in the New Year of 1945 gave a high-level presentation of the wide range of issues delegates were to discuss at the conference. The reports of the two commissions have a claim to be the best work for which the CJDP had been responsible. There was no fudging the issues where America itself was felt to be grievously at fault: the pervasive inequality suffered by blacks, and the price paid inside and outside the United States for unfettered capitalism.[33] The report of Commission II, "The Peace Strategy of the Churches," had a concluding section titled "The World Mission of the Church as Related to World Order" that can be read as a blueprint for the postwar development of the WCC.[34]

Dulles also presided over this National Study Conference. His opening address[35] was a passionate appeal—quite unlike him—to the churches, and to the American people generally, to commit the nation irrevocably to collaboration in a postwar international order, but with the condition that their eyes be open to the political maturity—unprecedented in their history—that that would require. A sufficient foundation had been laid in October 1943, Dulles claimed, at the Moscow conference, where it had been agreed to continue collaboration after the war through a general international organization. Any chance of building on this would be lost if Americans continued to demand feel-good paper declarations with high-sounding words, and then totally fail to support their elected politicians in the inevitably messy and inconclusive situations where such declarations might have cash value but in which other countries would also have their own ideas. American politicians' fingers had been burned too often. The price had been paid by other countries; in the case of Spain in the 1930s, "the democracies kept their hands and feet clean, but did so at a heavy cost to the Spanish people and in the long run to themselves." The difficulty for America "is internal. We cannot expect our Government to seek to co-operate on world problems unless that is what the American people want and unless they want it sufficiently to be tolerant of results which, in themselves, will often be unsatisfactory." And—a pointer to Nolde's future policy at the CCIA— "collaboration, to be acceptable, must be skilled" and sustained. The present opportunity was not one for playing games with "perfecting paper plans." His conclusion—"Christ taught that by self-development we could become channels for God's limitless power. Let us follow that admonition"—expressed very well the conative/vocational, striving, character that Nolde had put at the center of his claim for the special authority of intellectual and religious liberty within human rights.

The conference was a success. Its sixteen-page *A Message to the Churches* was published and widely distributed.[36] This recommended that "the churches support the Dumbarton Oaks proposals as an important step in the direction of world co-operation [and] urge the following measures for their improvement." There were nine of them. Three were specially relevant in giving a mandate to FCC consultants at UNCIO: "(1) A Preamble should reaffirm those present and long range purposes of justice and human welfare which are set forth in the Atlantic Charter and which reflect the aspirations of peoples everywhere; (2) The Charter of the Organization should clearly anticipate its operation under international law and should provide for the development and codification of international law, to the end that there shall be a progressive subordination of force to law; and (5) A special Commission on Human Rights and Fundamental Freedoms should be established." It was highly relevant to the postwar life of the ecumenical movement that the paragraph amplifying the churches' commitment to a human rights commission makes as its first statement: "We believe that religious liberty is basic to all human rights and that it should be accompanied by equal and unsegregated opportunity for all races."

In general, the *Message* was warmly welcomed in the churches and in the media. The *Presbyterian Outlook* recommended that "a copy be sent to all armed forces personnel so they could see how the folks at home felt about world order." A. J. Muste, the long time leader of the pacifist Fellowship of Reconciliation, felt it had sold the pass to "a military alliance of the big powers to run the world." The February 15 number of *Post-War World* was almost entirely devoted to reporting it. Attention then turned to Nolde's question on the agenda of the March 23 meeting of the JCRL: "What shall be the understanding of our relationship to the San Francisco Conference?"

THE ROAD TO SAN FRANCISCO

From the summer of 1944, when Nolde was invited to sit with the Human Rights Committee of the Shotwell Commission, until UNCIO convened at the end of April 1945, Nolde was allowed by the JCRL to define his (and its) work as relating to government. The Cleveland conference both gave Nolde, as representing the JCRL, diplomatic credentials on behalf of the FCC and the CJDP and also defined the objectives he was to work for at UNCIO. Nolde was anxious to bed these objectives in a common front with the Shotwell Commission, and in close contact with the ALI and its draft *Essential Human Rights*. After this group of lobbyists astonished themselves by their success at UNCIO, Nolde's landscape changed.

Particularly in the tumultuous days after UNCIO—with the first atomic bombs, the collapse of Japan, Stalin's grab for Europe east of the Oder, chaos and refugees everywhere, and a rising tide of anticolonialism—the new UN (yet to become an Organization) carried an unrealistic burden of hope. It was not a responsible moment for the churches to pull out from any care they could offer the infant they had helped to birth. So the JCRL continued to support Nolde's work. Perhaps it had little alternative. Nolde was after all not their employee. As long as he could convince the Lutheran Theological Seminary at Philadelphia that this area of work with secular powers, leading into work with the staff of the UN, was his vocation—as critical for the future well-being of God's world as he himself believed it to be—it would be politically difficult to stop him. He certainly convinced the JCRL.[37] With the Dumbarton Oaks conference, Nolde made the transition from being primarily a religious educator to developing his career as an unusually competent international diplomat; a member of a subset of clergy familiar enough in Vatican tradition, but in Protestant church history a shooting star.

Having secured his position as sole intermediary on behalf of the FCC and the FMC with the State Department, Nolde turned his attention overseas. With both Paton and Temple dead, it was hard to find a British interlocutor. He sent a letter to ten British church leaders via the newly established British Council of Churches, enclosing his JCRL Memorandum No. 3 (and his *Religious Liberty* pamphlet) to rally support for international church action on religious liberty "within the framework of the Dumbarton Oaks proposals" and to ask for information on what they were themselves doing.[38] This letter also went to his two roundtable contacts in Australia (who as a result wrote to Dr. Evatt, the Australian representative at San Francisco, assuring him of the churches' support for a Commission on Human Rights).[39] Nolde sent a letter also to all the national delegations to UNCIO as they were appointed. He sought out possible contacts; for instance a number of the Latin American delegations had members with a YMCA background. The Chinese delegation was especially open; indeed, it included a Presbyterian missionary.

It was, however, natural for Nolde to apply most pressure to the U.S. delegation. On March 8, he wrote to each of its members (copied to Rothwell in the State Department as "appreciative of the cooperative spirit in which you receive our representations") enclosing the JCRL's Memorandum No. 3. He recapitulated the

FCC's and the FMC's formal recommendations that an agency on "human rights and fundamental freedoms" be set up and a longer passage from the Cleveland conference. His concluding paragraph referred to the "substantial percentage" of citizens this support for a human rights agency within the Economic and Social Council represented; and asserted such a step to be "in harmony with our democratic traditions and principles." He concluded with what must have seemed to its recipients (and staff in the State Department) an unhelpful claim to inside knowledge: "I have every reason to believe that our United States delegation to the San Francisco Conference will concur in these purposes and will seek action to bring about the establishment of a Commission on Human Rights."[40] This confidence would be shown as mistaken when the conference gathered.

March 1945 was a time of frantic organizing activity. Rothwell, having been secretary of the policy-related State Department Committee on Post-War Planning, was appointed to San Francisco to take charge of complex physical arrangements for a large international conference in six weeks time. His absence from Washington reduced the weight of procommission opinion in the interim. President Roosevelt was anxious that there be a woman in the delegation and appointed Dean Virginia Gildersleeve of Barnard College. Dulles, who six months earlier could well have supposed he would be present as secretary of state, was appointed a consultant within the U.S. delegation, which included his admirer Senator Arthur H. Vandenberg of Michigan as its official Republican foreign policy spokesman. Dulles felt he had to resign as chair of the CJDP for the period of the conference. The State Department's great innovation—specifically from its group of Dartmouth alumni[41]—was, however, its decision to summon consultants from forty-two institutions of American civil society—the nongovernmental organizations. This changed the character of the conference and made it perhaps the first major diplomatic event to include a democratic element. In Secretary of State Stettinius's subsequent report on the conference to the president, he spoke of this as one of its most successful features. In other countries, too, there was hectic jockeying for an invitation and then selection of delegates.[42]

The FCC was informed that it was likely to be invited to send a consultant in early March; but arrangements were far from clear-cut. Van Kirk was nominated. Then one, and then two, assistants were invited. Nolde was alerted, to carry the JCRL concerns. The FMC had received no invitation, so James C. Baker, the Methodist bishop of Los Angeles, was invited late in the day to take the remaining FCC place. It was only on April 11 that Nolde received his official invitation. On April 17, Barnes wrote to the three on behalf of Bromley Oxnam, the FCC president, setting out their functions. Van Kirk was to lead with the media. Otherwise Nolde was given the substantial assignments; to "press the concerns of the churches" in human rights and religious liberty and to "call the attention" of U.S. delegates to positions taken by the FCC. The monthly meeting of the JCRL on March 23 indicates there had already been discussion of Nolde's role representing both the CJDP and the JCRL. It was minuted that his "competence has been established through a series of contacts with the State Department" and that "the churches are generally conceded to have a special interest" in religious liberty. Warnshuis and Barnes were eager to be empowered to offer him any help he would need.[43]

This same committee meeting had a full agenda. It seemed at last that finance could be found for Nolde's half-time New York secretary for the past year, Amelia Wyckoff, to be made full time. With the war coming to an end, items arose from many countries, including India. It is noteworthy how many were related to apprehension about activities of the Catholic hierarchy (though it is clear that there was increasing contact with individual priests, e.g., Fr. John Courtney Murray, S.J.). It was also the moment when Bates's book *Religious Liberty; An Inquiry*, the original JCRL brief, was on the verge of publication. In the event, it confounded earlier fears for its sales, and it was a resounding success at what could hardly have been a more timely moment. Decker reported that the National Council of Churches in China—one of the Sponsoring Powers—was especially looking forward to it, and that it had asked its government to support a human rights agency at the San Francisco conference.

NOTES

1. Four or five university centers became home to groups of refugee scholars of distinction from Europe. The quality of the papers discussed in the Princeton group was often very high. George Thomas, the first professor of religion at the university, gave a particularly insightful paper on April 9, 1944, "American Ideals and World Organization." John A. Mackay Papers, folder 39, Special Collections, Princeton Theological Seminary (PTS) Libraries.

2. Mackay Papers, box 40, PTS.

3. See JCRL Minutes from December 1943 through February 1944 for the remission of the question of extension and new definition of functions to the FCC and then to the FMC executive committees in January 1944.

4. The sections of Bates's book—*Religious Liberty: An Inquiry* (New York: International Missionary Council, 1945)—were set out in 1944: I. The Problems of Religious Liberty Today; II. The Problems of Religious Liberty in History; III. What is Religious Liberty?; IV. The Grounds of Religious Liberty; V. Religious Liberty in Law; VI. Conclusions and Proposals.

5. *World Organization* asserts "a basic choice," and favors an international organization "with American participation" which "in addition to such use of force under law as is a requisite of order discharges tasks which are curative and creative." It goes on to say, "[We] recognize that any international organization dealing with such matters may, at first, have to depend more upon moral than upon legal authority. But we do insist that international organization should be designed, not to maintain a [repressive] faulty world status, but to seek inventively to eradicate the political and economic maladjustments, the spiritual and intellectual deficiencies, the inadequacies of international law, which basically cause war." Franklin D. Roosevelt Library, OF 213.

6. Roosevelt Library, PPF 1628.

7. Roosevelt did not want to see a delegation led by Dulles after the Delaware conference in the spring of 1942, but he was anxious to receive this deputation to present him with the CJDP pamphlet *World Organization: Curative and Creative* in February 1944. Roosevelt Library, OF 213.

8. This may have been Nolde's first meeting with Rothwell. If so, it was important.

9. Nolde to Mackay, March 22, 1944, Mackay Papers, box 40, PTS.

10. See Appendix E for the text of the statement.

11. *Post-War World*, World Council of Churches Library and Archives, Geneva.

12. Cavert, the general secretary of the FCC, enclosed this to the president, April 18, 1944. Roosevelt Library, OF 213.

13. John C. Bennett (1902–95), who was born in Kingston, Ontario, was the son of a Presbyterian minister. After postgraduate study at Oxford and Union Theological Seminary, he was on the faculty at Auburn Seminary in New York (where Dulles's father taught; 1931–38) and then at the Pacific School of Religion in California (1938–43). From then until his retirement, he was on the faculty at Union Seminary in New York City, variously as Niebuhr Professor of Social Ethics, dean, and president.

14. F. Ernest Johnson, "Religious Liberty," *Christendom* 9, no. 2 (1944): 181–94.

15. Mackay Papers, box 40, PTS.

16. National Council of Churches Records, Federal Council of Churches Records, Presbyterian Historical Society, Philadelphia (hereafter PHS [FCC]), RG 18, box 67, folder 23.

17. Mackay Papers, box 40, PTS.

18. In the JCRL Minutes of May 24, 1944, there is an interesting reference to the joint statement by the Catholic "Sword of the Spirit" group and the ecumenical Protestants in London. This was apparently "drawn up but never issued" (presumably because of the hierarchy's objections) and sent to New York "with the understanding that it cannot be quoted." It was agreed that "Dr Nolde should have it."

19. This piece appeared in Reinhold Niebuhr's newsletter, *Christianity and Crisis*, June 26, 1944. At the end of the article, Nolde writes, "Within the scope of Christian responsibility lies the task of securing to all men their inalienable rights, rights which derive from the dignity of man as the highest of God's creation. Whether or not the hoped-for laws are written, Christians must seek, by processes of education, to bring themselves and those outside the Christian community to an appreciation of the highest standard of human liberty. In their own life and within the sphere of their influence, they must exemplify the principles of freedom which they are advocating. And, if need be, in the absence of protective law or a protecting society, they must be willing to suffer persecution for the convictions they hold."

20. PHS (FCC), RG 18, box 67, folder 2. *Essential Human Rights* was the work of "A Committee of Advisers Representing the Principal Cultures of the World," and was one of the most useful documents available to the UN Commission on Human Rights when it began its work. Nolde noted that "Freedom of Religion is accorded the position of Article I." Ellingston, the ALI's representative in New York, was, like the ALI's director, an active churchman.

21. The text of this document is included in appendix F.

22. According to *The Concise Oxford Dictionary, conation* is the "exertion of willing that desire or aversion shall issue in action." It has to do with "striving."

23. Nolde in *Christianity and Crisis*, June 26, 1944.

24. Mackay Papers, box 15; PTS; copy also in Roosevelt Library, OF 213.

25. The report on their activity ran: "The Methodist Church has completed the first phase of its Crusade for New World Order. Many thousands of Methodists in all parts of the country have written to their representatives in Washington in support of the following declaration: 'The peoples of the world must choose between INTERNATIONAL COLLABORATION, in which lies the possibility of enduring peace; and ISOLATIONISM, in which lies the certainty of continuing war. . . . As CHRISTIANS, we reject isolationism, which subordinates the well-being of the world to national self-interest, and denies the Christian doctrine that all men are children of one Father and are members of one family. JESUS CHRIST is the Saviour of the WORLD. THE WORLD IS OUR PARISH.'" The General Conference of the Methodist Church, meeting in Kansas City in May 1944, authorized the continuance and expansion of the Crusade.

26. However, in the Minutes of the JCRL, October 20, 1944, p. 3, there is the note "Dr Nolde reported that the United Lutheran Church had unanimously adopted the Religious Liberty Statement at its meeting in Minneapolis."

27. The correspondence between Under Secretary of State Stettinius and Van Kirk is revealing. On November 8, 1944, Van Kirk, as secretary of the CJDP, wrote Stettinius a friendly letter referring to the CJDP's plans to convene a national study conference in Cleveland in January, mentioning in his final paragraph that the assistant director of the Office of Defense Transportation had written him requesting he "cancel my plans for the Cleveland meeting. I am extremely reluctant to do this as I look upon the Conference as a 'must' if we are to get the churches behind the developing international situation." Stettinius replied on November 11 with a classic letter suggesting it might be helpful if Van Kirk called "Mr John Dickey Director of our Office of Public Information, who will be glad to go into the problem with you." On November 24, the State Department wrote to Van Kirk saying it "would like very much to have someone present at your Cleveland conference" and "I think you can safely count on either Mr Geirig or some other officer of the Department being present in Cleveland for your conference."

28. Mackay Papers, box 40, PTS.

29. PHS (FCC), RG 18, box 67, folder 19.

30. Dr. Luman J. Shafer, a New Yorker, was a minister of the Reformed Church in America and secretary for China and Japan (where he had been a missionary for twenty-three years) in its Board of Foreign Missions. In 1940, his *The Christian Alternative to World Chaos* was chosen as "Book of the Month" by the Religious Book Club. He was chair of Van Kirk's FCC department and in 1943 was given leave of absence to be cosecretary (with Van Kirk) of the CJDP. His special responsibility was for the Cleveland conference. It is interesting that Henry Smith Leiper had written a popular interpretation of the Oxford and Edinburgh conferences under the title *World Chaos or World Christianity?* (Chicago: Willett Clark and Co., 1937).

31. A single-sheet popular digest of the *Message* was produced for mass distribution. The core of this is the nine points of suggested revision.

32. O. Frederick Nolde Papers, Lutheran Archives Center at Philadelphia. The documentation of Cleveland is notably prominent among the papers Nolde retained personally.

33. Some papers from the WCC Study Department were also circulated. A salient concern was their perception of the central phenomenon of "massification" in modern industrial society. The goal, therefore, was to foster civil institutions. WCC Archives, box XIII, "Analysis of the Christian Attitude to the Social and Economic Bases of a Just and Durable Peace," June 1944.

34. This final section of the Report of Commission II is included in appendix G.

35. Nolde Papers, Lutheran Archives Center, Philadelphia.

36. The final typescript is in the Nolde Papers. A printed version is in WCC Archive, box OFN Papers, Articles, etc.

37. The minutes of the JCRL meeting of February 13, 1945, included "Dr Nolde can handle only governmental problems in the time he can devote to the Committee's work." After Nolde reported that the CSOP had appointed a subcommittee on the question of a Commission on Human Rights, it was minuted that "Dr Nolde's relationship to the sub-committee is entirely personal but he felt he was serving the purpose of the Joint Committee. It makes possible a measure of cooperation among all groups with a relatively common purpose." The JCRL was "delighted to have Dr Nolde to continue his personal efforts" and agreed "that the Joint Committee should press for a Declaration of Human Rights as far as seems expedient at San Francisco." PTS (FCC), RG 18, box 67, folder 3.

38. Nolde letter to A. C. Craig, December 29, 1944. PTS (FCC), RG 18, box 67, folder 19.

39. This was an effective example of action by the hitherto provincial "younger churches." They were now able to make their own contribution to a common policy in international affairs. The response by Wilson Macaulay and Bishop John Moyes to Nolde's request was a direct product of their attendance at Princeton in July 1943 and their having met there the American ecumenical leaders. Dr. H. V. Evatt was president of the General Assembly of the UN during the debates on the Universal Declaration in December 1948.

40. PTS (FCC), RG 18, box 67, folder 19.

41. Patrick Killough of Swannanoa, N.C., a former State Department officer, alerted me to the significance of this group.

42. E.g., Charles Malik spoke of Lebanon's declaring war on the Axis powers at the end of February, pressing to send a delegate to UNCIO in March, and pulling him [literally] out of his lecture room to become minister in the United States and delegate to UNCIO in April.

43. PHS (FCC), RG 18, box 67, folder 3.

CHAPTER 7

◆

The Charter of the United Nations Organization

PRESIDENT FRANKLIN D. ROOSEVELT, exhausted after his return from the Yalta conference in mid-February 1945, surprised his team by failing to recover his energy. He died on April 12. One of his last concerns had been what he would say in opening the United Nations Conference on International Order (UNCIO) in San Francisco on April 25.[1] He had insisted, against advice, that it was his obligation as host to welcome the representatives of the nations of the world to the United States in person, and to set the tone in which their task should be addressed.[2]

The president's commitment is illustrated in Jacob Blaustein's and Joseph Proskauer's memory of their visit to the White House on March 21. They represented the American Jewish Committee. During their visit, they spoke of the holocaust in Europe and of their world-order hopes for UNCIO. They also spoke specifically for a commission to draft an International Bill of Human Rights. The president said to them: "Go to San Francisco. Work to get those human rights provisions into the Charter so that unspeakable crimes like those by the Nazis will never again be countenanced by world society." In phrases reminiscent of those he had put into the Atlantic Charter, Roosevelt claimed such provisions would be "of the greatest significance, because they go to the root of what is fundamental to the well-being and the very lives of all people, namely respect for the dignity of the human being and protection for the human rights of each individual regardless of race, language, religion, and sex."[3] His leadership in guiding America's contribution to drafting the UN Charter might have been seen as a fitting culmination to Roosevelt's thirteen years of New Deal policymaking. Instead, these duties became some of President Harry Truman's first tasks.

The weeks before and during UNCIO were marked by liberation of one Nazi concentration camp after another. Photographs were published of Jewish inmates that still haunt our public memory. The war with Japan seemed by no means over, but the U.S. and U.K. leaders (and through the spy Klaus Fuchs, the Kremlin) knew that atomic bombs were almost ready for deployment. They also could assume that such action would win that war (with equally haunting photographs), within two months of UNCIO's conclusion.

Preparation for the convening and organization of UNCIO was in the end hectic. The U.S. State Department had compounded UNCIO's logistic problems by introducing a wholly new element into the conference personnel. Rothwell sounded out Alger Hiss about possible advisers for UNCIO, and on May 12, 1944, the president approved a list of individuals. Then, in addition, on May 19 he approved an additional list of national organizations "representing the principal groups i.e. agriculture, labor, women, business, churches, [sic] negroes."[4] Forty-two national nongovernmental organizations (NGOs) were invited to send representatives to serve as a body of consultants to the U.S. delegation and its advisers. The intention was to provide instant access to the opinion of the "communities" of civil society, and to ensure their subsequent commitment.[5] The consequences both then and throughout the post–World War II period were of the highest importance. In his *Report* on UNCIO to the president,[6] Stettinius calls their contribution "not only an innovation in the conduct of international affairs by this Government but also, as events proved, an important contribution to the Conference itself."

The curtain that was lifted at San Francisco on what was to be the post–World War II comity of nations revealed a scene where the old European empires had become politically and morally unacceptable to U.S. diplomacy.[7] The United States insisted that China be given a seat at the top table. India was hustled in.[8] Leaders in both the State Department and the Federal Council of Churches (FCC) had concluded that America's own structures of racial inequality had to be dismantled if it was to have any hope of drawing the postwar world along the path toward a global human rights order.[9] The FCC sent a letter to the U.S. delegates as they arrived that "the highest interest of the world and the highest interest of our nation coincide."

The conference opened on April 25.[10] It had been decided that the four "Sponsoring" Powers (China, the Soviet Union, the United Kingdom, and the United States) should discuss together the suggestions and criticisms that the Dumbarton Oaks proposals had attracted, and agree on revisions. It was apparent to those seeking changes, particularly the NGO consultants with the U.S. delegation, and to the smaller nations that were anxious for a bigger role, that there was a far greater chance of significant changes being accepted if revision proposals were submitted before the joint meeting of the Sponsoring Powers on May 3.[11]

It had become clear to journalists that the group of NGO consultants seen to be fighting for a human rights commission in the UN Charter had prepared an effective campaign. A press item of April 30 described this project as the work of the "Federal Council of Churches of Christ in America, the American Jewish Committee, twelve Catholic bishops, and the powerful Baptist Joint Conference Committee on Public Relations, which speaks for 11 million Baptists." It was reasonable, in 1945, to think that very few American citizens were left unrepresented by such an alliance. Because of the local and yet global character of the Christian denominations and, to an extent, the Jewish organizations, their consultants were to have ready access not only to colleagues in California (which to many American members of UNCIO, including Nolde,[12] was terra incognita) but also to an uncommonly effective network of contacts in many of the other national delegations.

The consultants were to meet each weekday under the chairmanship of James T. Shotwell, then doyen of American international peace studies. The core group consisted of Clark Eichelberger (American Association for the United Nations), Jane Evans (National Peace Conference), Nolde (FCC and Joint Committee on Religious Liberty, or JCRL), Proskauer (American Jewish Committee), and Shotwell (Carnegie Endowment for International Peace). The State Department had taken pains to ensure that the U.S. delegation and its advisers enjoyed easy and frequent two-way communication with this group. Regular debriefing sessions on the conference's progress were timetabled. At the consultants' first meeting on April 26, Archibald MacLeish, assistant secretary of state in charge of public and cultural relations, introduced the secretary of state, who "assured the group of his consultation plans," and he in turn introduced John S. Dickey[13] as "the principal contact man through whom they will work."

In the run-up to UNCIO, Nolde and his associates had agreed that their principal goal was to get the U.S. delegation to commit to a human rights commission in the proposals it would take to the Sponsoring Powers' draft-revision meeting on May 3. Nolde's San Francisco diary is tantalizingly short-lived. It began on April 29 and stopped after May 4. It records the intensity of the crisis committee's action during those hours before the U.S. delegation's meeting to finalize its position on revision proposals at 5:30 P.M. on May 2.[14] Perhaps those days proved to be too full for him to imagine it would be realistic to continue. Tuesday, May 1, is a very long entry. It starts at 8:30 A.M. "Consultants meeting—Fairmont [Hotel]. Present: [Virginia] Gildersleeve, [Harold] Stassen, Dulles, and about ten special advisers." There follows: "Dismay of consultants group when inference was made [by Gildersleeve to Eichelberger] that few changes were contemplated in Du[mbarton] Oaks. Raised specific question about provision for human rights. Implications given that no commission was to be urged by U.S. delegation. After three-quarters of an hour, delegates and Mr. Dulles left." The discussion continued. There were administrative questions to be decided (it was the beginning of the consultants' corporate work under Shotwell's chairmanship) such as the setting up of education and economics subgroups; and then, during a break, Nolde "sounded out various people— Shotwell, Proskauer, Eichelberger, etc. and found them disposed to push farther on human rights." Before 11 A.M. Nolde "briefly saw J. F. D[ulles] about feasibility of this and concluded to move." After clearing his schedule for the day, Nolde met with the core group.

They set out to divide contacts in the U.S. delegation between them so as to make it clear how seriously their constituencies viewed the proposed abandonment of a human rights commission. Friendly politician members of the U.S. delegation and State Department staff had to be lobbied with the message that the NGOs represented the communities that made up the American electorate; that these had come to a steady conviction of the necessity of a peace in which (by its commitment to human rights) the United States could be a wholehearted player; and that how the United States acted in this matter in these next hours would be decisive for the whole character of the new international order being crafted in San Francisco. It was also necessary to agree on a text for the message that the consultants hoped to present to the secretary of state, and to decide who would constitute the delegation and who would speak. It was decided to prepare a "statement on human rights to be signed by consultants and submitted to Stettinius," but not, it seems, at this stage in person. "Proskauer volunteered to prepare [a] short draft."

Nolde then went to a "luncheon given by Nelson Rockefeller [assistant secretary of state, adviser to the U.S. delegation], in honor of South Am[erican] delegates," at which, true to form, he "talked considerably about work of [the] churches in general on world order and particularly about human rights" and "found a sympathetic ear." There was a plenary session at 3:30, and then at 4:45 there came the critical moment, a "Human Rights (small group meeting)" of eight consultants at which Proskauer's draft was reviewed "with Eichelberger, Shotwell, Evans, Atkinson, Blaustein, and a Catholic."[15] The result was that they "substituted [the] form worked out by John W. Davis, Com[missioner?] in N[ew] Y[ork] (previously submitted to Joint Committee on R[eligious] L[iberty])" and "decided to make final revision next morning." Nolde then telephoned the delegation from China, the one possibly uncommitted Sponsoring Power, to arrange a lunch the following day.

The following day, Wednesday, May 2, was going to be the decisive encounter. A personal appointment with Secretary Stettinius was arranged, most likely by Isaiah Bowman, for the core group of consultants to present their letter and make their case. This was scheduled at 5 P.M., the last possible moment for effective action. The U.S. delegation's meeting at 5:30 had in the end to begin without Stettinius in the chair.

Meanwhile the group had to finalize its draft and lobby as many fellow consultants as they could find for their signatures in favor of its initiative. This was not easy to do without notice because there were a hundred or so scattered around the city. Nolde and his associates canceled engagements and began phoning around and sending off a flurry of notes. At 10 A.M. there was a short meeting with the church people involved with the conference (not only the invited "consultants"). Nolde noted "good feeling, broke down barrier between consultants, associates, and others; reported on recent developments on human rights, etc." This entry includes the only reference to "prayer." The consultants' group then met at 10:30 A.M. at the International Center, where they "shaped up document and signed [by twenty-one consultants]; Jane Evans to get further signatures."

At noon Nolde had lunch with the Chinese delegation. He brought together Foreign Missions Conference colleagues who had contacts and special expertise in China (Bishop Baker, Cameron P. Hall, Charles F. Boss, and Sue Wedell). He notes: "discussed religious education, missions, [the] progress of [the] Conference, human rights. Secured strong expression of support on [the] latter. Appreciation of Chinese amendments to Du[mbarton] Oaks." He continued with dictation of letters, and then attended the plenary at 3.30 P.M. Nolde had "brief meeting with Shotwell [and] Proskauer" prior to joining the rest of the consultants' delegation. At ten minutes to five, they asked him "to make [the] formal presentation of human rights document to Stettinius to be followed by Proskauer." Nolde was known for his talent in speaking from the back of an envelope.

At 5 P.M. they met Secretary Stettinius, who was accompanied by MacLeish and Bowman. Stettinius[16] began the meeting by stressing how hard Bowman (and by implication he himself) had pushed for human rights at Dumbarton Oaks, and how they were unlikely to be more successful at the San Francisco conference. Nolde said that during this MacLeish "came down to my chair and urged me to get to my feet immediately upon the completion of the Secretary of State's remarks," and introduce the consultants' letter.[17] Nolde did this briefly and soberly, stressing that its positions were "not the product of hasty construction here" but had been drafted by "jurists and churchmen," "business and labor." Only time had prevented more signatures. "We would like to let know the people we represent that our American Delegation is taking a lead in this respect," he said, and handed Stettinius the letter.

Judge Proskauer then rose "to say a few words." They were clearly the masterpiece of a gifted advocate's art. It was a historic moment as well, for the delegation's agenda that evening included consideration of how VE (Victory in Europe) Day was to be celebrated at UNCIO. He spoke from the heart and deployed what he called "an extemporaneous argument." He claimed that the proposals "reflected fundamental desires of the vast majority" of the American people. Recalling his appeal to the secretary of state, he later wrote: "I said that the voice of America was speaking in this room as it had never spoken before in any international gathering." And then later, to the American delegation: "If you make a fight for these human rights proposals and win, there will be glory for all. If you make a fight for it and lose, we will back you up to the limit. If you fail to make a fight for it, you will have lost the support of American opinion—and justly lost it. In that event you will never get the Charter ratified."[18] That last political stick was a powerful one.

Shotwell, a principal conspirator, then followed up with solid, commonsense advice on how to press the matter if the delegation took it up. Next came Philip Murray of the Congress of Industrial Organizations, who had not signed and whose position was not known. Proskauer sighed with relief when he "subscribed wholeheartedly." He was followed by Walter White of the National Association for the Advancement of Colored People, who "emphasized the importance of including colonies and other dependent peoples within the concept of human rights"; by Father Edward Conway, S.J., as a Catholic;[19] and then Eichelberger, who "stressed the primary significance" of a commission on human rights because "an agency would thus be set up to work for the ideals which could not be fully specified in the Charter." Finally Blaustein made the point that all that was needed at that point was the general principle of a commission.

According to Proskauer, "Mr Stettinius rose to his feet impulsively and exclaimed that he had no idea of the intensity of the feeling on this subject and would immediately put the matter to the American delegation." Shotwell's recollection is even more positive: "Secretary Stettinius instantly promised that he would do all he could to have the human rights clauses inserted in the Charter." It was by then 5:25. Stettinius shook Nolde's hand warmly and left the room.

Nolde's diary entry is brief and states only that Shotwell (the chair of the U.S. consultants) introduced him, and Proskauer followed him. He notes: "Apparently well received," in the context of Stettinius's earlier remark that "in order to be usable in the US recommendations" the deadline was 5:30, and ends that, Stettinius having "left to take the letter to the American Delegation," he had a "discussion with Isaiah Bowman." In Nolde's *Remarks* at the tenth anniversary meeting of the consultants (which he chaired)[20] in San Francisco on June 20, 1955, he recalled this discussion, in which Blaustein took the initiative. Bowman raised in detail the "difficulties to be encountered in securing adequate provision for human rights in the Charter," to which Blaustein's reply "strongly emphasized the importance of a provision for a commission on human rights, even though concrete particulars might not be attainable at this time." This deferral of commitment to any definition of "human rights" proved an important factor in making the proposal acceptable. "Dr. Bowman gave firm evidence of agreement with this point of view."[21]

This barrage of intense conviction had left the secretary of state shaken. The official record of the U.S. delegation meeting that began at 5:30 on May 2 is far from full.[22] Stettinius was pleased that "the previous evening with Mr Molotov, Mr Soong, and Mr Eden had been marked by the best spirit" so far, and this had carried through to the morning. That evening, however, when "views would be exchanged on amendments to the Dumbarton Oaks Proposals" would be "a very important meeting." He wanted, before discussing the amendments that the United States would bring to the Sponsoring Powers that night, "to report on the meeting of the Consultants." "He thought it had been an excellent meeting and he had been deeply impressed by the discussion." The secretary mentioned Nolde's and Proskauer's speeches, and read out the consultants' letter.[23] He reported that he had promised them that he would "take up the matter of expanding and defining in greater detail what the functions of the organization might be" in respect of human rights. And he added that "even if the US Delegation failed in its attempt" to "obtain agreement on giving much greater emphasis to human rights," the delegation could "put out a statement that it had tried and this would carry a great weight with American public opinion."

For an urgent (though unprepared) debate on how to act in a matter of consequence, the reported discussion appears curiously desultory and unfocused. The secretary noticed it would soon be 9:30 in Washington, and he wished to phone the president to tell him of the sincerity and force of the consultants' arguments;[24] and that he personally "felt the Delegation should make public its position" and "take a public stand after tonight," which was supported by Senator Arthur Vandenberg of Michigan. Representative Sol Bloom of New York continued to be irritated by the phrase "human rights" that "means nothing." After Stettinius had made his call, the discussion resumed on a proposal (apparently already made by Commander Stassen) that reference to a human rights commission should be inserted in paragraph 2 of Chapter IX. A consensus agreed to take it to the Sponsoring Powers' meeting. The delegation meeting drew to a conclusion with a feeling that more attention needed to be given to a preamble "setting forth the motives which lie behind the Charter," and an urgent interruption from MacLeish asking what he should say to the press at their Friday conference, for the "journalists were eager to be told first about the American proposals."

The State Department held a conference for NGOs on October 31, 1947, on the state of its preparations for an International Declaration of Human Rights. Walter Kotschnig, then acting chief of its Division of International Organization Affairs, gave the first talk, and began with his vivid memories of this meeting of consultants with the secretary of state "in the Blue Room of the Fairmont Hotel at the top of Nob Hill" in May 1945. It was Proskauer's bravura performance that filled his memory of that afternoon, of his pointing at Stettinius and charging him personally with his duty "to take the lead in this matter . . . to live up to what is best in our traditions, to write into the charter a provision which would give meaning to the articles which pledge the nations of the world to promote human rights and fundamental freedoms."[25]

Kotschnig continued: "I accompanied Mr Stettinius at the end of that meeting to a meeting of the American delegation. We went straight there. And all the way up in the elevator, then way down the long corridor on the fifth floor, down to the corner room, where the American delegation was meeting, he didn't say a word. He was obviously moved. But he did speak strongly and convincingly at the delegation meeting. It was that afternoon that the Commission on Human Rights was born. It took several more weeks before Article 68 was given its final form. But, upon the proposal of the United States delegation, that article asks specifically for the establishment of a commission for the promotion of human rights. Thus began one of the major undertakings of the United Nations, an undertaking which to my mind is fundamental to the success of the organization."[26]

It was the following year in Cambridge that Dulles referred to the substantial contribution made by the FCC team (in which he included himself) to the UN Charter agreed on in San Francisco. The team certainly did not hide its pride in helping midwife the Commission on Human Rights. Cuttings kept by Nolde from the San Francisco and Philadelphia newspapers show clearly that this knowledge was widespread.[27]

CLAIMING A PLACE AT THE UN

After the Sponsoring Powers' revisions of the draft UN Charter on May 4, Nolde personally was in a very different position. He was pictured in the media nationwide as a principal figure in setting a new image for what was being formed as the UN— its purpose, its structures, and above all its "global ethos." He had begun to walk and work with foreign ministers and celebrities of many nations. His voice was listened to in the remaining weeks of UNCIO on other topics than human rights, particularly in advancing the smaller nations' cause and the role of NGOs within the UN structures. For instance, he was chosen to take the lead in speaking to commend the role for NGOs that was agreed on in Article 71. Of course he made many personal contacts that were to prove useful later in relating to the Commission on Human Rights. It seemed unthinkable to waste these. The JCRL was now known through him rather than the reverse. He had to hurry back to Philadelphia to cram in the courses he had been unable to give during UNCIO, but there is no indication that anyone—least of all he himself—assumed he would return to his pre-JCRL life at the Lutheran Theological Seminary at Philadelphia in the fall.

The Protestant churches' achievement at UNCIO was remarkable, but it was certainly not a solo performance. Dulles and Van Kirk clearly, but also the continuing backbone names of the JCRL, had worked with sustained determination. Barnes and Ernest Johnson of the World Council of Churches (WCC), Alfred W. Wasson and (until 1944) Mackay of the Foreign Missions Conference—these deserved campaign medals. But above all, perhaps, Warnshuis was responsible; for as joint secretary of the International Missionary Council, he had first proposed the JCRL's role on a much more than North American basis, and he had taken a principal part even after his retirement. They encouraged Nolde to continue.

The JCRL met on May 16 with Nolde away in California. It was delighted at what he had been doing. Visser 't Hooft had come over from Geneva, and was anxious that all communication with Europe should now be via his office. His presence was valuable in discussing the range of acute problems presenting themselves, not least those arising from the blackout of news from Soviet-occupied Eastern Europe. Decker, too, was able to present firsthand news of India and China after his recent visits. At the end of June, Richard Fagley convened an ad hoc meeting of church social and international affairs officers in New York to respond promptly to the UNCIO decisions, specifically to support Senate ratification "without reservations." Remarkably, the Senate did so.[28] All churches were urged to read the FCC statement on the UN Charter on Sunday, July 22. For the fall, ambitious programs were drawn up for the Commission to Study the Bases of a Just and Durable Peace (CJDP) to produce education materials, prayers, and film strips for use in supporting the UN. Nolde's short paper, "Human Rights in the World Charter," quoting liberally from Stettinius's estimate of the central importance of UNCIO's human rights provisions, also carries this date.[29]

The September meeting of the JCRL was the first (and also with Nolde present) since May.[30] The minutes are found also in draft. Their final form has two appendixes that are powerful evidence of Nolde's systematic work as executive secretary. One is a four-page detailed listing of JCRL activities from the JCRL's authorization of its *Statement* on March 3, 1944, to congratulatory letters sent to, and received from, U.S. delegates at the successful conclusion of UNCIO in July 1945. The other is the file-classification of the JCRL archive—"on human rights"—set up by Inez Cavert in the FCC office in New York and later managed by Nolde's secretary, Amelia Wyckoff.[31] Recurring throughout the meeting were expressions of appreciation to Nolde for achieving so much more than they could have anticipated at UNCIO; and a deep sense of group satisfaction at their accomplishing both that and the publication of Bates's book in the same summer. They now had a worked-out exposition of religious liberty in a world perspective. The first reviews of *Religious Liberty* had been good.[32] A second edition and translations were already being called for.

Emory Ross had been in England in the summer, and he reported on the formation of the joint British Council of Churches–International Missionary Council committee on religious liberty in London. This was welcomed, but a sentence from his report in the draft minutes that was excised had noted the absence in the United Kingdom of a "sense of urgency, on a broad scale, about matters of religious liberty and inter-faith relationships, as in this country."

Center stage, however, was the question how to follow up on the ground won at UNCIO. Three points were made. First, Warnshuis (in the chair) made the point that circulating the JCRL's material to "church groups in countries abroad" had had a measurable impact on UNCIO, so it was important that the churches' international network on religious liberty and human rights should be kept alive and developed. Second, several members (not least Nolde) were emphatic that a principal avenue of the JCRL's UN-related work should now be in education. The UNCIO human rights provisions depended on that to be effective. The JCRL (together with the CJDP and the Commission to Study the Organization of the Peace) should seek contact with the UN Educational Scientific and Cultural Organization (UNESCO) that was to be formed, and this should have human rights education specified as a central element in its remit.[33] Third, and at the top of Nolde's mind, was whether the post-UNCIO situation called for another memorandum in the series following the 1944 *Statement* from the JCRL to the State Department.

In July William Draper Lewis, the director of the American Law Institute (with which the JCRL had been working so closely before UNCIO), had written to Nolde inviting him to contribute an article to the *Annals of the American Academy of Political and Social Science*, of which he was the editor.[34] This was published as "The Commission on Human Rights, Possible Functions" in a special number (January 1946) "devoted to the problem of human rights through international co-operation." As a spin-off from this, Nolde brought along to the September JCRL meeting a draft of his article, presenting it as something useful for the JCRL to do (though not mentioning its potential destination in the State Department). It could serve as a ready-to-hand text for revision if that were agreed on.

In his report on UNCIO to the JCRL meeting, Nolde began by distinguishing two categories of work proper to the JCRL: "First, Remedial or Curative—tense situations and solutions which seem possible; Second, Preventive or Constructive—guarding against problems." He asserted—very interestingly for understanding his approach to later work on the Universal Declaration—that "the provisions of the United Nations for human rights fall in this second category." He then went on to note that the UN Charter "leaves unanswered two very crucial questions: It does not say what human rights shall be sought; nor does it say how they shall be promoted. A first step would therefore seem to be that of bringing the Commission on Human Rights to the acceptance of certain functions; a second, to indicate how the functions shall be fulfilled." He ended by asking whether the JCRL would continue to recognize a "study of matters involved in the Commission on Human Rights" as "part of its responsibility?" It agreed; but the resulting action by Nolde—approved only to be "informal and unofficial"—was not to be "study" but an escalation of lobbying those in government.

This became evident at the end of October. Nolde had established a close relationship over the past eighteen months with Easton Rothwell, first as his principal interlocutor in the postwar planning group at the State Department, and then in San Francisco as the officer in charge of UNCIO. On October 25, the day before the monthly JCRL meeting, Nolde had a substantial phone conversation with him, and the implication is that this was not the first that autumn.[35] Rothwell had just returned with Stettinius from a conference in London on the UN. Nolde wanted to find out what the plans now were (he discovered that a human rights person would be included—as member-presumptive of the commission—in the U.S. delegation to the forthcoming General Assembly in London in December), but above all how best he could get the JCRL's encouragement and his "specific recommendations" concerning the Commission on Human Rights to the attention of the State Department.[36] Late November was Rothwell's recommended time for any memorandum; and he suggested the next "effective contact" be when the commission "assembled for organization."

The JCRL meeting on October 26 was again chaired by Warnshuis.[37] Managing sales of Bates's book was still important. The high profile of the JCRL's work that summer was reflected at meetings in determined bids to discover fresh funds that might be tapped. There were reports of "the impact which the work of the Joint Committee was making on a considerable number of ministers." Nolde was expanding that impact overseas; he had sent a package to "130 leaders in 65 countries." This contained covering letters from Henry Smith Leiper, the FCC's "ecumenical secretary" and the WCC's North American representative, and Wynn Fairfield, "chair of the Secretarial Council" of the Foreign Missions Conference. It also included a digest of Bates's book, and a letter from Nolde asking for overseas church support and networking for religious liberty and, in particular, for establishing the functions of the Commission on Human Rights. Other bids for a JCRL voice included approval of Nolde's draft, "after consultation with the State Department," of a letter to Archibald MacLeish (the NGOs' friend at UNCIO), who was to head the U.S. delegation to the UN "Educational and Social Conference" in London on November 1. He asked that human rights education be specified in its constitution. Yet another draft letter was approved, this time to Secretary of State James F. Byrnes on the inclusion of human rights provisions in all peace treaties, with special reference to Italy and religious liberty—the 1929 Vatican Concordat was not acceptable. And, looking ahead (and underlined), "Should the Joint Committee seek to have consideration of Human Rights placed on the Agenda [of the WCC Provisional Committee in Geneva in February 1946]?"

For Nolde, however, the key item was that on his proposal "to prepare a Memorandum [to the State Department] dealing with the functions of the Commission on Human Rights." He referred to his article for *Annals*. It was felt to be "highly desirable," and he was authorized to complete and submit it.

Thus, on November 14, the State Department received a rather bald covering letter from the JCRL, whose central affirmation was "We are primarily concerned with religious liberty as it stands in its proper and indissoluble relation to all other human rights." Enclosed was the nine-page Memorandum No. 4—titled "Memorandum suggesting a Program of Action for the Commission on Human Rights of the United Nations Organization"—together with copies of the three previous JCRL memoranda and their foundation document, the *Statement*.[38] This memorandum set down six requirements (in a distinctly didactic tone, and each with an expanded "comment") if the Commission on Human Rights mandated in the UN Charter was to become progressively more effective internationally. It forms "our conception of [its] composition and competence." Nolde was to feel—and be told—that this time, too, his work had had a perceptible influence on how the first meeting of the Economic and Social Council (after the assembly) came to its decisions on the commission.

Meanwhile, domestically, the exhilaration following rapid ratification of U.S. membership by the Senate after UNCIO gave way to other concerns. There were immense practical problems in switching industries and the returning armed forces to the concerns of peace. The churches and the YMCA found that their members' interest in "postwar world" issues fell away very quickly. Their leadership worked hard to retain it. A particular initiative of the CJDP from early November onward, characteristically well prepared, was the FCC program for the media and local churches in Lent 1946, "Christian Action on Four Fronts for Peace." The first, the "Inner Front," was led by Dulles—"Let us seek to cleanse our hearts of the evil contaminations of war and pray God to renew a right spirit within us"; the second, the "Church Front," was to be led by Bishop Bromley Oxnam—"Let us seek unity of effort, by all men of good will, at home and abroad, in order that their influence may accomplish the task that lies ahead"; the third, the "Peace Treaty Front," led by Harold Stassen—"Let us seek peace treaties which embody principles of justice and which will promote the general welfare"; and the fourth, the "United Nations Front," led by Virginia Gildersleeve—"Let us seek that the United Nations Organization develop its curative and creative functions so that, through common effort against the common threats to mankind, the peoples of the world may find fellowship." It was very worthy (and wordy). It was understandable returned servicemen should seek more immediate satisfactions.

But Dulles's expositions of these "Four Fronts" were not only powerful and valid. They were also moving. On the UN, for instance, he began that it "is an asset of incalculable value"; that it includes all that was foreshadowed and hoped for in the "Six Pillars of Peace"; and that it "has the power and opportunity to establish a peace that will accord with Christian principles." And "furthermore, it is available for use now when it is most needed."

Dulles's final paragraph, over a note commending the fine FCC *Statement on the Control of the Atomic Bomb*, foreshadows the Marshall Plan: "The functioning of the United Nations Organization presupposes a civilized world. In great areas that civilization is now imminently threatened by starvation, privation and consequent chaos. Therefore, pending the time when the United Nations Organization can function and, indeed, in order to make that functioning possible, the people of our nation should take whatever remedial and sacrificial action they can to alleviate the appalling conditions which are the aftermath of war."

NOTES

Another account of the events in these pages is given in J. S. Nurser, "The Ecumenical Movement Churches, Global Order, and Human Rights: 1938–1948," *Human Rights Quarterly* 25, no. 4 (2003): 841–81. *Human Rights Quarterly* is published by the Johns Hopkins University Press.

1. The press conference he held aboard the *U.S.S. Quincy* on the way home from the Yalta conference gave ample evidence already of UNCIO's prominence in his thinking. For instance, "The United Nations [a name coined by FDR in 1941 for the countries fighting the Nazis] will evolve into the best method ever devised for stopping war, and it will also be the beginning of something else to go with it" (*The Public Papers and Addresses of Franklin D. Roosevelt*, vol. 13, *1944–5, Victory and the Threshold of Peace* [New York: Harper, 1950], 557). The content of that "something else" was understood as economic development and human rights. Cp. Charles Malik of Lebanon, the future president of the UN Assembly, annotated his copy of the U.S. Department of State's Dumbarton Oaks Documents on International Organization of February 1, 1945, in red pencil. He wrote, "Freedom of Truth and conscience," "positive content of civilized existence," and "justice must be included . . . mere peace and security are more or less privative [*sic*] and static terms" and underlined FDR's "the creation of the conditions that make for peace" (Library of Congress, Washington, D.C., Malik Papers). The last address FDR prepared was for Jefferson Day on April 13. The draft moves from Jefferson's "brotherly spirit of Science—widely dispersed throughout the different quarters of the globe" to "The work, my friends, is peace." He added by hand his final sentence: "Let us move forward with strong and active faith" (*Public Papers and Addresses of Franklin D. Roosevelt*, vol. 13, item 148, pp. 613–16). See also, "Memorandum for the Secretary of State, April 6, 1945: Is someone drafting a proposed speech for me for the San Francisco Conference? F.D.R."—filed with note, "No accompanying papers." Stettinius's reply of April 7 says, "Mr. MacLeish is preparing a draft" which will be "ready by the 12th" (the day on which FDR was to die). Franklin D. Roosevelt Library, MS 4725.

2. Townsend Hoopes and Douglas Brinkley, *FDR and the Creation of the UN* (New Haven, Conn.: Yale University Press, 1997).

3. *To Reaffirm Faith in Fundamental Human Rights*, ed. Felice Gaer (New York: American Jewish Committee, 1995), 5. This booklet, published by the Jacob Blaustein Institute in New York, is an edited version of the anniversary address "The UN and Human Rights 1945 to 1995," which was given by Mrs. B. B. Hirschhorn, Blaustein's daughter, using her father's memoirs. Mrs. Hirschhorn commented, "I shall never forget the buoyancy with which he told his family of his visit to the President and the President's endorsement of including human rights in the UN Charter."

4. Hoover Institution, Stanford University, Stanford, Calif., Papers of Easton Rothwell, box 43.

5. It is noteworthy that the ecumenical churches had included "community" in their overall theme "Church, Community, and State" for the 1937 Oxford conference.

6. "Report to the President on the Results of the San Francisco Conference," State Department, Washington, D.C., 1945, p. 27.

7. The State Department's Division of Special Research, set up in 1941 "to do some general planning for what the shape of the world would be after the war," had "dependent

areas"—originally "colonial"—as one of its four sections. C. Easton Rothwell, "On the Formation of the UN," p. 4; Dag Hammarskjöld Library, United Nations, New York (Oral History). The final question to FDR at the post-Yalta press conference referred to Churchill's speech that "he was not made the Prime Minister of Great Britain to see the empire fall apart," on which FDR commented, "Dear old Winston will never learn on that point. He has made his specialty on that point. This is of course off the record." *Public Papers and Addresses of Franklin D. Roosevelt*, vol. 13, p. 564.

8. "We insisted that India be considered an independent nation when the UN was formed, and the British gave in to that . . . from the beginning India was its own master at the UN." UN Library, Rothwell, p. 15.

9. Life and Work's Oxford conference in 1937 had put race in the forefront of its thinking about international issues. The logical implication of this for the American color bar at home and as a factor in international relations is a continuing theme in the discussions of the FCC's Commission on a Just and Durable Peace. Ralph Diffendorfer of the Methodist Board of Missions wrote to the secretary of state on September 18, 1944, to press that "dependent African peoples" be put on the agenda at Dumbarton Oaks against presumed British resistance. Color discrimination and exploitation should be promoted as salient postwar issues. Hoover, Rothwell Papers, box 43.

10. Van Kirk and Nolde prepared a six-page radio script, "Impressions from the First Plenary Session." It is noteworthy how modest their expectations then were of the part to be played by the NGO consultants: "By invitation of the government the churches were to have a part in the Conference as observers, maybe as advisers; they were to have no organic relationship with the Conference nor any assignment in the way of any political decision. Exactly what function the consultants are to perform has not yet been defined. Their very presence behind the delegates bespeaks an experiment in democratic procedures; in a sense it offers a demonstration of the reality of democracy." National Council of Churches Records, Federal Council of Churches Records, Presbyterian Historical Society, Philadelphia (hereafter PHS [FCC]), RG 18, box 66, folder 25.

11. "Between April 25 and May 4 such a remarkable degree of unanimity was reached among the four (France became a fifth during UNCIO) delegations concerned that they were able to present jointly to the Conference their unanimously approved suggestions for some thirty amendments to their Dumbarton Oaks Proposals." Edward R. Stettinius, *Diaries of Edward R. Stettinius*, ed. T. M. Campbell and G. C. Herring (New York: New Viewpoints, 1975), 3.

12. He told a friend later that on the long train journey west he wondered what he was getting into. He had not been west of Ohio before UNCIO.

13. Dickey was one of a group of Dartmouth College alumni in the U.S. State Department who took the lead in advocating this new role for representatives of civil society in U.S. foreign policy.

14. World Council of Churches (WCC) Library and Archives, Geneva, Nolde's "San Francisco Diary #2."

15. This was probably Fr. Edward Conway, S.J.

16. Accounts of this meeting come from three of the consultants. Blaustein's is recounted by his daughter Mrs. Hirschhorn (see note 4 above); Proskauer's in his autobiography, *A Segment of My Time* (New York: Farrar, Straus, 1950); and Nolde's is in his "San Francisco Notebook #2" in the WCC Archives and in O. Frederick Nolde, *Free and Equal* (Geneva: World Council of Churches, 1968), 21–25. Proskauer's recollection shortens the period by twenty-four hours. Nolde's diary record is more credible.

17. See appendix H. There is a copy under the heading, "Proposals regarding Human Rights; submitted to the US Delegation by a Group of Consultants representing Church Bodies, Business, Labor, Civic Organizations, etc." in box 191 (US Gen 42) of the UNCIO papers in the National Archives II, Maryland.

18. *To Reaffirm Faith*, ed. Gaer, 8.

19. Richard Fagley's two letters of 1990 to J. S. Nurser mention Conway's role as significant at San Francisco, though Conway's name does not appear in the list of Catholic consultants of April 26 (viz. from the Catholic Association for International Peace or from the National Catholic Welfare Conference). However, there were many unofficial "associates" present at UNCIO. Fagley wrote "At the UN founding conference in San Francisco Fred Nolde . . . and my Jesuit colleague from Denver, Ned Conway, pushed this particular objective [international safeguards for human rights]." Fagley expands this: "He [Conway] and . . . Nolde persuaded . . . Stettinius to support the establishment of a Commission on Human Rights, citing the second of the *Patterns* [*of Peace*] principles." This principle ran: "the dignity of the human person as the image of God must be set forth in all its essential implications in an international declaration of rights. States as well as individuals must repudiate racial, religious, or other discrimination in violation of those rights."

20. The invitation to chair this meeting is an indication of the prestige Nolde had won at UNCIO.

21. Lutheran Archives Center at Philadelphia, Nolde Papers, Speeches, box A.

22. *Foreign Relations of the United States, Diplomatic Papers 1945, Vol. I, General: The United Nations* (Washington, D.C.: U.S. Government Printing Office, 1967), 528–41.

23. The State Department minutes of the meeting with the consultants are noted as "not printed."

24. Possibly this indicates that President Truman had advised Stettinius to be cautious in following through FDR's enthusiasm in this matter.

25. Department of State, Transcript of Proceedings, Conference on the International Declaration of Human Rights, October 31, 1947, Washington, D.C., p. 5, Roosevelt Library.

26. Department of State, Transcript of Proceedings, pp. 6–7.

27. "Phila Man Wins Charter Change," *Philadelphia Inquirer*, May 4, 1945, and "Story behind Human Rights Plan," *San Francisco News*, May 16, 1945. WCC Archives, box 428.3.23, with duplicates in box 428.3.25.

28. The *Congressional Record–Senate* of July 23, 1945, pp. 8087–88, includes tables showing organizations and individuals that had testified for and against Senate ratification of the UN Charter. The "For" organizations with the largest memberships were the FCC (25 million), the American Federation of Labor (6.6 million), the Congress of Industrial Organizations (5.5 million), and the American Legion (1 million). The largest of those "Against" had 25 members. A Mrs. Marie Lohle was "against," whose "daughter purports to represent the younger generation." Senators Connolly (Dem.) and Vandenberg (Rep.) made powerful speeches, Connolly going so far as to claim a vote to ratify the UN Charter would be like the shot at Concord Bridge hymned by Emerson, and "resound round the earth."

29. WCC Archives, box OFN Papers, no. 45.

30. PHS (FCC), RG 18, box 66, folder 25 (the draft) and RG 19, box 67, folder 3.

31. There are four sections: I. Administration; II. Data (A. by countries, B. general); III. Philosophy-Theology of Religious Liberty; IV. State Department. Under II. A. there are forty-nine countries listed plus thirty-three of the states of the United States. Under II.B. the listing runs: Church and State, Church bodies, freedom of press, inter-faith [Catholic–Protestant] relationships, IMC on religious liberty, racial tensions, Roman Catholic church [no less than eighteen headings], and YMCA. There were many press cuttings and offprints. Nolde reported that over 200 news and journal titles were taken. It is unclear what happened to this collection after Nolde retired and the CCIA office was moved to Geneva.

32. A complimentary copy was to be sent to Fr. Courtney Murray, who had been kind enough to send offprints of two of his articles on religious liberty to the committee.

33. Charles Malik, the Lebanese delegate at UNCIO, consistently emphasized the education aspects of human rights in his speeches. Nolde's contact with him at UNCIO led to their close collegiality in the work of the Commission on Human Rights, where Malik was rappor-

teur. For Malik's contribution, see Mary Ann Glendon, *A World Made New* (New York: Random House, 2001).

34. PHS (FCC), RG 18, box 67, folder 7.

35. PHS (FCC), RG 18, box 67, folder 19.

36. It was a trademark of Nolde's diplomatic work to make an approach—a visit, a paper, a speech—only at a time and in a context that he had first ascertained as most favorable to its reception.

37. PHS (FCC), RG 18, box 66, folder 25. These minutes are also in RG 18, box 67, folder 3.

38. PHS (FCC), RG 18, box 67, folder 3, and also RG 18, box 67, folder 23. There is a similarly structured paper dated October 22 as from the Commission to Study the Organization of the Peace titled "The Commission on Human Rights—Program and Composition," though it is less full and less forceful; PHS (FCC), RG 18, box 67, folder 21.

CHAPTER 8

◆

An Ecumenical Instrument

FROM THE EARLIEST DAYS of the World Council of Churches–in–formation (WCC), its constituting churches were emphatic in announcing two aspects of what had happened at its birth in 1938. It was, they claimed, both an event of world-historical importance and also one that made no difference to the ecclesial sovereignty of those who would come to participate in it. This was, and remained, a paradox. The word "council" in the post–World War II Council of Europe has harbored similar practical difficulties, though in the latter's case the increasing significance of the council's setting up a common Court of Human Rights at Strasbourg is now established. It is transnational, and citizens can appeal to it against their own state, but each state claims that its sovereignty is unimpaired.

The WCC also established a body whose executive officers claimed that it had a uniquely "substantive" character among the WCC's instrumentalities. By this they intended to signify a qualified executive autonomy with regard to the authorities of the WCC's constituent churches. This was the Churches' Commission on International Affairs (CCIA), set up at the conference called by the WCC—in association with the International Missionary Council (IMC)—at Girton College, Cambridge, in August 1946. A precedent had already been established by the churches of the FCC—together with their mission societies—empowering one person, Nolde, to act on behalf of the bedlam of Protestant voices in representing their interests in religious liberty to the U.S. government in 1944, and then at the San Francisco conference in 1945 in acting to help swing international opinion in favor of radical revision of the Dumbarton Oaks draft UN Charter. This achievement was built on at Cambridge, and Nolde was again empowered; this time he was to represent the Protestant world-level organizations, the WCC and the IMC, as their "ambassador" to the newly functioning UN organization in New York. It is evident from the CCIA files in Geneva that the work of the UN Commission on Human Rights (CHR) was the CCIA's principal concern in its first years, and that the adoption by the UN General Assembly of the Universal Declaration of Human Rights was perceived as a successful policy outcome.

The CCIA leadership pairing of Sir Kenneth Grubb[1] and Nolde was established in Cambridge, and they remained in office for more than twenty-two years. In 1954, at the Evanston Assembly of the WCC, their pioneering work was sufficiently recog-

126

nized that the CCIA was given the resources to build up a remarkably able and cohesive team. Its achievements over two decades—when the cold war was at its height and new Asian and African states by the dozen were beginning their life— deserve the serious historical attention they have not yet received.[2] After Visser 't Hooft retired as its general secretary in 1965 (when popular hopes for the UN's potential for a new world order had largely evaporated), the WCC let lapse its earlier symbiotic relation to the UN as the principal legitimizer of world organizations and began to redefine what functions the CCIA should serve.

At the high point of Nolde's period as its director, the CCIA had two offices, one in London and one in New York adjacent to the UN. The core staff of six met regularly in London, Geneva, or New York.[3] During the sessions of the UN Assembly, there would normally be up to twenty men and women working from the CCIA office in New York. In the 1960s the WCC brought a diminished and restaffed CCIA office to join its other departments (including the recently integrated IMC) under one roof in the rather grand new WCC building on the outskirts of Geneva.[4]

International affairs were extraordinarily prominent in what the first generation of leaders of the ecumenical movement (and none more than Visser 't Hooft himself) believed they were doing. Not only is that in itself noteworthy, but so is the persistence with which, from before World War II, they nourished the idea of a conference on the theme of "global order" as soon as was conceivably possible after the cessation of hostilities.

When the "International Conference of Church Leaders on the Problems of World Order" took place in Cambridge—only twelve months after VJ (Victory over Japan) Day—the memories of many of those present went back to the Oxford conference that had generated the WCC in an English university vacation context only nine years before. The Cambridge conference was the conclusion of preparations for the constituting assembly of the WCC in 1948 in Amsterdam, which had been delayed by the war, and foreshadowed the "ever-closer union" between the WCC and the IMC that was to be consummated in 1961 at its New Delhi Assembly. For those who had been together in Oxford and then Edinburgh in 1937, meeting again in Cambridge was an emotional experience. The partial overcoming of boundaries of denomination, language, and continent in building personal friendships and trust over the six weeks or so in that summer had been something new in the history of the Reformation churches. "Let the church be the church," "Una Sancta" (the one church dispersed throughout the world), and "evangelical catholicism" were banner phrases that delegates had taken back with them.[5]

The 1930s had seen populist fascist nationalisms and an equally populist Communist International. The ecumenical leaders also were internationalist, believing that being a baptized one-world Christian conferred a group identity more compelling than the holding of a state's passport.[6] Two years (for Americans, four years) after the Oxford and Edinburgh conferences, the world's states had relapsed into the mutual hatred and destruction of World War II. The years apart during the war saw strenuous (and often heroic) efforts to keep alive the 1930s experience of ecumenical unity in Christ among those who could not meet each other. It is not

surprising that many who were able to make their way to England in 1946—
especially those who had been active in the Resistance—still lived on their nerves.[7]
What was remarkable—in contrast with the 1920s after World War I—was the
heartfelt desire for reconciliation between Christian leaders of former enemy
nations,[8] who this time included Asians.

BUILDING ON SAN FRANCISCO

For the UN secretary general (Trygve Lie) and his colleagues, who had been
entrusted with the task of constructing a functioning diplomatic entity out of the
United Nations Conference on International Order (UNCIO), it was a difficult
twelve months. The UN's major godfathers quickly fell to quarreling in public. The
administrative structure, the buildings, the working languages, and the staffing of
the new organization all had to be set in train from scratch in New York, a city that
had no experience of diplomacy or of a world organization. Meanwhile the well-
oiled diplomatic machines of major states were engaging—in their national interests—with a succession of crises, and a great many nations were still in chaos. Putting the UN together began at a series of meetings in London at the end of 1945,
leading on from the first assembly to the setting up of the Economic and Social
Council (ECOSOC) and then in the spring to the small group charged by ECOSOC
with its UNCIO mandate as a Commission on Human Rights (CHR). Mrs. Eleanor
Roosevelt, the U.S. nominee, was elected its chair. It is not surprising that matters
arising from Article 71 of the UN Charter, relating to the role of nongovernmental
organizations (NGOs) in the work of ECOSOC, took some time to attract attention
and resolution.

The Federal Council of Churches (FCC) and the YMCA were determined not to
allow the end of hostilities to diminish their commitment to questions of global
order. The Four Fronts program was kept in high profile, and the FCC conference
in Columbus, Ohio, in March 1946 adopted seven "Program Suggestions on World
Order," including the annual keeping of "World Order Day" on the Sunday nearest
to October 24 "when the UN Charter became the law of nations." The paper produced for that section looked forward to the Cambridge conference and made two
complementary points of particular interest. The churches were "dedicated to the
progressive realization of the dignity and worth of man" and to "the world-wide
achievement of man's individual freedom, under God, to think, to believe, and to
act responsibly according to the dictates of his own conscience." And, remarkably,
the churches were now called upon to demonstrate—set in competition with communism—that a Christian society, confessing its past failures "to solve the social
and economic problems of our society," can in fact "enable all men to enjoy a fullness of life to an extent which not only equals but surpasses that which any other
faith can accomplish."[9]

From October 1945 on, there was widespread concern to exploit the potential of
Article 71. Dulles, Van Kirk, and Nolde in particular (with the enthusiastic assent of

Visser 't Hooft in Geneva) decided that the way to exert influence on the UN and its various subordinate entities was to find a way for one body to be empowered to represent the Protestant churches of the world (and the mission societies associated with them) on their behalf, and for this body to be recognized by the UN. From an early stage it was envisaged, at least by the Americans, that the person to represent this body would be Nolde. Concentration in the first place on the CHR would make sense in terms of Nolde's special interests. His record meant that he would satisfy UN requirements for an "observer" or "consultant."

It is unlikely (in the context of relations with the Catholic church in the 1940s) that it escaped the attention of Protestant leaders that this project would give their churches an instrument that could function for the first time, admittedly only in certain areas of concern and limited to the UN, in ways analogous to the Vatican's diplomatic service. What was of great practical importance was that in the procedures envisaged in the UN Charter it was only through its own state that any approach could be made to the UN by a citizen or a national organization (e.g., a church). Protestant churches were nationally organized (and often small), and their governments were indifferent or even hostile to them. It would therefore be advantageous to have an international and accredited instrument available as an alternative access to ECOSOC (and the UN generally). Such international organizations had been recognized in Article 71, which Nolde at Cambridge claimed "came into existence as the result of the insistence of the NGOs, chiefly in the United States."[10] Nolde had already come to the conclusion in October 1945 that the situation would call for a WCC-related body at the UN with one empowered representative.

The Commission to Study the Bases of a Just and Durable Peace (CJDP), of which Nolde was now a central figure under Dulles and Oxnam, wrote to the FCC to press its judgment that the coming meeting of the WCC's Provisional Committee in Geneva in February 1946 should have international affairs as a principal agenda item.[11] The WCC (and then the IMC's) Executive Committee met before the Provisional (Central) Committee, which received and approved the proposal that a Commission on International Affairs should be set up jointly, and that a Conference on International Affairs for at least sixty persons be held in London (later moved to Cambridge because of accommodation difficulties) in the following August, set between a range of other WCC and IMC meetings in England. This would economize on travel expenses. That summer, it was by no means certain that an international journey, once made, could easily be repeated; and it required high diplomacy, and management of Swiss neutrality, to get any German delegates at all to be present.

It is clear that the substantial delegation of Americans and Visser 't Hooft together pushed the Provisional Committee to these decisions. There were elements of faits accomplis in both the decision to set up a CCIA (which later on in August was deemed—rather curiously—to require the conference to repeat the process) and in the hijacking of a long-premeditated conference's agenda for the benefit of this particular proposal. The American delegation in Geneva in February— effectively the CJDP—offered to prepare the materials for the conference, organize it (with the assistance of Oliver Tomkins in London), and to a very considerable extent fund it, particularly its travel costs.[12] In the current state of the rest of the world, that was a straightforward condition of the event's happening at all.

Meanwhile, in the spring of 1946, Nolde continued with the procedures that had served him so well at UNCIO. His papers were full, rehearsing precedents and authorities, and largely factual in character, leading to a clear policy desideratum. He had given a blanket distribution of material to all the participants at UNCIO, and he repeated this to those attending the first UN Assembly in London.[13] And he continued to nourish his existing contacts with useful officials (and discouraged any thought of others striking up confusing parallel conversations). From early 1945 on, the appendixes Nolde attached to the minutes of Joint Committee on Religious Liberty (JCRL) meetings multiplied out of recognition—not least because Nolde had suddenly become a lead player in his own right. When, for instance, he wrote to Archibald MacLeish, the U.S. official responsible for setting up UNESCO, Nolde received a helpful reply with warm references to working together earlier throughout UNCIO. He was able to get frank personal advice from Easton Rothwell in the State Department about how best to influence the UN Assembly in London. When in April 1946 Nolde wanted to speak directly to Stettinius, then the U.S. representative to the UN, about the latest JCRL memorandum, he received a "too busy" reply citing the name of the officer he should speak with—which was presumably the result he hoped for.[14] Having had a high-level introduction to Chester Williams, Nolde went on to nourish close informal relations with other State Department officers—Durward Sandifer, James P. Hendrick, Walter Kotschnig, and Lyman White—who also were to be Eleanor Roosevelt's team in the work of the CHR.

One paper that Nolde drew up in June 1946, listing his contacts with the State Department over the previous two months, is particularly impressive.[15] The specific thread for these is the responsibility Nolde had taken on to write Paper III for the Cambridge conference, titled "The Churches and the United Nations: Problems of Liaison." When it finally appeared,[16] it had been reviewed by the relevant U.S. and UN public officials (as well as the churches) and thoroughly revised.[17] Nolde and Van Kirk were central in preparing the documentation for Cambridge on behalf of the WCC, which must have been quite galling for the Study Department in Geneva.[18] Nolde's role was helped by his membership in the continuation group of UNCIO veterans that worked under the auspices of the American Association for the UN, the Commission to Study the Organization of the Peace (CSOP), and the Carnegie Endowment in New York for optimum implementation of the CHR and NGO provisions in the UN Charter, and began to discuss draft bills of human rights.

It became clear in the spring of 1946 that the hoped-for churches' voice at the UN could not wait for the Cambridge conference in August; this may have been why the WCC Provisional Committee minuted in February that, in association with the IMC, it had set up the CCIA. Nolde was asked by the FCC to draft a letter of appointment to the UN, which was used (with appropriate changes) to produce four "to whom it may concern" letters at the end of April from the officers of the

FCC, the Foreign Missions Conference (FMC), the IMC,[19] and the WCC.[20] The four bodies also agreed to provide $1,500 in funding, shared equally, for six months' necessary expenses.

Nolde's first formal encounter, so equipped, with the CHR was on May 13. The "continuing informal committee" on human rights of CSOP had written to Mrs. Roosevelt as chair of the CHR on May 2 indicating the four points they wished to press: implementation, rights of minorities, freedom of communications, and an international bill of rights. A hearing was granted, and Clark Eichelberger presented nine "witnesses,"[21] of whom Nolde spoke first, true to form distributing copies of the JCRL's work—the *Statement,* two memoranda, and Bates's book—and making nine clear-cut proposals for the commission's agenda.[22] The preparatory ("nuclear") CHR, set up by ECOSOC in February, was to make its initial report to ECOSOC on May 25. In his weekly NBC radio program of May 18, Van Kirk spoke of "history being made" when "spokesmen of religious groups have appeared in person before any UN body for the purpose of recommending a given course of action," that is to say, "the inclusion of a UN Bill of Rights as a part of international law, enforceable by direct court action."

Among Nolde's concerns in the months before the Cambridge conference, establishing positions on the putative CCIA's status at the UN, two specific issues had arisen. One was to do with peace treaties: how should provisions for religious liberty be phrased? This had a particular focus for the imminent treaty with Italy. There the ancient Waldensian Protestant church was apprehensive about too easy a revalidation of the Vatican's ecclesiastical privileges granted in the 1929 Concordat with Mussolini. There was, however, a more generalized antagonism to the phrase "freedom of worship," which kept appearing in drafts throughout 1946, and was stubbornly promoted by the USSR. Dulles fought—equally stubbornly—at Moscow for the wording to be changed to "freedom of religion," which at least held open a richer range of interpretations.[23] The contrast between a one-dimensional "worship" provision (whose outworking had for twenty years been evident in the USSR), which at first seemed the probable wording, and the final text of Article 18 in the Universal Declaration of Human Rights is striking.[24] It was to be another major achievement of the JCRL and, subsequently, the CCIA.

A second issue that had to be resolved immediately was the form in which "religious liberty" should appear in UN trusteeship documents. Nolde was anxious that the door should be kept open in these provisions for the fullest development of liberty in the colonial and trusteeship territories. It had long been an IMC grievance that the authorities in the Congo had discriminated by funding Catholic mission schools and hospitals but not Protestant. It was gratifying that the Socialist postwar Belgian government had been quick to change this practice.

What, however, in this area was a step change confronting Western mission bodies was the principle enunciated, rather aggressively, by Nolde in a letter to Emory Ross of the FMC. It followed from his contention that religious liberty is the key to, but dependent on its position within, a general assertion of human rights. He was seeking the FMC's final agreement to the draft of the "Memorandum on Human

Rights and Fundamental Freedoms in Trusteeship Agreements with Particular Reference to Religious Liberty" that he issued on March 29.[25]

The principle that Nolde wished to assert as JCRL policy was that the memorandum should be written (he underlined) "from the standpoint of the inhabitants of trust territories," not "of missionary work." For "whatever missionaries may be permitted to do by way of entering territories, travelling, residing, holding property, erecting buildings, and so forth, will have to be inferred from the rights of the inhabitants 'to freedom of access and exposure to the cultures, ideas, and beliefs of other peoples, and freedom of cultural exchange.' Personally, I believe this form provides the kind of broad base on which missionary freedom should rest."[26]

GIRTON COLLEGE, AUGUST 1945

The delegates to the Cambridge conference began work on Sunday, August 4, and were together for four days. They were a disparate group. Those on the executive of the WCC had been involved in meetings immediately beforehand, with Oldham as host, in a rural farmhouse in Surrey. The Americans—and the two Canadians—had worked together closely in a relatively normal world throughout the war, had mastered their papers, and had traveled together. The British had undergone the strains of wartime scarcities and the blitz, but they had not had the experience of enemy occupation. They felt that they had shared both in forging the Allied victory and in the patterns of conversation throughout the war that had resulted in the conference, but that their assent to the CCIA proposal had yet to be secured, and assumed they could well veto it. The Geneva staff saw this as a first public opportunity to put into effect the vision of what the WCC had been founded to become. And the rest, individuals from a surprising range of continental European nations (plus one each from China and Australia), had arrived amid the gardens of Girton College direct from years of chaos, brutality, and starvation and not best prepared to debate the finer points of the American CJDP's papers or of a CCIA constitution.[27]

For Nolde, it began as a depressing first visit to Europe. He arrived in Cambridge, to be turned back by Visser 't Hooft and told he was not expected. That problem was sorted out, but the group did not jell together, and the American leadership began to sense possible shipwreck. Dulles and Nolde had registered that whiskey would not be easily available in postwar Cambridge, and they had brought their own supplies. They met to take refreshment and mutual encouragement in Dulles's room. At the end of the first two disappointing days, the atmosphere changed. Bromley Oxnam maintained in his diary that the turning point came when he told the conference of the success of the Methodist Church's Crusade for World Order campaigns; that, contrary to delegates' expectations, it was entirely possible to educate and enthuse congregations on issues of international peace and justice and human rights.[28] This was important, for Oldham, the patriarch of the whole movement, had been almost fatally cool in his response to the proposal in the early sessions—that it was overly ambitious in the light of the realities of the churches' life and of dubious utility.

It was difficult for the key Americans—notably Nolde—to talk through the questions being raised with those coming new to them as if it were possible the answer was undecided. After all, they had consulted at the highest level and continually revised their documentation for the previous six months. It was not likely that anyone else at the Cambridge conference had had comparable conversations with the leader of his national delegation to the UN, his foreign service's staff, and the officers of the UN. As long ago as May 22, Roswell Barnes had written on behalf of the FCC to give John G. Winant, head of the U.S. delegation to the UN, a confidential sight of Nolde's Paper III on Liaison with the UN for the Cambridge conference; to convey to him that Nolde had been appointed as their representative at the UN by the FCC, the FMC, the IMC, and the WCC together; and to claim that the churches expected to be given a consultative status at the UN not inferior to labor groups.[29] Real damage, and not just red faces, would be the consequence of failure to endorse what was already well in train.

The conference began on Sunday morning with a tradition-locating survey by Visser 't Hooft, who put forward names for approval; Dulles (United States) as chair, Boegner (France), Grubb (United Kingdom), and Francis Wei (China) as vice chairs, and Van Kirk and Visser 't Hooft as secretaries. Emil Brunner[30] chaired the Drafting Committee. The conference Message was to go out under the names of Boegner and Bishop Baker, the chairs of the WCC and the IMC.

The draft record of daily proceedings is in the Geneva archive, together with the *Message* published afterward in New York with an optimistic essay by Henry Smith Leiper titled "The Meaning of the Cambridge Conference."[31] Dulles, as chair, began and ended the conference. He started from the decision to establish the CCIA. He proposed four aspects that needed to be covered. The new body should not only be competent but Christian in its membership; it should also pay serious attention to disputed "facts" and work toward building a common understanding of them among Christian groups;[32] it should secure "a recognized standing in relation to the UN"; it should consider "parallel action" with Catholics and Jews in appropriate cases. The only specific issue he raised was that of relations with the Soviet Union, and the tensions that were now evident in every sphere. The conference was to have a report followed by discussion on "Russia and her satellites," and on other problem areas: Germany, Japan, Korea, China, the Balkans, and Indonesia. Dulles's advice on Russia was that "this was a problem that should not frighten the conference." "The Christian democracies," if they approached the matter with "clear vision and calm mind," could find a way to "lessen the tensions which now existed."[33] Dulles ended by voicing the general emotion at being in each other's company after the traumas of war. Clearly, Cambridge represented to him the taking up again of the 1939 conference in Geneva. Many of those present then had since suffered, and contact among them had often been minimal, except in regular intercessory prayer for each other and for the postwar world.

When the time came for Nolde to speak late that evening, it is doubtful how attentive the non–English speakers could by then have been. He spoke to the opportunity provided by Article 71 of the UN Charter for the churches to relate to ECO-SOC, and more generally to the UN. He briefly explained what had been set out in masterly detail in his Paper III on Liaison. It was rather technical. Nonetheless, he put his case. The conference should welcome the setting up of the CCIA; it should indicate areas of work (e.g., human rights and religious liberty) it considered important for the churches; whatever it did should be assured of the resources to perform competently; it should take seriously the appointment of a full-time executive secretary to build a network of personal contacts at the UN; and it should contemplate the advisability of an expanding network of national CCIAs. Characteristically, he found basic documents he might rehearse. The CCIA should appropriate Oxford and Madras. He concluded: "The approach begins with Oxford—e.g., the statement concerning international law (law must represent that which in the main they have already accepted—a world ethos). It would not be difficult to relate this to the General Assembly of the UN. Perhaps if we attack a great problem such as this, we may be able to find agreement. I am convinced that the Church has a testimony to make."

As these few days came to an end, and delegates began to be convinced they should endorse the CCIA, there was the usual end-of-conference high (which many of those present had not had to take into account for seven years). Even Oldham, who earlier had drizzled cold water on the project, came to the party and as the gathering's Grand Old Man gave it his blessing. He voiced the bass rumble that had (understandably after Hiroshima) underlain other speakers' words: "Nobody knows how long the world will go on, or the human race survive," but went on (after his initial irritability at the very notion) to endorse the CCIA proposal with enthusiasm.[34]

The decision was made to approve a draft constitution for the CCIA, for forwarding to special meetings of the WCC and IMC for formal confirmation within two weeks. There were to be two offices (in London and in New York). Grubb was invited to be director and Nolde associate director (with responsibility for developing relations with the UN). The CCIA was saddled with responsibility for preparing Section IV (International Affairs) of the constituting First Assembly of the WCC in 1948. This was also to entail editing the preparatory volume of studies. The only information about a budget was that it would be discussed by the Americans.

Grubb had the reputation for a somewhat mercurial temper, and he makes it clear in his autobiography that, so soon after discharge from his senior wartime role in the Ministry of Information, he had enough commitments in mind earning a living and enjoying some family life. He was, and remained through the autumn, unwilling to give a definite yes or no to the offer of director (which had no specified income attached). Clearly it was a field that attracted his sense of vocation greatly—in a semidetached way. But his hesitancy did not help the CCIA, which was due to be constituted on January 1, 1947. He finally accepted the title of director late in the year, but in the spring of 1947 it was agreed that Grubb should become chairman of council and Nolde be director. This was after an autumn of consider-able tension between them, including remarkably fiery letters from Grubb. It was, in fact, unreasonable to ask Nolde to refer decisions in connection with the UN back across the Atlantic. Grubb was persuaded—not before time—to cross to New York to take part in consultations with the FCC and FMC in December, which low-ered the temperature greatly. In fact, Nolde and Grubb soon took to each other and became for twenty years a familiar and complementary duo on the international and church scenes.

Grubb took responsibility for establishing CCIA's work with UNESCO, whose office was being set up in Paris under Julian Huxley as secretary general. There was a general presumption that this, rather than the UN, would become the appropriate forum—concerned with education and culture—for the churches' contribution to international affairs.[35] At the Cambridge conference, Sir Alfred Zimmern (who had been a major churches figure in the League of Nations world) was strongly of that opinion, and he emphasized the institutional autonomy of UNESCO, which unlike the UN had nothing to do with "the Powers." For whatever reason, however—Parisian *laïcité*, Grubb's working from London (and his tetchiness), Huxley's scien-tific humanism—the CCIA never managed to get an enduring foothold there. And it is evident that when in late 1947 UNESCO made its bid for philosophical authority over human rights, to be worked out in humble practical ways by the UN's CHR, it was quickly shown the door.

Grubb brought a great deal of lay experience of operating at leadership level in a government department, as well as in the world of mission societies. He and Nolde—presenting himself always as a seminary dean of graduate studies on sec-ondment—made a credible delegation on behalf of the churches in the "corridors of power." Neither of them could be described as "churchy"; Grubb took pleasure in his image of an adventurer back from the Amazonian forest, and Nolde came across as a rather Germanic "good fellow." Both of them were fiercely effectiveness oriented. After Grubb had accepted the invitation to be director, and had had his arm twisted to visit Nolde and the American Committee for the WCC, he wrote a report to Visser 't Hooft.

It shows his qualities. Major decisions had been made for the future of the CCIA: what were to be the shape and chapter topics of the book to be edited for the WCC's first assembly in Amsterdam; that CCIA contact with national governments would only be through national Christian councils; and that, as a joint creation of the WCC and the IMC, the CCIA's own "principles" for its positions on religious lib-erty would have to be grounded in the Oxford (WCC) and Madras (IMC) state-ments taken together. More immediately important, Grubb wrote: "I was able to achieve a wider measure of provisional agreement with Nolde than I had antici-pated. I think we can count on the enthusiastic support of the American group, and on the serious counsel of Mr John Foster Dulles."

Memories of the energy and staff work of the American panzers at Cambridge led Grubb to enjoy some mutual Old World quizzicality with Visser 't Hooft. This sheds light on differing perceptions of the conference's achievement then and later.

Grubb wrote: "What impressed me more than the actual formalities of discussion was the tempo of it. Many of our American friends actually believe that the Commission can play a positive part in developing harmonious international relations. It was difficult to make them see that we in Europe would regard it as a major mercy if the Commission was merely instrumental with other forces in avoiding or deferring major evils." And, "finally, I did my best to keep constantly in mind in the course of these discussions the requirement of a) Continental[36] Christianity, Protestant and Orthodox, and b) the Younger Churches. Americans are very ready to respond to either of these appeals, but unless they are kept to the fore, they are apt insensibly to drop off the stage."[37]

An analogy to this "dropping off the stage" can be seen in comparing the objectives set out for the CCIA—its "Charter"—with its actual achievements during its first twenty years under Nolde as director. The nine aims set out are prefaced by an emphatic assertion that "the primary responsibility of the CCIA shall be to serve the Churches, Councils, and Conferences which are members of the WCC and the IMC" in various ways. These were set out in order as "stimulus and knowledge," "medium of common counsel and action," and "organ in formulating the Christian mind on world issues and in bringing that mind effectively to bear upon such issues." The first of the aims was to foster national commissions, and then followed various aspects of resource gathering, conferences, study, coordination, ringing alarm bells on emerging problems. It was only at this point that the new body's attention was directed away from the essentially inward-looking church-serving functions that were in the event to take up so minor a portion of the CCIA's time. The seventh aim, from the context of Barthian imperatives in church "statement-making," makes an important provision. Nolde's Paper III on UN Liaison had made it clear that the UN Secretariat needed the churches to have one person commissioned internationally to speak with authority on their behalf. The source of the CCIA's early claim to be "substantive" was the provision in this seventh aim for the CCIA to "speak in its own name" when the WCC or IMC were not in session, provided it was made clear this had not been endorsed by the parent bodies. Then, at last, in the eighth aim came representation of the WCC and IMC "in relations with international bodies such as the UN and related agencies," and in the ninth, to work together with other organizations for "particular ends."

It would not be too unfair to Nolde to conclude that he had brought (with exemplary preparation) his own blueprint to Cambridge for a CCIA defined as relating to the UN and took it back to New York as the officer commissioned by world Protestantism to deliver—stamped with sufficient approval. Of course he was never offered the finances that alone might have funded major study projects. And in the decade after the WCC's Evanston assembly of 1954, the CCIA staff was expanded to be deployed in a ministry crisscrossing the globe to sit with academics and officials at conferences, and in personal discussion with leaders of increasingly antagonistic (and numerous) states. This led to the writing of many influential papers and to an important study on nuclear disarmament.[38] However, the CCIA's objectives in relating to international bodies, spelt out in the seventh aim, were certainly taken as normative for its work throughout the period. These were: "progressive development and codification of international law," human rights (with "special attention being given to the problem of religious liberty"), regulation of armaments, international economic cooperation, the well-being of dependent peoples ("including their advance towards self-government and the development of their free political institutions"), and the general field of UNESCO "enterprises."

When the matter of titles had been sorted out with Grubb, Nolde found himself early in 1947 the executive of an organization quite without precedent in Protestant Christianity. It had become shaped—largely through the whole-hearted continuing commitment of the faculty of his Philadelphia seminary and of his wife—around his personal availability and his understanding of what it was now possible, after UNCIO, for the "evangelical catholic" churches to work for in following their vocation. A "global ethos" of human rights had come to be seen as a credible goal whose achievement would benefit men and women of any faith, and which would be the precondition of a durable "global order." It seemed at the time reasonable that "everyone" could agree on what were the ingredients of a "good society." What would then be the case—in this new understanding of "Christendom"—was that the consequent protection of religious liberty under international authority might allow Christian witness and scholarship to take their opportunities in free competition without hindrance or privilege in every community in the world.[39]

It needs explanation why the Cambridge conference and its founding of an ecumenical instrument for international peace and human rights should so soon have been let lapse from celebration, and then even memory; for many of those present there had seen it as a moment of radical hope, worth bracketing with Oxford, Madras, and—to come in 1948—Amsterdam. Perhaps the answer lies in the apparent inability of the UN to fulfill in one generation the hopes raised at UNCIO. Perhaps it was the shifting of ground under mainline American Protestantism during the long struggle for civil rights and then the Vietnam war. Perhaps it was a sense of relief that the post–Vatican II Catholic Church had taken over responsibility for a Christian voice in favor of peace, justice, and human rights in international affairs. Perhaps it was the uneasiness with the concept of human rights that became prevalent among Protestant theologians. Perhaps it was the determination of the 1960s generation and after in the west to decouple religion from any questions of public morality, so that concern for human rights had to be given a secular frame (as in Amnesty International, with its limitation of vision to questions largely of imprisonment and torture). Perhaps it was the bifurcation of Protestant mission into a concern for community development in the "developing world," downplaying religious conversion, on the one hand, and one-dimensional, Bible-focused evangelism on the other. For whatever reason, Nolde did not rate an entry in the first edition of the *Dictionary of the Ecumenical Movement* published by the WCC in 1991.

NOTES

1. Kenneth Grubb (1900–80) was the son of a Church Missionary Society (CMS) missionary clergyman and, like Nolde, sought to claim some Scandinavian ancestry. He came

from an Ulster Irish family. His formative years were spent in Latin America, in work for missions among remote indigenous tribes, and on business. During the 1930s, he directed the Survey Application Trust in London, a fruit of the ambitious Protestant mission programs of the early 1920s. This involved managing sociopolitical research and consequent church publications. He was invited to join the Ministry of Information of the U.K. government in charge of its Latin America Section in 1939 and became its overseas controller in 1941. Appointed director of the CCIA at the 1946 Cambridge conference, he was uncertain whether to accept; in 1947 he became its chair of council and remained in that post until 1968. Among his leading roles in English Protestantism he served as president of the CMS and chair of the Church Assembly, House of Laity, Church of England. In 1970 he became a knight commander of the Most Excellent Order of Saint Michael and Saint George, an honor traditionally bestowed on diplomats. His vivid autobiography, *Crypts of Power* (London: Hodder and Stoughton, 1971), has a chapter on his engagement with the CCIA (pp. 163–200).

2. E.g., It would be valuable, now that state archives have become available, to have a study of the effect of the CCIA's contribution to the intense debates on nuclear proliferation and disarmament generally. Both Grubb and Nolde made a point of being present and available at the major East–West conferences on these topics. Nolde (and therefore the WCC) was in a privileged position from 1952, when Dulles became secretary of state. As an old colleague from the 1940s, he was able to get direct access to him.

3. The members of the CCIA team from 1954 to 1968 included Nolde and Grubb (who respectively ran the New York and London offices); Alan Booth, based in London working principally on disarmament; Richard Fagley, based in New York; and Dominique Micheli and Elfan Rees, working in both Geneva and New York. By the time of the Uppsala Assembly of the WCC in 1968 (following the radical Study Department conference on "Church and Society" at Geneva in 1966), all six were routinely castigated for being too white, too old, too "establishment," too anglophone, etc.

4. There had been a rapid expansion of the WCC's work. Up to 1945, the WCC office was in the Crêts de Champel, and it housed a maximum of seven or eight staff. The pressures of postwar relief work led to a considerably larger office being made from two houses on the rue Malagnou. The present office building occupies a whole block on the route de Ferney (Ferney was Voltaire's home village just across the border in France). Its internal garden-space is maintained from a trust fund raised to commemorate J. H. Oldham, in whose honor is a modest sundial outside the library. Many of the offices are currently leased to other bodies.

5. In opening the Cambridge conference, Visser 't Hooft emphasized its origins in the Life and Work conference of 1937 at Oxford. They "were meeting once again, as in that year, in a historical English university city." He paid tribute especially to the lay element at Oxford, and to William Temple and William Paton (who had convened "a peace aims group" at the beginning of hostilities); he then referred to the American CJDP's continuing work during the war years, "which had probably gone further to enlighten public opinion from the basis of the Church than almost anything that the Churches had done at any other time." World Council of Churches Library and Archives, Geneva, box 428.0.01.

6. Howard Schomer recounted that in a postwar meeting of the WCC Executive Committee, Bishop George Bell, its chair, came in waving a newspaper saying, "At last they've got it right." He was pointing to his photo alongside the headline, "Bishop puts loyalty to World Council Churches above Britain" (personal communication).

7. David Garnsey, later the Anglican bishop of Gippsland, was the Australian delegate at Cambridge. One of his principal recollections was of chain-smoking delegates and frequent overexcited confrontations (personal communication).

8. Two vivid moments in the reception of German church leaders into postwar ecumenical fellowship can be cited. In October 1945 the WCC brought an international delegation to meet a group of German church leaders in the flattened city of Stuttgart. Their *Declaration*

of guilt and reconciliation was of great importance, and much influenced by the martyr's death of Dietrich Bonhoeffer six months earlier. Soon afterward, a Lutheran conference was held in Lund, Sweden, to which a delegation of German church leaders arrived by train. The Scandinavian reception party on the platform included Bishop Berggrav, a hero of the Norwegian resistance. Neither group had met during the war years. An awkward silence was broken by Berggrav's asking, "Wie bist Du, Hans?" In America, the FCC had organized a conference with Japanese church leaders in California shortly before Pearl Harbor. A visit by American churchmen to Japan to renew the contact with the churches was organized soon after VJ Day.

9. National Council of Churches Records, Federal Council of Churches Records, Presbyterian Historical Society, Philadelphia (hereafter PHS [FCC]), RG 18, box 67, folder 22.

10. Both Dulles (in his opening speech as chair) and Nolde spoke at Cambridge in a frank way about their understanding of World War II. Hitler, Dulles declared, had been broken by "the moral forces of the world" and "the thought of Christianity." "There was today the United Nations Organization. This was primarily because of the religion of Christian people of Britain and the United States"—there had been no reference to "a world organization" in the Atlantic Charter. The "character of the UN Organization was very largely determined by the organized Christian forces which worked at San Francisco." WCC Archives, box 428.0.01.

11. At its meeting of November 8–9, 1945, the CJDP resolved "that the Chairman (Mr John Foster Dulles) appoint a committee to prepare a memorandum for submission through American members of the Provisional Committee of the WCC at their meeting in February proposing an international conference of the churches on world order." Dr. Samuel Cavert, the general secretary of the FCC, had been seconded to work with Visser 't Hooft—at his invitation—in the WCC office in Geneva in that postwar winter.

12. The North American delegation to Cambridge was numerous—twenty out of a total of sixty (including five Geneva staff). A press photo shows them at La Guardia Airport, climbing into a Pan-Am Constellation put at their disposal. Thirty-six of those present were native English speakers.

13. Nolde reported to the JCRL meeting of January 26, 1946, that he had personally submitted the JCRL Memorandum No. 4 plus a copy of Bates's book to officers of the State Department on November 14, 1945, and to Mrs. Roosevelt, "just prior to her departure for the UNO meeting." In January a letter with the Memo had gone to John G. Winant, the U.S. delegate to the first meeting of ECOSOC, and to Dulles. Sixty copies of the "Essential Human Rights" issue of *Annals* that included Nolde's paper were flown to London for heads of delegations at the London UN General Assembly. Five hundred copies for each of their members followed by the *SS Queen Mary*, and 200 packs had gone to the WCC at Geneva, containing the *Annals* issue, the current issue of *Christendom*, and the *Information Service Digest* of Bates's book. There is more than a suspicion that Nolde chafed at not being present in person at London as he had been at UNCIO in San Francisco. Certainly the British churches neither intended nor were equipped to mount a comparable effort.

14. Nolde was sufficiently self-confident to ask Trygve Lie, the new UN secretary general, for an appointment, but was not successful. PHS (FCC), RG 18, box 67, folder 19.

15. Nolde's systematic and wide-ranging pursuit of contacts is given prime illustration in his report "The Churches and the United Nations. Problems of Liaison." On October 25, 1946, he submitted this report of his activities from the beginning of April to the JCRL. He attached his Cambridge paper III, a list of five "ends accomplished," and a "chronology of procedures . . . to illustrate in a general way the manner in which the investigation was carried on." Grubb's name is notably absent. These documents are in PHS (FCC), RG 18 67 22.

16. This paper was substantial (23 pp.). Papers I and II related to a questionnaire—a familiar tool of the academic educationalist. PHS (FCC), RG 18, box 67, folder 22.

17. E.g., Cavert wrote to Nolde on May 20 that he had "done an excellent job," but advised against Nolde's use of the phrase "the Evangelical Catholic churches." Cavert had two reser-

vations. The first was that Nolde had presumed that the CCIA would relate only to the UN, but other fields of work should also be addressed. The second was that too little prominence was given to "study." He doubted whether any contemporary churches (other than in Britain and the United States) would be able to submit well-informed and persuasive views to the UN. Effectiveness would depend on the WCC's doing "a first-rate job of education within its own constituency." PHS (FCC), RG 18, box 67, folder 22.

18. Nils Ehrenström of the WCC's Study Department had written rather plaintively to Cavert on August 27, 1945: "The time is now come when the World Council Headquarters can and must resume a definite responsibility in stimulating and coordinating the thinking of the churches on international problems." WCC Archives, box 24.162.

19. Decker, the IMC's New York secretary, wrote to Nolde on April 26, explaining the situation: He had consulted the chairman and committee members of the IMC, who "had been very enthusiastic" about the proposal that Nolde should represent the IMC at the UN; he had written to Goodall, his cosecretary in London, asking him "to cable if he saw any reason for dissent," but had had no reply; so, giving Goodall a few more days, he said "Go ahead." Decker finished: "The IMC considers itself exceedingly fortunate in having you as its representative in establishing and using the prospective relationships with the UN." PHS (FCC), RG 18, box 67, folder 20.

20. The text of the WCC version of this standard letter ran: "I hereby request O. Frederick Nolde, Ph.D., to explore possible avenues of relationship between the World Council of Churches and the United Nations, to communicate through my office to the World Council of Churches information concerning arrangements proposed by the United Nations for relationships with voluntary agencies, and to make such representations to the United Nations as may from time to time be authorized by the World Council of Churches." Interestingly, the letter on behalf of the WCC Provisional Committee in Geneva was on 1943 notepaper of the "American Office" in New York, and signed by its long-time "Secretary in America," Henry Smith Leiper, as "Associate General Secretary of the Provisional Committee of the WCC." PHS (FCC), RG 18, box 67, folder 22.

21. The delegation consisted of Nolde (the FCC "and other Protestant bodies"), Proskauer (American Jewish Committee), and Fr. George B. Ford (Church Peace Union); and also included representatives of the National Women's Trade Union League; the American Bar Association; the National Conference of Christians and Jews; the National Association of Broadcasters; the Motion Picture Association; and the American Civil Liberties Union, represented by Roger Baldwin, who also presented a letter from William Draper Lewis (American Law Institute) and a communication from the International League for the Rights of Man (of which Henri Laugier, a French secular socialist, now deputy secretary general of the UN, was president). PHS (FCC), RG 18, box 67, folder 21.

22. In his submission Nolde speaks "in behalf of the FCC and the FMC, working through their JCRL, but also in behalf of the two church-constituted world bodies, the WCC and the IMC." He goes on: "By inference from the documents [prepared by the JCRL for submission to the State Department and now to the CHR] I suggest a few actions that may properly receive consideration in these early meetings of the nuclear commission." His concluding paragraph assured the commission of the churches' wish to be related to the CHR "in such manner as will be deemed appropriate." He claimed that "through political instrumentality conditions favorable to the observance of human rights can be created." PHS (FCC), RG 18, box 67, folder 21.

23. A letter from Nolde to Secretary of State Byrnes of June 6, 1946, repeats the objection to defining religious liberty as "of worship," this time in the context of the draft Finnish peace treaty as "probably the pattern of a paragraph on human rights to be written into all peace treaties." PHS (FCC), RG 18, box 66, folder 26.

24. The draft International Bill of Rights prepared in April 1946 by the CSOP Human Rights Committee (of which Nolde was a member) proposed as Article I an antidiscrimina-

tion clause (including religion) and an Article II, "every person is entitled to freedom of conscience and belief and freedom of religious association, teaching, practice and worship." The newly established British JCRL (whose chair was Sir Ernest Barker and secretary, Max Warren) had begun to produce a "Declaration on Human Rights" that had a powerful influence on the text later put forward by the U.K. government. By October, the CSOP committee—"a research affiliate of the American Association for the United Nations"—had revised and expanded its proposals, so that the discrimination article was now Article II and religion was Article V, followed by a new Article VI (in which it is hard not to see Nolde's hand): "Every person has the right to form and hold opinions and to receive opinions and information made available from any source." PHS (FCC), RG 18, box 67, folder 3.

25. PHS (FCC), RG 18, box 67, folder 3.

26. PHS (FCC), RG 18, box 67, folder 19.

27. Girton, then the senior Cambridge college for women, on the outskirts of the city, was presumably chosen because one of the two bursars (Mrs. Marjorie Hollond or Miss K. Murray) was known to the staff of the British Council of Churches. *The Girton Review* of Michaelmas 1946 refers to the Old Students' Weekend in July as highlight of the Long Vacation and to "conferences of less immediate interest to the college"—including the World Council of Churches—bringing "many distinguished and colourful visitors."

28. Bromley Oxnam's diary for Monday, August 4, records the nadir of the conference and Dulles's depression about the outcome. Oxnam is surprised and distressed that even Oldham "has taken a most reactionary view." Like "all the British here throughout," Oldham "tried to tear into shreds the recommendations that we coordinate the work of the churches." So Oxnam "found it necessary to reply very, very respectfully to him pointing out what had happened in the US as the CJDP had moved with power at San Francisco. I outlined in detail our Crusade for a New World Order. The response was almost electric. Professor Brunner came to me afterward. He said 'We had never dreamed that any such work had been done by churches anywhere. This is the way.' It seemed to be the turning point as far as the Commission was concerned." Library of Congress, Oxnam Papers, Diary 1946, vol. 2, box 15.

29. PHS (FCC), RG 18, box 67, folder 20.

30. Emil Brunner (1889–1966) was professor of theology at Zurich (1922–53). Brunner was a "dialectical theologian," opposed to theological liberalism but, unlike Barth, open to natural theology. He was much used in YMCA and World Student Christian Federation circles in the 1930s and 1940s.

31. WCC Archives, box 428.0.01.

32. *The Cambridge Modern History* (1902–10), so influential on both Shotwell and Dulles, had its starting point in the thesis expounded by Lord Acton, its founding editor, that a fundamental step could be taken to heal the ongoing conflict between Catholic and Protestant myths of the sixteenth-century Reformation. Historians of both parties should work to establish those "facts" in their stories on which they could agree, and build out from that experience.

33. Dulles discouraged the conference from associating itself with the current Vatican "crusade against Russia" and its "hostility to the Orthodox communion." In Leiper's essay on the conference's "meaning," he goes out of his way to explain that this was not to be misinterpreted; there was in general "a strong disposition to find ways" of working together with the Roman Catholics.

34. The closing of this conference was an emotional moment for Dulles, the realization of a dream. His words revealed the vision that had driven him since his acceptance of the chair of the CJDP. Extracts from his and Oldham's concluding speeches are reproduced in appendix I.

35. Most lay well-wishers in the diplomatic world, as well as European churchmen, assumed that the organization to which the churches might most appropriately relate was UNESCO.

36. Grubb, as was general at the time, did not include Britain in "the Continent," which could so easily be "cut off by fog in the Channel."

37. Grubb to Visser 't Hooft, December 19, 1946. WCC Archives, box 428.0.02.

38. Alan Booth, *Not Only Peace: Christian Realism and the Conflicts of the Twentieth Century* (London: SCM Press, 1967).

39. A comparable situation is envisaged by David L. Edwards in the chapter on a "Common Market in Religion" in his *Christians in a New Europe* (London: Collins, 1990).

CHAPTER 9

♦

Finding a Text

THERE WERE MANY situations in late 1946 in which the World Council of Churches (WCC) and the International Missionary Council (IMC) might have used the instrument that they had set up in Cambridge for action at a global level. It seemed a long year since the San Francisco conference had ended with assertions of a twentieth-century "peace on earth and goodwill toward men" from all present. Not least, there were anxieties (for different reasons) about the immediate future of the Christian churches in India and China. The continental European churches were wholly preoccupied with unprecedented numbers on the road to somewhere (whether demobilized servicemen, returning prisoners of war, or displaced populations), with widespread hunger, and with the reconstruction of organized society. Those with responsibility had to come to terms with what the Soviet military presence was likely to mean for Eastern Europe, and in Western Europe, governments coming to be dominated by Kremlin-controlled parties of the left in France, Italy, and Greece in particular. The Vatican's hostility to Soviet Russia was focused close to home—on how to prevent the disaster of an elected Communist government in Italy. The principal concern of the saintly George Bell, the bishop of Chichester in England and heir to William Temple's role as chair of the WCC, was world reconciliation, and especially the reception of a "new" Germany. However, the field of vision of the Commission of the Churches on International Affairs (CCIA) was largely confined to the potential offered by the UN.

The leaders of national Protestant churches and mission societies were unable to give time, either individually or together, to shape the CCIA's work. Whatever work that would be, there was no indication at first that it would have substantially more resources than an initially halfhearted (and very part-time) Grubb in London, and Nolde in New York,[1] still juggling an ostensibly full-time teaching load at his seminary in Philadelphia. By early 1947, however, it was possible to have an administrative secretary, Sartell Prentice Jr., and a stenographer join the New York office, from which the finances were managed, with Philip Eastman serving half time in London. The annual budget of April 1947 was $50,000. Financially, the WCC and IMC shared costs as generously as they could, and prospects for effective action improved when John D. Rockefeller (a close friend of Dulles) made one of a sequence of substantial donations to the postwar WCC for this work.

Where the national churches did give practical help in the first months of the CCIA was in finding candidates—principally laypeople—from a number of countries who could be invited to serve as the CCIA's international commissioners. Interestingly, these were recruited by the London and New York offices according to the traditional IMC division of territories. And in a few countries, it was possible to begin to put together a body of nationals for the commission officers to feed and be fed by.[2] Getting this initially rather overly complex and clanking international machine constituted and serviced, and providing it with a common sense of its conventions of operation, was a major time-consuming task.[3] Nolde undertook it.

The Joint Committee on Religious Liberty's (JCRL's) secretary, Miss Amelia Wyckoff, who had been employed principally to help Nolde set up the New York resources center and archive, found herself "by arrangement giving some time to the commission with special attention to UN documentation." She was soon transferred to the CCIA as "documentation secretary." A challenging quantity of additional paper descended on her from the UN. Nolde had registered the CCIA with the UN Department of Public Information directly after the Cambridge conference. This replaced the previous subscription service to UN publications and press releases. Such access, Nolde reported, was "imperative if the CCIA is to keep the churches informed about what is happening and at the same time identify issues on which the Christian conscience should be registered." The CCIA, at this stage, was the only church-recipient of UN materials, and the UN was discussing whether other centers in the world might receive "limited documentation." In the four months so far, poor Miss Wyckoff had become dizzy with the weight of paper she was attempting to control and the categories she had to establish to make it accessible for use.[4]

Grubb had been persuaded to take time out to fly to the United States in December 1946 for the first substantial discussions on how the CCIA was to be run. Happier with his role after that, he made a further visit in the spring of 1947. This led up to the CCIA Executive Committee[5] meeting on April 25–26 at the Federal Council of Churches' (FCC's) traditional center for its conferences at Buck Hill Falls in the countryside north of Philadelphia. This was an occasion that set the CCIA's future course. Grubb ceded the title of director to Nolde (which made day-to-day sense in the context of the UN), and he himself became executive chairman.

It is clear that Nolde made himself familiar in the corridors of the UN from the beginning. He made contacts—and even friendships—with both staff members of other nongovernmental organizations (NGOs) and the State Department officers prominent in establishing the UN world. He initiated conversations about what category of representation it would be possible for the churches to be granted. On September 17, 1947, the secretary general wrote to Grubb informing him that the CCIA had been granted consultative status in category (b)—which was what had been hoped for—and that a condition of this was that the previous status of the IMC at the UN should be folded into the CCIA. Grubb replied asking that all future communications be addressed to Nolde's office in New York.[6]

Ten years later, the CCIA had become an impressive international network. A real problem was to surface, however, as the judgment of the national commissions, composed largely of lay retired diplomats and distinguished academics with a few theologians, was rarely able to mesh fruitfully with the ecclesiastical bodies that had invited them to serve. As a result, there was little educational benefit to national churches. Congregations were rarely encouraged by clergy to pay attention as Christians to international problems or routinely directed to their national CCIA for information and guidance. Clergy who felt called to be "prophetic" on what they and their friends deemed to be "the issues" often preferred not to bring in alternative authorities, especially ones who were knowledgeable and elderly—and lay.

The upshot was that the first two years of the CCIA can be described—with little remainder—as preoccupied with human rights. Because Nolde was the man already on deck at the UN working from carefully prepared positions, and (with the support of the American JCRL) was entirely persuaded that this was the strategic pressure point for Christians in the current range of international problems and opportunities, the UN came to define the CCIA. No one important objected that religious liberty, for instance, was only a secondary issue, or that the UN had very little practical significance. Because even Nolde had only limited energy, what Nolde did not choose to do was rarely done.

There is in consequence an executive directness and coherence in what was achieved in those two years. One of Nolde's techniques was an extension of his practice of citing the cumulative background of previous documents in any new report he was called on to write. In his many speeches and articles, he would reuse whole paragraphs from the past; the personal-computer commonplace of cutting and pasting would have been a godsend to him. Editing a book on international questions in a series for Christian students in America[7] was helpful in shaping his postwar horizon. Then came his central article in the preparatory volume—principally edited by Grubb—for Section IV (International Affairs) of the WCC's First Assembly at Amsterdam in August 1948.[8] Finally, the Assembly Report gave emphasis to its freestanding statement on religious liberty[9]—extremely timely in the context of that autumn's hammering out of the UN Universal Declaration of Human Rights—which was thereby given the specific international authority of both the WCC and the IMC. It shared family features both with the JCRL *Statement* of 1944 and the UN Declaration as it emerged in December.[10]

Nolde was frequently invited to preach, give speeches, and write papers in these years. But above all he was a presence, in personal lobbying and presentations, during the drafting of the Universal Declaration of Human Rights and its passage through the Commission on Human Rights (CHR; and its Drafting Committee), then the Economic and Social Council (ECOSOC), then Committee III, and finally the General Assembly of the UN and its approval without a dissenting voice on December 10, 1948, in Paris. Its provision for freedom of conscience, religion, and belief had been substantially affected by the direct and indirect influence of the CCIA. At the height of the intense efforts to prevent last-minute amendments in Committee III to the CHR's draft Article 16, Visser 't Hooft wrote to thank Nolde in Paris for his report. He took pleasure in news of the back-and-forth of diplomatic chess. "But," he wrote, "I am writing especially to congratulate you warmly on your own work. I know enough of the situation to realize that article 16 [the eventual Article 18] would probably be a heap of ruins by now if you had not worked so hard and so intelligently to protect it from all onslaughts. If it becomes international law, you will always be able to feel that this is in a very special sense *your* article."[11]

In 1948, in Amsterdam, Nolde was appointed associate general secretary for international affairs of the WCC, to go alongside the title on his calling-card of dean of graduate students of the Lutheran Theological Seminary at Philadelphia. He had already begun (largely by pressure of time) to drift away from the roots in the American JCRL that had given him a base and his principal colleagues of reference, and this connection was severed. From that point on, the work of the CCIA became much more multistranded and international, and it deserves a level of attention—especially since the Soviet archives have become available[12]—it has not so far received. The suggestion that the UN might invent "peacekeeper" observers at the time of the Korean War was, for instance, the CCIA's.

PREPARING THE GROUND

There was a good deal of confusion in the Commission on Human Rights in the first half of 1947 as it began work. The Moscow conference of foreign ministers in March had shown the hard realities of contention within which the world of international affairs—even for those states that wanted to be a "Third World"—now had to be carried on. George Marshall, the U.S. secretary of state, drew a new sharp line between "police-states" and "freedom." His statement in Moscow on March 14 made points very close to Nolde's position on human rights.[13] Dulles was converted to the view that relations with the Soviet Union were by no means hopeless but would have to be conducted—if possible peacefully—as with a determinedly hostile aggressor.[14] This meant that those charged with establishing what the UN Conference on International Order (UNCIO) had had in mind in 1945 could not expect harmonious give-and-take. It is a remarkable tribute to Eleanor Roosevelt in chairing the CHR that she managed to control its business, build the affection and respect of its members, and deliver the text of a declaration that was in the end approved with abstentions but no contrary votes.[15] At every point in the process, the Soviet group of states made plain its opposition to a large part of what was being undertaken—by their tactics, lobbying, and speaking. Observers spoke admiringly of the outstanding intellectual quality of those chosen to make the Soviet case.[16]

A public self-consciousness took over of a United States organizing itself militarily, ideologically, and economically for confrontation with the USSR. From the point of view of the FCC and its associates, this threatened to subvert their wartime achievements in swinging opinion behind involvement in new institutions of global order.[17] The FCC, YMCA, and YWCA had determined that—once hostilities had ended—they would not slacken off the urgency of their grassroots campaigns to keep American opinion focused on playing its part in establishing a "moral" global order, and in particular a "curative and creative" UN. In January 1947, for instance, the Executive Committee of the FCC published a congratulatory statement on the recent first General Assembly of the UN, picking out six "concrete achievements," and calling on "the American people and our Government" to "bend every effort to the end that this great new world institution shall, in fact, function for peace and justice." But events were not helpful to keeping open a space for that hope.

In the *Houston Press* of March 27, for instance, Elliott Roosevelt was writing of his time at the Tehran conference, reporting his father and Churchill as supine drunken dupes of Stalin. The beginnings of McCarthyism took root. Some of the most honorable and publicly visible leaders of the FCC's international policy, like the Methodist bishop G. Bromley Oxnam—and similarly leaders of the YMCA— were accused of being soft on communism. In general, the ecumenical leadership was accused of insufficient enthusiasm for red-blooded economic capitalism. They were accused of "east-coast elitism." It was not unremarked that Alger Hiss had served as the secretary general of UNCIO in 1945. Another contributing factor was the virulent hostility of Protestants of the Carl McIntyre school to international bodies or ecumenical entanglements, dating from the 1920s controversy about biblical authority within the Presbyterian churches.[18] For whatever reason, Eleanor Roosevelt felt in mid-March that she had to offer her resignation as U.S. representative on the CHR to the State Department.[19]

The growing commitment of the FCC (and the CCIA) to the "fight against racism" within American society (and soon against apartheid in South Africa) led to disaffiliations, and thus a smaller constituency to endorse FCC statements. The ecumenical leaders continued to make the point that America could only hope to inspire a "moral" world order that rivaled the attraction of communism if it was prepared to clean up its own backyard. That was not at first a widely welcome idea. What became a more popular apologetic (in America as elsewhere) for the "free world" was that it led not so much to an outward-looking "good society" as to higher personal disposable incomes.

For Nolde, February 1947 was a full month. He produced two more of his memoranda. The one on the German peace treaty was dated March 5 and addressed from the JCRL to the U.S. secretary of state.[20] It was principally concerned that the precedent of using the phrase freedom of "worship" in the Italian treaty should be broken. He cites the bad consequences in Russia of such phrasing. Remarkably, Marshall and Dulles succeeded in breaking down determined opposition from Molotov to a change to freedom of "religion." The second, dated March 4 and addressed from the CCIA to the director of the UN Secretariat's Human Rights Division (John P. Humphrey),[21] was a "Memorandum on Provisions for Religious Liberty in an International Bill of Rights."[22]

Nolde realized this was a critical moment, and that the churches needed to make a move. But he felt the absence of any CCIA group that might empower him to act. An initial draft of a Bill of Rights was being prepared by Humphrey (who "in all probability will play a large part in what is produced at this level") for circulation to the CHR on April 1. But what action, Nolde asked Henry Smith Leiper (the representative of the WCC in North America) on February 25, should he take, and by what authority (as still only "associate director")? Rather, should the JCRL be the source of any memorandum?[23] Nolde sent the memorandum on behalf of the CCIA to Humphrey on March 4 and then on the following day, after a meeting of the JCRL, another copy on behalf of the JCRL. In that letter he explicitly gives priority to the JCRL as having "formally approved" it, and he refers to the background of the JCRL's track record on behalf of religious liberty at the San Francisco conference. With regard to the CCIA, he can only cite "a measure of formal endorsement" and assure Humphrey of the CCIA's interest in the CHR's work and "our desire to lend assistance in every appropriate way." This offended Nolde's principles of representation.

The contents of this memorandum on "provisions for religious liberty" form another of Nolde's building blocks, based principally on the formal reports of the WCC and the IMC in the 1930s and on the JCRL *Statement* ("extensively used by church leaders in other lands"). Two principles for ensuring religious freedom are advanced. The first is that the "rights and freedoms necessary to the full exercise of religion" should be spelled out[24]—or at least not be potentially open to constriction by a general phrase; the danger posed by simply using the word "worship" was still a real one. The second was the principle dear to Nolde's heart, that religious rights should be seen as only an element in the wider package of rights on which their exercise depended. An attempt was made to change an important sentence in his draft, but he repulsed it. The question of foreign missionaries was always at issue: It was why mission societies were interested at all, and it was a major cause of governmental unwillingness to get involved. So "freedom of missionary persuasion" was proposed to Nolde as an addition. Nevertheless, the memorandum text followed his position. It ran: "Freedom to carry on missionary activities involves all or many of the other freedoms. Its bases may be found, on the one hand, in freedom of access to information or freedom of cultural exchange and, on the other, in freedom to express one's convictions anywhere in the world."

Three related draft documents appeared at the same time as this memorandum; from the U.S. State Department, the Human Rights Committee of the Commission to Study the Organization of the Peace (CSOP), and the British Council of Churches. The first, a draft Bill of Rights from the State Department, was forwarded to Mrs. Roosevelt by its legal adviser on March 14.[25] His enthusiasm for a proposed bill was limited. He saw it as of little practical value without "a strong means whereby the individual may be protected in the rights which are recognized." The draft had nine articles. The first, remarkably, used the phrase "endowed by their Creator with certain natural, inherent, and inalienable rights." Religion followed as Article 2: "All persons are entitled to enjoy freedom of religion according to individual conscience, of public and private worship, of speech and of the press. The full and free dissemination of knowledge and information may not be denied or abridged."

CSOP (for this purpose, the "Research affiliate of the American Association for the UN") published its own *Draft International Bill of Human Rights* with a prefatory note by James Shotwell.[26] More than forty organizations were listed as endorsing it, including the JCRL. Its Human Rights Committee had some seventy names, including Nolde. Shotwell placed the committee's work firmly in the tradition of the UNCIO; it was "a direct continuation of the work of the Consultants of the American delegation," "culminating in the proposal for the erection" of the CHR. He stressed the "economic rights of the common man," "the extension of the field of human rights to cover the normal conditions of living has been a matter of genuine concern to all those who have worked upon the problem of human rights." As chair of the UNCIO consultants, Shotwell's conclusion was significant; that the proposed bill was rooted not in theory but in both "universal history" and the "needs of the world today." He sees it with one leg in the Institutes of Justinian and the other in the "Anglo-Saxon insistence on the rights of man" within his local community that "found expression in Magna Carta." The proposed articles on religion related to nondiscrimination, general freedom of association, and Article 5: "Every person has the right to freedom of conscience and belief and freedom of religious association, teaching, practice, and worship" (to which should be added Nolde's missionary concern, Article 6: "Every person has the right to form and hold opinions and to receive opinions and information from any source").

The British JCRL, in the short time it existed with Max Warren as its secretary, was able to produce *Human Rights and Religious Freedom*.[27] This was not a draft bill, but its thinking was influential on the draft the British government put before the CHR. Most of its members were clergy. The claim this weighty essay advanced was that "religious freedom is the fundamental human freedom in which alone the true dignity of human personality can be fostered and its highest capacities flower [cp. Maritain's "blossom"]. The right to it is therefore inalienable at all times and in all circumstances, and ought to be acknowledged and duly safeguarded by the State." Seven categories of civil rights for its protection were proposed and outlined, together with three more specifically Christian requirements relating to changing religion, aspects of associations, and religious education. Considerable attention was given to religious minorities, but of course no treatment of minorities of any kind found its way into the final declaration.

Any protection being sought for religious liberty should emphatically be for all religious faiths equally. Interestingly, the British statement, at Grubb's suggestion,[28] was forwarded to Humphrey via Nolde at the CCIA, a first consequence of the decision that he become director.

Eleanor Roosevelt, as chair of the CHR, decided in June that a smaller body would be needed to hammer out draft texts, whether for a declaration or a convention (which would have legal force). Australia, China, Chile, France, Lebanon, the United Kingdom, the United States, and the USSR were appointed forthwith to a Drafting Committee to work on the basis of a draft bill to be compiled by John Humphrey (and then reordered by René Cassin,[29] the French representative and jurist). To a surprising degree, these eight representatives each made powerful, valid, and complementary contributions. Their personal commitments became a collegial group commitment—even for its Soviet members—whose sense of vocation spilled out, to give the process of making the declaration a dimension approaching exaltation at its climax in the General Assembly. It was an experience that was—and perhaps remains—without parallel in the history of the UN. For those also playing committed roles offstage, like Nolde, the period from June 1947 to December 1948 was a drama and a battle that was consuming and unforgettable.

It was partly from this sense of engagement that UNESCO was sidelined. The continuation group of American NGOs after UNCIO had been anxious for members of the CHR to be selected for their personal experience and wisdom. When the time came, they were in fact nominated by their states. When UNESCO put its query about the basis of human rights out for responses from the nations of the world, it approached individual "philosophers."[30] They were idiosyncratic choices. From the point of view of religious liberty, it was fortunate that the report[31] presented by UNESCO to the CHR—with high hopes of receiving the respect and continuing involvement due from the executive arm to the heirs of Plato—was largely ignored. In it, reference to religion had been studiously avoided. It is very evident that members of the UN Drafting Committee—especially Malik, Andrei Vyshinsky, and T. C. Chao—saw their dialectical exchanges as essentially philosophical and as needing no outside help. Dean Acheson had sent a robust message to Julian Huxley on April 25 informing him of the State Department's insistence that UNESCO should not involve governments beyond informing them of its approach to individual philosophers. It was through the CHR that governments would communicate on "the political and legal issues involved in establishing [an] international bill"; and nothing should be done that "might be interpreted as duplicating [its] work."[32]

A meeting of the JCRL immediately preceded the CHR Drafting Committee session of June 9–23. S. A. Morrison from Cairo, the IMC's principal figure in Moslem discussions, and Rallia Ram and Rajah Manikam, secretaries of the Indian National Christian Council, were present, and particular attention was paid to India and its Constitution after independence. The first draft of Nolde's paper on religious liberty for the Amsterdam volume had been circulated for comment. There was continued good news about sales and translations of Bates's *Religious Liberty*, and it was agreed that two copies of each language edition should be deposited at the UN. Nolde's report on developments at the UN included his satisfaction that one of the proposals of the JCRL's Memorandum No. 4 had been followed up (that it would be helpful to have a compilation of "law and usage relating to human rights" in all member states); this was now in the press, to be published as the UN *Yearbook on Human Rights*. The Commission to Study the Bases of a Just and Durable Peace was preparing a statement (adopted June 20), "Crossroads of American Foreign Policy," for submission to the FCC.[33] But there was still alarm at the possibility of "freedom of worship" slipping through at the UN as the easy solution to a religious freedom requirement in the international bill.

This anxiety was justified. The Drafting Committee was circulated on June 12 with the Secretariat's promised document, tabulating Humphrey's Draft Outline, the U.K. Draft, and the U.S. Proposals. The British draft was full. The Secretariat's was brief: "There shall be freedom of conscience and belief and of private and public religious worship." Nolde's response was swift. On June 15, he sent Mrs. Roosevelt a telegram (from Delaware University) in the name of the CCIA, which he claimed somewhat exaggeratedly as representing "the Protestant and Orthodox churches throughout the world."[34]

On June 19, James Hendrick, the principal State Department officer attached to Mrs. Roosevelt and frequently consulted by Nolde, sent her a memo suggesting she might wish to summarize Nolde's telegram (as she had done for the memo from the Jews[35] on June 18) to the committee. He proposed: "It is the opinion of the CCIA that religious freedom involves more than the right to worship; that the rights of teaching, preaching and persuasion and the right to carry on activities of value to the community and the right to change one's religion are also important." Dulles was also in play. He wrote informally to Mrs. Roosevelt on June 24, about a family visit, and wanting a chance to talk, and making the point against freedom of "worship."[36]

At the end of the session, Mrs. Roosevelt had no illusions about the probability that any text would have to be "fought out with the USSR paragraph by paragraph," and that it would only be "very late in the proceedings" that the USSR would show its hand on acceding to a convention.[37] In his brief report to the CCIA, Nolde was still uncertain as to how opinion was shaping on the "worship" issue, and on the question of freedom to change one's belief.

Nolde found himself in a very different community of discussion when the WCC's "Study Commission IV (CCIA)" convened outside Geneva on June 24–26 preparatory to Amsterdam the following year. Grubb was forced to show his skills as chair. Twelve were present (including both Visser 't Hooft and Van Dusen), the majority from Europe. Papers for the publication had been circulated, and debate— recorded in thirty-two pages of notes—was wide-ranging and intense.[38] The discussion of Nolde's draft revealed the degree to which many continental Europeans (especially those from what were to become the Warsaw Pact states) felt the UN was somehow an "unreal" entity, that there was great risk in "reducing" Barthian theological language for use in supporting the juridical protection of human rights, and that the proposals advanced for church action were only imaginable in an American context. Nolde said he would take these criticisms on board, and the text was lightly revised.

Three comments made in the discussion were particularly noteworthy: Nolde asked—possibly naively, but the "global order" he sought would depend on the answer—"as a moral premise, should we not say to all nations, and particularly to the United States, that they must base their foreign policy on a conception other than self-interest?" The Dutch Baron Van Asbeck (the first president of the CCIA) asserted emphatically that religious liberty was more than for "the highest development of [our] personality" and the "well-being" of our fellow-men—its "first and most important part was that a man might find his way open to follow God and hear His Voice." And Nolde asserted the eagerness of those working at the UN to receive the CCIA contribution.[39] A small cloud on the horizon presaged later storms over both the CHR and CCIA. A young Indian theologian, M. M. Thomas, was at the Geneva office; he had sent via Visser 't Hooft an aggressively root-and-branch attack on the whole Section IV enterprise, which began from his being asked to comment on papers by Jacques Ellul and Reinhold Niebuhr. He declined, however, to attend. As an "Asiatic Christian," he proposed that the CCIA be dissolved, in the light of its widening the "social chasm" between "the Left" (and "dependent peoples") and Christianity itself.[40]

Nolde's days in Geneva, and then in Canada at an IMC conference, allowed him to return to New York equipped to write yet another memorandum, which he sent to Humphrey on July 21, and which was approved by the CCIA Executive Committee after "personal consultation" with "two groups of church leaders from many countries."[41] This was a corporate response to the findings of the Drafting Committee in June. It pressed for both a declaration—"carrying an obligation on all member states to comply with its provisions"—and a covenant. And it returned to the two particular needs to specify a freedom "to change beliefs" and to avoid any possibility of constricting language, such as for "worship." Overall, there was a need to relate religious freedom to the provisions of all the articles involved in its exercise.

Humphrey thanked Nolde with some warmth for the CCIA's continuing "deep interest in its work." The next meeting of the CHR would be in Geneva. Nolde was forced to concede that he could not be there, and he asked the New Zealander, H. W. Newell, who had recently joined the Geneva staff as assistant to Visser't Hooft, to take his place. He mentions Charles Malik to him as "particularly helpful"; and J. P. Hendrick (Mrs. Roosevelt's chief adviser) as "well-posted on our outlook." In more detail he reports to Warnshuis, now running Church World Service, on his work in relation to the Bill of Rights. It is impressive. All meetings of the Drafting Committee had been attended by Nolde (or Prentice). He had "conferred personally" with every member of it, except the Russian, and had had "numerous conferences" with "Dr Malik of Lebanon." At a time of danger, he had telegraphed Mrs. Roosevelt. The CCIA had submitted two memoranda. And after the committee adjourned, he had "a rather long conference with Mr J. P. Hendrick." Finally, a mysterious hint of grand policy—the drafting of the bill was being "elevated" to major importance in U.S. foreign policy and "we [Nolde and representatives of the FCC and Foreign Missions Conference] held an entirely off-the-record conference with Mr Truman" followed by the "establishment of contacts with the highest officers of the Department of State."[42]

ESTABLISHING A TEXT

The autumn of 1947 was used to prepare for the next meeting of the CHR in Geneva in December. There was a growing sense that it would be foolish to have Newell of the WCC staff rather than Nolde present at what was likely to be a decisive moment, granted his tenacious attendance at earlier meetings and his mastery of its agenda.

So Barnes fixed it. This proved to be worthwhile. A formulation was agreed on that during 1948 needed only to be defended against attack.

The UNESCO trawl of world philosophers in the summer on the Rights of Man led to a distinguished series of articles in the UN *Weekly Bulletin* from mid-October, stimulated by their responses.[43] A grouping of NGOs with consultative status and offices in Geneva was set up, which was to flex its muscles in the last weeks before the vote on ratification of the declaration. Its meeting on October 17 was attended by the two responsible UN officers of the NGO sections in Geneva and in Lake Success, New York. Appreciation was expressed of the "progressive and helpful" attitude of the UN in this regard, an "immense advance" on previous relations between governmental and NGO organizations.[44]

When the CHR began to gather at the beginning of December, antagonism between the United States and the USSR had sharpened greatly since June. Events in Prague, with the Communist takeover and Masaryk's death, were taken throughout Europe as ominous. It became known that the U.S. State Department had instructed Mrs. Roosevelt and the U.S. delegation to stop any further discussion of a convention or covenant. This was unwelcome news to Nolde at Geneva and to others, including Van Kirk, who wrote to Dean Rusk at the State Department, referring to their talks at the recent "high level" meeting, voicing the strong concern of the FCC that this would give the impression that the U.S. government had abandoned leadership in forwarding human rights, and putting it on the same level as the USSR.[45] It is doubtful from previous occasions, however, whether Mrs. Roosevelt had in fact much personal investment in the immediate usefulness of a binding covenant. Nolde, however, was determined to do what he could to loosen the State Department position. In his draft memoirs, he took satisfaction in recounting how some NGOs met in Geneva.[46] Colleagues "attempted to get in touch with high officials in Washington," while he phoned FCC leaders in New York to request them to write the letters, and he reinforced the attack by telephoning London, where Dulles and the secretary of state were at "a meeting of Foreign Ministers." The consequence was that instructions were "liberalized," and the United States voted in favor of a covenant as part of the bill. Nolde wrote to Dulles that "the impression given by the U.S. delegation in its various positions is much improved" and "our various recommendations have been largely sustained."[47]

It was the throwback to raw brevity in the treatment of religion in the draft declaration then proposed by the United States, however, that exasperated Nolde, and was the turning point of the drafting process (though its Article II introduced an astonishing element—that "everyone" has the freedom to petition not only his government but also the UN). This article's bundle of freedoms included "religion, conscience, and belief," but that was all the reference to religion in the entire document, apart from its inclusion in aspects of nondiscrimination. Nolde had written formally to Humphrey at the beginning of the CHR session to set out the four CCIA objectives: a declaration, a convention, freedom of individual and corporate belief, and freedom for their expression—in inclusive terms if general, and comprehensive terms if specific.[48]

On December 6, he wrote to Mrs. Roosevelt conveying observations by CCIA groups on the June drafts, from America on the proposed declaration, and from the WCC staff at Geneva on the covenant. As regards the U.S. draft article for this latest declaration, he wrote: "You will not misunderstand me, I trust, when I say that it is difficult to find words which will convey a sufficiently strong adverse reaction. The statement gives no idea of what is involved in freedom of religion." He closes by implying that he understands the immediate pressures she is under from the State Department.[49]

On December 10, he wrote again.[50] The point had arrived for "vital" issues to be resolved. He makes the pertinent point that the consultative status with ECOSOC held by religious organizations required "the assumption that they have something to contribute to a society of order and justice." This went to the heart of the whole Christendom project embraced by the ecumenical movement from 1937 on. Whether it was true of, or latent in, all religious organizations was then, and remains, doubtful. There are sheep and there are goats. It was certainly doubted by many national governments.[51] It is a tribute to the CCIA that it won its right to be heard.

What was achieved at the Second Session (which divided into three sections to deal with the separate elements in a bill—a declaration, a covenant, and their implementation) were agreed-on drafts.[52] Priority was to be given to defending the draft declaration through the necessary hoops in the hope that it at least could be ready for voting on during the December 1948 General Assembly in Paris. At the concluding press conference, one of the committee's leading figures (probably Charles Malik) reviewed the Session's achievements, particularly noting the draft covenant, against their "central problem . . . that the realization of world-wide respect for the rights of man must be attained by *international agreement.* There is no world-state, no single sovereignty, no universally valid *constitution* into which our Declaration can be integrated." His comments ended with an urgent plea for an ending of cold war policy assumptions as a new human right. He spoke of Western Europe and its "primacy of human personality" and of Slavic Europe and the "primary importance of man's economic (and social) status." Collaboration between them "has itself become a 'practical right' which today all humanity demands."[53]

Nolde also produced a "statement" on December 18, reviewing the session just ended. He faces the fact that it might be a long time before the three elements of the bill would be completed. But he points up the educational value of recent engagements: "If respect for human rights is to be effectively promoted, ultimate reliance must be placed on education rather than on legislation. Good will is imperative. Whatever forms may finally be accepted, they will be of little avail unless they are undergirded by sympathetic understanding and integrity."[54] He also produced a valuable ten-page Report on the Session for distribution,[55] noting that he was able to make formal statements to the committee. He claimed that in its discussion of the convention, the committee referred the shaping of Article 15 to Nolde's judgment at one point. The right to "persuade" caused much discussion, particularly from the

Moslem aspect, and Nolde was prepared to disappoint his mission society constituency by not pursuing it.

He observed with understandable satisfaction, "that all the recommendations advanced by the CCIA are reflected in the new text." When it came to the declaration, Nolde was satisfied with the draft—"a considerable gain has been registered." But he was emphatic in warning against any expectation that it was now "final in any sense." There was evident pressure to shorten it—whether in another session of the Drafting Committee or at ECOSOC in May, or then in Committee III of the General Assembly—but "if the Declaration is adopted, presumably by a two-thirds vote, it will carry a moral obligation on Member States to comply with its provisions." The churches needed, therefore, to study these materials urgently, and bestir themselves to act effectively to support the CCIA by educating their membership and lobbying the government, especially if it was a state represented on ECOSOC. The task had "basic and long-range importance."

Back home on December 31, Nolde compiled a file on the Geneva session for his records.[56] It contains a page on the declaration's Article 16, with the underlined observation—"The manner in which freedom of conscience and religion is set forth should be commensurate with its importance"—and citation of various texts proposed in the discussions. It was a time when Article 16 had two paragraphs; the first of which had been agreed on. He proposes three alternative forms for the second paragraph. The last of these is effectively that which appears in the committee's final draft, and is presumably his.[57]

There is little doubt that it was during the intensity of discussions at Geneva in December 1947 that Nolde established the wide international relationships of trust (his reputation at UNCIO had principally been with fellow Americans) and the authority of competence in his field that were to prove so effective during the following year. Working in Geneva as he was during this session, the staff of the WCC was able to gauge his quality. He introduced Visser 't Hooft to Charles Malik, who soon accepted an invitation to become a commissioner of the CCIA. Malik[58] and Eleanor Roosevelt in particular, and also John Humphrey (who was not a churchman), became close colleagues. His talents lay in formulating a realistic goal, preparing a documented case to support it, and then by personal persuasion convincing a group of individuals to act.

NOTES

1. Ehrenström's memo of his conversation—on behalf of the WCC Study Department—in London on January 15, 1947, is evidence (1) of his preoccupation with preparation for the Amsterdam Assembly and resentment at the "substantive" status of the CCIA and (2) of Grubb's lack of conviction at that time about Nolde's work patterns at the UN and of Grubb's marked preference for the CCIA to deal with UNESCO, whose director, Julian Huxley, was a friend. World Council of Churches Library and Archives, Geneva, Switzerland, box CCIA E1.

2. The foundation theory of the CCIA was that there would be in each country a national body that would have exclusive responsibility for engagement with the government of that state. The CCIA—unsurprisingly—was never able to develop such a convention of empowerment. So, if there was a general conviction among Protestant churches on an issue in international affairs (e.g., as happened over South African apartheid, nuclear disarmament, and development in poor countries) the matter was in fact pressed on governments either by Councils of Churches or by overtly secular groups such as the Campaign for Nuclear Disarmament, Oxfam, or Amnesty International, whose founders were active Christians.

3. "As you doubtless know I am giving much of my time to the newly constituted CCIA. The work involved in getting this Commission under way, in establishing relations in its behalf with the UN, and in devising lines of contact with the churches throughout the world, is exceedingly time consuming." Nolde letter to Paul Henry, February 19, 1947, National Council of Churches Records, Federal Council of Churches Records, Presbyterian Historical Society, Philadelphia (hereafter PHS [FCC]), RG 18, box 67, folder 7.

4. The CCIA had already been forced to borrow shelf space in the main FCC Library.

5. Those present were Marc Boegner (chairman); Kenneth Grubb, O. Frederick Nolde, and Sartell Prentice (officers); John Decker and Norman Goodall (IMC); W. A. Visser 't Hooft and Henry Leiper (WCC); George Adams Brown (North America); G. H. K. Bell (the bishop of Chichester), Martin Niemöller, and Alphonse Koechlin (Europe); and R. B. Manikam, G. Baez Camargo, and T. C. Chao (Younger Churches). Dulles and Bromley Oxnam apologized. Minutes of Executive Committee, CCIA, April 25–26, 1947, WCC Archives, box CCIA.

6. WCC Archives, box 42.6.049.

7. The American Inter-Seminary Movement (an offshoot of the World Student Christian Federation and YMCA) held a major conference in the United States in 1947. The volume preparatory to its Commission III was *Toward World-Wide Christianity*, ed. O. Frederick Nolde (New York: Harper, 1946). In an appendix were reprinted the "Messages" of ecumenical conferences from Lausanne 1926 to the constitutions of the WCC and IMC.

8. These preparatory papers for Section IV in Amsterdam on international affairs were published, together with the report of that section of the conference, under the title *The Church and the International Disorder* (London: SCM Press, 1948). The contributors were Grubb, Roswell Barnes, F. M Van Asbeck, Dulles, Josef L. Hromadka, Emil Brunner, and Nolde.

9. See the text in appendix L.

10. Four recent monographs give a solid base for a better understanding of the history of the Universal Declaration. These are Paul Gordon Lauren, *The Evolution of International Human Rights: Visions Seen* (Philadelphia: University of Pennsylvania Press, 1998); William Korey, *NGOs and the Universal Declaration of Human Rights: "A Curious Grapevine"* (New York: St. Martin's Press, 1998); J. Morsink, *The Universal Declaration of Human Rights: Origins, Drafting and Intent* (Philadelphia: University of Pennsylvania Press, 1999); and Mary Ann Glendon, *A World Made New: Eleanor Roosevelt and the Universal Declaration of Human Rights* (New York: Random House, 2001). Morsink's treatment of the drafting of Article 18 is inadequate.

11. Visser 't Hooft to Nolde, November 17, 1948. WCC Archives, box 428.3.25. Visser 't Hooft's foreword to Nolde's *The Churches and the Nations* (Philadelphia: Fortress Press, 1970) chose to speak of Nolde as a churchman who had lived "on the frontier between the church and the world" and had "influenced the formulation of important articles in the Universal Declaration of Human Rights."

12. As with Molotov's readiness to accept virtually overnight the inclusion of a CHR in the Sponsoring Powers' revision of the draft text of the Charter at UNCIO, it would be fascinating to discover whether the opening of Soviet-era Moscow archives has shed light on the decision not to vote against the Universal Declaration of Human Rights.

13. "To the American Government and citizen [democracy] has a basic meaning. We believe that human beings have certain inalienable rights, that is, rights which may not be given or taken away. They include the right of every individual to develop his mind and his soul in ways of his own choice, free of fear of coercion—provided only he does not interfere with the like right of others. . . . There are personal freedoms and access to information, and right and opportunity to exchange and propagate thoughts and beliefs, so that that there can be, on an individual basis, genuine reflection and sober choice by minds and spirits that are both free and developed by use."

14. Dulles's experience in Moscow led him to see Soviet policy as merely the working out of Stalin's prewar writing on the future of Communism. Nevertheless, in sending an advance copy of his June 18 Commencement Address at Northwestern University in Evanston, Illinois, to Eleanor Roosevelt, he said he was seeking "to clarify our national attitude in certain respects where it seems to be unduly aggressive and imperialistic." Franklin D. Roosevelt Library, box 3281.

15. As early as July 23, 1947, at the conclusion of the first session of the Drafting Commission, Secretary of State Marshall wrote to express his own as well as the department's gratitude to Mrs. Roosevelt "that the principal objectives of the United States were accomplished and that so large a measure of harmony was achieved in the Drafting Committee itself are matters of national gratification and a real tribute to your ability as the US Representative and Chairman." Roosevelt Library, box 4587.

16. Personal communication from Howard Schomer, September 1999.

17. This threat was given a paranoid edge when in 1949 the government of China fell into the hands of the Chinese Communist Party. A significant proportion of the leaders of Protestant Christianity in the United States had personal experience of work in China, and Chinese church leaders had been prominent in the interwar church conferences, and on American campuses.

18. As late as December 1958, Dr. McIntyre complained in *The Christian Beacon* (on the occasion of the tenth anniversary of the Universal Declaration) that Dr. Nolde "is said to have represented 'the Protestant Churches' in Paris. . . . The trouble with the Universal Declaration . . . is that, along with many fine personal and individual political rights which are fully recognized in the thirteen amendments to the Constitution of the United States, is an entire package of socialistic Communist rights."

19. Roosevelt Library, box 4587.

20. PHS (FCC), RG 18, box 67, folder 4.

21. John P. Humphrey (1905–95) was born in New Brunswick, Canada, and after practicing law joined the law faculty of McGill University in 1936. He had close links with Latin American left-wing constitutional lawyers. From 1946 to 1966, he was director of the Human Rights Division of the UN Secretariat. He was active in launching Amnesty International Canada. See his *Human Rights and the United Nations: A Great Adventure* (New York: Dobbs Ferry, N.Y.: Transnational Publishers, 1984). The title refers back to Henri Laugier's comment about human rights, "Ce sera là une grande aventure." Humphrey's chapter on 1948 is titled "The Magna Carta of the World."

22. PHS (FCC), RG 18, box 67, folder 21.

23. PHS (FCC), RG 18, box 67, folder 21, and RG 18, box 67, folder 4; also WCC Archives, box 428.3.24.

24. The Memorandum, p. 2, lists twelve requirements of religious liberty.

25. Roosevelt Library, box 4587.

26. PHS (FCC), RG 18, box 67, folder 4.

27. London, March 1947, 12 pp. PHS (FCC), RG 18, box 67, folder 4.

28. Grubb was chair of the British Council of Churches' International Affairs Committee. Nolde to Humphrey, April 30, 1947. PHS (FCC), RG 18, box 67, folder 20.

29. René Cassin (1887–1976), a notable jurist, many of whose maternal Jewish family members died in German concentration camps, was a French delegate to the League of Nations

(1924–38) and to the UN (1946–58). He was a permanent secretary of De Gaulle's Defense Council and commissioner for justice and education in the French government in exile during World War II. He received the Nobel Peace Prize in 1968.

30. E.g., neither of the two Australians invited to respond was a university philosopher (though it was a particularly strong discipline at Sydney University). One, A. P. Elkin, was a university field anthropologist; and the other, Ernest Burgmann (his friend), was the Anglican bishop of Canberra and Goulburn, a European-style "savant," and a lifelong associate of the Australian Labor Party leaders then in power. Burgmann was particularly close to Dr. H. V. Evatt, who led the Australian delegation to UNCIO and became prominent for his assertion of human rights and of the smaller powers' place in the UN. Burgmann had been a principal figure in the interwar Australian Student Christian Movement. Peter Hempenstall, *The Meddlesome Priest: A Life of Bishop Burgmann* (St. Leonards, N.S.W.: Allen & Unwin, 1993).

31. "The Grounds of an International Declaration of Human Rights" (Report of the UNESCO Committee on the Philosophical Principles of the Rights of Man to the Commission on Human Rights of the UN), Paris, July 1947. Roosevelt Library, box 4587.

32. This was done via the U.S. ambassador in Paris. Roosevelt Library, box 4587.

33. This seven-page statement was prepared by Georgia Harkness, Hocking, and Reinhold Niebuhr, with Dulles as chair. Its four topic headings were "I. The US should contribute largely to the relief and reconstruction of a dislocated world"; "II. The hope of peaceful relations with the Soviet Union lies in making clear to all that the basic international issue is the simple issue of the police state as against a free society"; "III. The US should avail itself of the great possibilities of the UN, and particularly its Assembly, to mobilize the preponderant moral sentiment of the world"; and "IV. It devolves primarily on our Christian people to assure policies which rely upon moral rather than merely material power." Mackay Papers, box 15, Special Collections, Princeton Theological Seminary Libraries.

34. Roosevelt Library, box 4594; copy in WCC Archives, box 458.3.23.

35. Maurice Perlzweig submitted a memo to the CHR Drafting Committee on behalf of the World Jewish Congress on June 16. This, too, harked back to the foundational work of the NGOs at UNCIO. He makes a powerful claim for the protection of the human rights of religious minorities. Roosevelt Library, box 4587.

36. Roosevelt Library, box 3281.

37. Memo of conversation, July 3, 1947. Roosevelt Library, box 4587.

38. WCC Archives, box 24.225.

39. Nolde said, "It should be made known that our views are being solicited by officers in the United Nations because more and more they are beginning to see that what we ask is not just for ourselves, but for the whole world." WCC Archives, box 24.225, p. 26.

40. M. M. Thomas: "The oneness and universality of the Church is not so manifest as to speak one word and to act in unison in this sphere, and the attempt to do so when we are not ready has only been done by the domination of a certain kind of politics, which may be called Anglo-American." WCC Archives, box 24.225, p. 26.

41. WCC Archives, boxes 428.3, 23, and 24.

42. September 4, 1947. PHS (FCC), RG 18, box 67, folder 21.

43. These were E. H. Carr, M. H. Gandhi, Benedetto Croce, Arthur H. Compton, Aldous Huxley, and Salvador de Madariaga.

44. These organizations, convened by the Inter-Parliamentary Union, also included the Carnegie Endowment for International Peace, CCIA, International Abolitionist Federation, International Social Service, International Student Service, International Union for Child Welfare, International Committee of the Red Cross, International Council of Women, World Federation of UN Associations, World Jewish Congress, World YWCAs, World's Alliance of YMCAs, and the World Alliance for International Friendship through the Churches. The impression given is very anglophone.

45. Letter of December 5 (also formal letter of same date from Cavert and Fairfield to Mrs. Roosevelt). WCC Archives, box 428.3.23.

46. Documents and Analyses relating to Consultation in behalf of the CCIA, Second Session UNCHR, December 17, 1947, Geneva (folder collected by Nolde), including two pages, "Action on position taken by the US Delegation in the matter of a Convention"; also, O. F. Nolde, "Draft Memoirs, Section II," p. 27. O. Frederick Nolde Papers, Lutheran Archives Center at Philadelphia.

47. WCC Archives, box 428.3.23.

48. December 3, 1947. WCC Archives, box 428.3.23.

49. WCC Archives, box 428.3.24.

50. See appendix J.

51. Nolde made a list, titled "Incidental Notations of Points of View Advanced by USSR and Related Countries." This list is included in the Report for the CCIA (dated December 31, 1947) produced by Nolde on the Second Session of the UN CHR. WCC Archives, box 428.3.24.

52. "First drafts of the International Covenant and Declaration on Human Rights as published on 17 December 1947 at Geneva by the UN Commission on Human Rights," *UN Bulletin*, vol. 4, no. 2, January 15, 1948.

53. Roosevelt Library, box 4587.

54. WCC Archives, box 428.3.24.

55. WCC Archives, box 428.3.24.

56. WCC Archives, box 428.3.24.

57. A personal conversation in 2001 with John Garrett of Sydney, who was on the staff of the WCC in Geneva in the 1950s, indicated that H. F. E. Whitlam of Canberra (father of the Australian prime minister), an active Presbyterian who served as the legal officer of the Australian representative on the CHR, helped Nolde with drafts for the article on religious liberty in the Covenant.

58. On the Drafting Committee, Eleanor Roosevelt and Charles Malik were active lay Christians, and there was considerable church influence in both the U.K. and Australian delegations. Malik, a Greek Orthodox (with two brothers who became priests in Catholic religious orders), was theologically informed as well as a Platonist professor of philosophy; he had been educated at Harvard University under Hocking and Whitehead, and under Heidegger in Germany. He was often irritated by Nolde's assumption that questions of religion had to be explained to him.

CHAPTER 10

◆

Declaring Human Rights

THE INTERNATIONAL ATMOSPHERE in early 1948 did not encourage easy optimism. The executive of the American Federal Council of Churches (FCC) met in January and chose to make a substantial statement reaffirming the commitment of their churches to the UN and "wholly disagreeing" with "those who spread disillusionment and defeatism." The work of the Churches' Commission on International Affairs (CCIA) figured prominently, and not only with regard to human rights. Its stands on genocide and on freedom of information texts were also mentioned. The FCC went so far as to assert its support for a Covenant on Human Rights and "accept a measure of international concern in what has hitherto been considered a purely domestic field."[1] By April, Nils Ehrenström could write from Geneva: "The world situation is indeed dark. As before '39 we must again take all possible alternatives into account in our planning. Hardly anybody discusses any longer whether war is likely to come or not, but rather whether it will come in four years' time or in 1949."[2]

It was perhaps the tension of the time that helped Nolde make the claim plausible (at least to himself) that he was acting at the Commission on Human Rights (CHR) as in some sense representing the religions—not just of Protestantism or of Christianity—but of the world. John E. Merrill, an altogether too perceptive minister active in the Foreign Missions Conference (FMC) committees, wrote to Nolde on March 30, intrigued by his role at the UN. He asked whether Nolde was a consultant "invited to assist in the drafting of articles" on religious freedom. If so, how "honored and responsible!"—or did he act as a "pressure group seeking to have the opinions of Protestant Christians brought to attention with a view to their reflection in a Bill of Rights?" If so, Catholic, Jewish, Muslim, and other groups are doubtless doing the same thing. Or, is he a lobbyist, "seeking to bring influence to bear on the UN Commission so that the right of Protestant missionaries to proselytize in Muslim and other non-Christian countries may be written into international law?" Merrill put his own view: "Protestant theory aims to train Christian men and then expect them to put Christian principles into practice in common life, political affairs, international relations, in the positions held by them." This was the individualist Reformed tradition of pre–social sciences days, against which Dulles's energy in founding the CCIA had been directed.

160

Nolde replied on April 21, somewhat needled by these comments. He needed more leisure than he had at the moment. But he set out his own view of his role clearly. He rehearsed the granting to the CCIA under Article 71 of the UN Charter of Category B observer and consultant status, under which it enjoys the privileges "allowed many other NGOs [nongovernmental organizations]." He goes on: "The CCIA does not operate as a lobbying or pressure group. In the area of human rights it seeks to communicate to the CHR the mind of its constituency in so far as that mind has been formed. Use is made of the Oxford and Madras Statements, with necessary adaptations." Account is taken of conferences and committees; and contact is maintained with individual leaders and national councils in many lands, "to reflect the view of the Commission's constituency. Every effort is made to see to it that the stand taken before the UN is objective. What Christians seek for themselves they must equally grant to all others. In taking a stand of this kind, we believe that we contribute not only to the observance of human rights, but also to the promotion of world order."[3]

THE MAY 1948 DRAFTING COMMITTEE

Nolde had come to the conclusion in December that it would increase his influence if he could generate practically useful information from his ex officio world constituency.[4] His principal activity preparatory to the reconvening of the Drafting Committee in early May and its final revision of drafts for the Third Session of the CHR (May 20–June 18) was to set up a questionnaire. Mrs. Roosevelt replied on May 13 to Nolde's sending her the results: "This is a very interesting finding and I am extremely glad to have it before me."[5]

What Nolde had done at the end of January was to send out copies of the Second Session drafts of the covenant and declaration, and his own report on that session, with a covering letter asking four questions. The recipient was to convene a group to discuss and assess the CHR's drafts and return its conclusions to the CCIA office. The International Missionary Council (IMC) network was invaluable in this exercise, for every continent could thus contribute. Nolde reported to the JCRL on February 25 that 200 letters to forty countries had gone out via Sartell Prentice from the CCIA offices in London and New York, and that 900 had been sent within North America via Van Kirk by the FCC and FMC.[6] The first question was as to whether the draft declaration article should be retained or changed; the second, similarly as regards the covenant article; the third question whether the addressee has additional comments; and the fourth, whether any representation has been made to his national government.

With the CHR due to reconvene, the NGOs in New York, London, and Geneva were asking for position papers from the CCIA. Nolde's action paper of April for New York concluded by looking forward to replies from his survey. A memorandum[7] produced by the CCIA for the NGO group at Geneva in mid-May was still expressing a preference for work on the convention (even if only a number of like-minded states ratified it—a position put by Dulles to Mrs. Roosevelt in June)[8] over the declaration. It hoped, too, that provision for minority communities might be included, and was rash enough, putting religious freedom in the context of other freedoms, to make the claim "on which they in turn depend."[9]

The Drafting Committee began its work in Lake Success, New York, on May 3. Mrs. Roosevelt, Charles Malik, René Cassin (from May 10), and Hernan Santa Cruz (Chile) provided the core of long-term representatives. There were four alternates present. In its report to the CHR of May 21 on its work, representatives of specialized agencies (UNESCO, International Refugee Organization, and International Labor Organization) were listed, and also the NGO consultants present.[10] Nolde took care to present the results of this CCIA survey of church opinion on the December drafts in a full letter to Malik on May 2,[11] and to Mrs. Roosevelt. He wrote to Grubb in London and to Dulles at the same time, sending a copy of the tabulated results with a digest of their recommendations for "consultation with the UN CHR."

The message was, he told Malik, clear, and "highly significant." He underlined that "our constituency considers the provisions in the Geneva drafts to constitute the minimum of practices that have been tested in experience and found essential to the observance of religious freedom." So defending the Geneva text became Nolde's concern. If there were to be any changes made at all, they should be in the direction of strengthening provisions. The letter closes with renewed appreciation of Malik's role as standard bearer for "the pre-eminent importance" of conscience and religion (and volunteers any help Malik may wish for). The Drafting Committee finished its work, leaving Article 16 virtually unchanged.[12] It had given its principal attention to a covenant. In September, the CHR was to reverse that order, and to begin with the Universal Declaration. Long discussions in the CHR meant there was only time for that work. But it was completed. This proved to be a fact of great consequence; it was a precondition of the General Assembly of December 1948 achieving any part of the anticipated bill before the cold war permafrost.

When, on June 30, Nolde wrote his wide-ranging "Report on the Third Session of the CHR (at Lake Success, May 24–June 18),"[13] he ascribed considerable impact to his communication to Mrs. Roosevelt on May 6 of the results of the CCIA world-church survey. The approaches made by churches to their national governments had also been of considerable help to Nolde in his approaches to their representatives at Lake Success. He states baldly, "the work of the CCIA and of national church groups between December 1947 and May 1948 was a major factor in sustaining provisions for religious liberty at the present stage of drafting." Mrs. Roosevelt herself may not have been content with the policy laid down for her by the State Department, but Nolde had reported to Grubb[14] on May 17 that both the United States and France were seeking much briefer texts. Nolde's letter to Mrs. Roosevelt enclosing the survey results had been intended "to counter this move." Somewhat mysteriously, Nolde reported that this letter was distributed on May 25 to all delegates in digest form by the UN Secretariat. But it is clear that the survey, whatever its intrinsic interest, was invaluable to Nolde in his "many conferences with individual delegates and committees or groups" throughout May and June. In the event, he saw the work of the Third Session as having been very positive, and not only with regard to Article 16. A matter for regret was the removal of the article on minorities.

PRESERVING THE DRAFT ARTICLES

Nolde's final comment to his constituency was to foreshadow the meetings of the UN Economic and Social Council (ECOSOC), of which Malik had recently become president, in Geneva beginning on July 19; and then, on September 21, of the decisive Third Session of the General Assembly. The CCIA would, he promised, be present. He was still hoping for a covenant; though he granted that his immediate agenda had to be the Universal Declaration, which does not pretend to "guarantee these rights, but can have value as an expression of the goals to which world society should work." The CCIA would continue to need the pressure of churches on national governments; and the ongoing practice in their societies of "study, teaching, and example."

For whatever reason, ECOSOC found little time for human rights and remitted the work of the CHR, en bloc and as it stood, for consideration in September by the General Assembly. From the point of view of Nolde and Dulles, who were deeply involved in the World Council of Churches' (WCC's) constituting First Assembly in Amsterdam, this was a happy state of affairs, as it was perhaps for Malik, its president.[15] Because the draft Universal Declaration was the only text in the CHR package ready for consideration by the General Assembly, and as it immediately gripped the attention of the member states (most of which of course had had no representatives taking part in the discussions of the Drafting Committee or of the CHR), it together with the draft Convention on Genocide were to prove agenda enough. These matters fell under Committee III, of which, again, Malik was chairman.

When the assembly gathered in Paris in September under the presidency of Dr. H. V. Evatt of Australia, a politician and a nation deeply involved in human rights issues from 1945 at the United Nations Conference on International Order (UNCIO), it received heavyweight coverage. The crisis over Berlin, scarcely resolved by the Anglo-American airlift, was not an obvious time for debate about articles on universal human rights with no formal claim for practical implementation. The WCC assembly in Amsterdam (August 22–September 4), followed by the meeting of the committee of the IMC (September 7–10), had at least given a powerful impetus to the authority and clarity of what the CCIA could contribute on behalf of the world's Protestant churches in Paris.[16] Nolde was made associate general secretary of the WCC and was given the international affairs section of the assembly report and its declaration on religious liberty to work with.[17] Also, the WCC and the IMC passed identical resolutions on human rights to be remitted via the CCIA to the UN secretary general as the assembly opened on September 21.[18] Their message (presumably drafted by Nolde) was that human rights were a matter of such deep concern to the churches that a declaration was a minimum, and the churches would support progress toward enforceable provisions in general, and also the Convention on Genocide and the Convention on Freedom of Information and the Press. When the Committee III hearings began, Nolde sent a personal letter to delegates, giving the background of the WCC concern for human rights and its survey of constituency opinion in the spring, enclosing the Amsterdam resolutions and declaration, and offering the opportunity to meet for conversation. The much-increased number of national delegations involved at this stage meant that Nolde was having to build up many new relationships.

The opening days of the assembly included a fine address by Secretary of State George Marshall surveying the major problem posed by the USSR in general, and the many particular flash points. He chose to put a case for hope that included the initiative for European economic development that carries his name, but centered on human rights. His first paragraph celebrated the fittingness of Paris as the scene for "a new declaration of human rights for free men in a free world." His second delineated these freedoms, "the elements that combine to give dignity and worth to the individual."[19]

Mrs. Roosevelt gave a public address, "The Struggle for Human Rights," at the Sorbonne on September 28 that set out her credo, from her husband's New Deal and then through the San Francisco conference to her own work shepherding the CHR to the draft bill that the assembly had now received.[20] The shape of her argument is worth noting. She begins by asserting the utter centrality of "human rights and fundamental freedoms" to the UN Charter (which would certainly have surprised the Dumbarton Oaks–era State Department). She goes on to mention the draft declaration: "without [these rights], we feel that the full development of individual personality is impossible"—and then the so far incomplete draft covenant. She makes the interesting point that the passage of the declaration should "encourage every nation in the coming months to discuss its meaning with its people so that they will be better prepared to accept the Covenant." She meets the Soviets full face over trades unions and the press. Her own position follows: "Among free men the end cannot justify the means. We know the patterns of totalitarianism—the single political party, the control of schools, press, radio, the arts, the sciences, and the church to support autocratic authority; these are the age-old patterns against which men have struggled for three thousand [sic] years." And, of the various freedom articles: "these are not just abstract ideals to us; they are tools with which we create a way of life in which we can enjoy freedom." It was not a formula when she ended, "I pray Almighty God that we may win another victory here for the rights and freedoms of all men."[21]

As chair of Committee III, Malik knew he would have to steer the draft Universal Declaration through weeks of passionate debates (many of them going over the ground already well trampled in the CHR) before its presentation in plenary session. He summoned help in this task from an old friend, who had been his assistant earlier during the Second Session of the CHR in Geneva.[22] Howard Schomer had been at the Divinity School when Malik was engaged at Harvard on his doctorate.[23] They had both studied under W. E. Hocking. In 1946 Schomer and his wife had been sent by his church to help staff a remarkable French Protestant community at La Chambonne sur Lignon in the remote Cevennes, set up during the war partly to harbor Jewish young people. From there he could drive to Geneva to be the U.S. Congregationalists' representative on the WCC's interchurch aid committee. Malik contacted him to ask if he would serve as his personal assistant for the assembly session. He accepted, with a brief to research historical questions for Malik. During the whole of the Universal Declaration's passage through Committee III, Schomer sat immediately behind Malik, where he could observe and be available to go out and speak with delegates and consultants. He also wrote Malik's major speech of September 27 to the initial plenary session.[24]

This speech, again, is a long and powerful statement of the architecture within which the decision to be made on human rights was perceived as critical. ECOSOC was "the faint glimmer of design" that could be emerging from "the dismal recent past of international anarchy and national autarchy." Rights need to be grounded, not on a Supreme Being, but on a "Lord of History." If ECOSOC continues to be dominated by "the brutal clash of national politics," it will be a "derogation of the original integrity of the Council as a constructive, co-operative, deliberative, technical, supreme organ of the UN." The UN "must feel creatively concerned for the material and spiritual welfare of their less fortunate fellow Members."[25] Malik asserts that World War II was "fought in part because fundamental human rights were trampled on by Nazi Germany. . . . We can therefore say that the UN is itself the outcome of a war whose whole moral climate was saturated with the issue of human rights. [It is impossible] to displace the question of human rights from the centre of our vision." The UN Conference on International Order had left a lacuna: what exactly are these human rights that were so repeatedly asserted? The Universal Declaration will be the answer; "the ordinary citizen throughout the world will be able to say, 'Now the ambiguity is removed; this is what my government pledged itself in San Francisco to have faith in and to promote and encourage and respect and observe and realize.'" So there, having defined universal human rights, is the key to solving all the great political issues of the day. Defining human rights requires attention to "the order of truth," the "mind and spirit of man," his "proper worth and dignity." "What," he concludes, "is the use of a peace and a settlement in which man is left ambiguous, estranged from himself and the truth?"

These speeches from the two principal officers of the CHR, immediately before the decisive battle of the campaign was to be fought, indicate the ground of their essentially "religious" conviction that the passage of a Universal Declaration would be an event of major consequence for history. This conviction was shared by the future Pope John XXIII, who as the papal nuncio resident in Paris was active and influential in promoting the Universal Declaration.[26]

After it had become clear that the attention of this session of the assembly was to be focused on the Universal Declaration, the CHR material was referred to Committee III and a snowstorm of 150 amendments was generated. Each of the fifty-eight member states contributed. Nolde's focus was on defense of the draft of Article 16 and on concern for Article 1.[27] Article 16 came up for debate in early November.

The Soviet group had made clear its dissatisfactions, and what made Nolde nervous was that other blocs, too—notably the Latin Americans[28] and the Muslim states[29]—had already formed and could, as the crunch votes drew near, trade support with each other. In the end, there were 5 major amendments, from the USSR, Saudi Arabia, Peru (withdrawn), Sweden, and Cuba. All were defeated. The days before these votes were Nolde's finest hour. Until the early hours of the morning, he attended subcommittees, he cajoled delegates, he wrote notes.

Particularly interesting evidence of the close relation Nolde had built with Mrs. Roosevelt arises from his letter to her of November 6 about the proposed amendments.[30] "Knowing how busy" she is, he begins, he chooses to write rather than speak. He sets out his views in a paragraph on each of the amendments: that they are "weak and inadequate." So the CCIA hopes "very much that the draft text of Article 16 [the eventual Article 18] will be retained." But he goes on to suggest to her—in light of the "danger of negative combinations"—that "much would be gained if, after the amendments have been introduced, you were to make a general statement in support of the draft text." It is possible that, in response, she asked Nolde to produce the "Draft Statement on Article 16," which can be found in that same box of the WCC Archive. It uses the language of Nolde's letter, is as from the U.S. representative, and is noted in longhand (neither Nolde's or hers): "E. Roosevelt, Paris, Committee III, 1948."

On November 8 he wrote to Senator Warren R. Austin of Vermont, the U.S. delegate to the UN, forwarding the WCC/IMC Amsterdam resolutions, as from Samuel Cavert on behalf of the FCC. On the same day he sent the CCIA objections to the amendments (in the same form as he had earlier expressed them to Mrs. Roosevelt) in letters to various delegates—in the case of United Kingdom's Mrs. Corbet, adding assurance of the British Council of Churches' support.[31] On November 9, he was able to cable Miss Wyckoff in New York (who forwarded the message to "Drs. Leiper, Decker, Barnes, Van Kirk, Boyd, and Fairfield"): "Article sixteen sustained intact after intensive debate."

THE PASSAGE OF THE DECLARATION

The debate moved on to other articles. Nolde planned to take his wife back to New York for a few days' break, but before he left attended a meeting (over which he was asked to preside) of the NGOs represented at the assembly, whose convener was Max Gottschalk of the American Jewish Committee. This meeting decided to draft a memorandum (to be agreed on November 22 at the Carnegie Endowment's Paris office) for transmission to the UN secretary general and to the national delegations. This "respectfully urges that the UN fulfil its pledge to strengthen and secure the observance of human rights by promptly enacting the Declaration and Conventions" on its agenda.[32]

While he was on his short break, Nolde was not idle. On November 19 and 20, he wrote notes to the leaders of the eighteen CHR members' delegations. Each one was handcrafted for its recipient, expressing amazement at the quality of his most recent speech and so on, going on to a common paragraph, and ending with the urgency of the assembly acting now, and sustaining the full text of Article 16. The key sentence of the paragraph stressed that freedom of thought and conscience, together with freedom to change religion, "recognizes a principle which will allow peaceful competition of differing convictions and ideologies. In an ever-shrinking world, the impact of one system of thought upon another makes the application of this principle an imperative requisite for world peace and order." The letter to Mrs. Roosevelt was dated November 18.[33] She notated it "I hope it will be," and her reply ran, "I hope it will be sustained in its full text."[34]

In Nolde's letter to Visser 't Hooft of November 23 (on his break away from Paris), he says he will be returning there earlier than planned.[35] And that it had already become known, before he left, that "pressure was being exerted on some delegations to have important provisions of the Article on religious freedom deleted when the Declaration appears for action in the plenary session. Good friends, some of whom you know personally, claimed that my return to Paris at the time when the debate in Committee III ended was imperative: I was told that 'neither personal convenience nor professional preoccupation should interfere.'[36] Arrangements were made to keep me informed about developments. Today I received the following cable from a man who holds a high post in the human rights division: 'Friend replies despite unchanged situation your presence necessary insurance against possible damage.' The friend referred to is the man with whom you and Dr. Cavert had dinner one night last summer at Geneva." Possibly the contact was Humphrey, and the friend probably Malik or Schomer.[37] At once, Nolde contacted the WCC and IMC leaders in New York, who said he should go. The threat was either a last-minute deletion from the article or postponement of the declaration to the next session.

On December 7, the rapporteur of Committee III, from Haiti, presented its report to the plenary. It began what was never going to be an "all passion spent" or harmonious final act to the drama. When the point of decision came, fears resurfaced. No contribution was more significant than that of Sir Mohammed Zafrullah Khan, the foreign minister of newly independent Pakistan, and a distinguished lawyer trained at the London Inns of Court. Mrs. Roosevelt had entertained him to dinner on November 26.[38] It is said that Malik had pressed him hard the day before he spoke, for the bloc of Muslim countries could well have voted against or abstained. In the event, there were no votes against at all. Only Saudi Arabia abstained, in the company of South Africa and the Soviet bloc. Khan warmly commended the article on freedom of religion, maintaining that his subordinate had made a silly mistake earlier, for because Islam is a missionary religion, how can it object to an individual's right to change his religion?[39]

Malik's own speech to the plenary on December 9 was principally a recapitulation of the process by which human rights had traveled from UNCIO to their present point of decision. He pinned his faith—confirmed by events—on the steady transforming influence of the Charter on reality: "the Declaration will serve as a potent critic of existing law and practice," and so they will be "gradually modified."[40] And Mrs. Roosevelt, after putting the personalist case against the Soviet amendments, that "this Declaration is based upon the spiritual fact that man must have freedom in which to develop his full stature," went on to stress to those fearful of practical commitments that what was at issue made no pretense to be a law or a treaty, but "a common standard of achievement for all peoples of all nations." But its passage would nonetheless be "a great event in the life of the UN and in the life of mankind. This Universal Declaration of Human Rights may well become the international Magna Carta of all men everywhere."[41]

And so the vote was taken on December 10, with none of the fifty-eight states then members of the UN prepared to vote against it.[42] Howard Schomer recalled that "as Mrs Roosevelt, Dr Malik and I gathered our straggling papers and—the last ones out—headed for the elevator, I saw in her face the lines both of strain and happiness. 'It *was* a long day!' I said. 'Yes,' she responded, 'A bit fatiguing, wasn't it? But worth it!' "[43]

POSTLUDE

The passage of the Universal Declaration on December 10 was indeed a date to remember. If it is not now part of the syllabus for every schoolchild in the world, as specifically mandated in its Article 26(2), that is a very serious charge against government ministries of education and the teaching profession (especially against those who work in schools under religious auspices). It is a charge on behalf of children kept in ignorance of its provisions. Its inclusion is part of "the pedagogy of the oppressed," to cite the phrase used as the title of Paolo Freire's famous account of his work in Brazil.[44] It has become standard to preface monographs on human rights with the assertion that, however apparently toothless, the Universal Declaration has increasingly become embedded in discourse about the good society across the world. Via the Council of Europe and the European Convention of Human Rights, the transnational institutions and legal frameworks of postwar Europe in the twenty-first century have become its vehicles.

Nolde's dogged presence—recalled by Schomer as characteristically having a smile on his face—through every twist and turn of the CHR's engagement with an International Bill of Rights, gave him the right to satisfaction when the declaration element of it was delivered. In a practical sense, international affairs—global order—have from that moment had a fresh dimension. There was a considerable literature of reflection upon that in WCC circles and in American Protestantism as the anniversaries of 1948 were celebrated. But that is another story, of a period that leads up to and comes to terms with the achievements of the Second Vatican Council. From the time of John XXIII, the popes have been the most coherent and assertive speakers of the language of human rights among Christian leaders. The Vatican Council's *Declaration on Religious Freedom* (1965) could have been as congenial to the American Joint Committee on Religious Liberty of the World War II years as had been its champion, Father John Courtney Murray, S.J. And the shade of Lord Acton, too, may well have murmured his *Nunc dimittis.*

There was one occasion shortly after the Paris general assembly that expressed a particular sense of thanksgiving and rededication. A "Symposium on Christian Responsibility in World Affairs" was hosted by the CCIA at Union Theological Seminary, New York (in those days, where else?), on April 29, 1949.[45] Dulles presided, and the Episcopal bishop of Albany, New York, Ashton Oldham—veteran of countless interwar committees for peace and light—was responsible for the invocation before dinner. Nolde introduced the symposium speakers afterward. Arnold Toynbee's subject was "the role of Christianity in international affairs"; Charles Malik's was "the spiritual implications of the Human Rights Covenant [*sic*]"; Charles Ranson's (general secretary of the IMC) was "Christian missions and world order"; Visser 't Hooft's was "the ecumenical approach to Soviet–Western tension"; and Dulles's was "the churches and the United Nations." There followed a discussion on "the task of the CCIA." Those involved could properly be described, in Oldham's famous phrase, as among their generation's best minds. They were also uncommonly effective in the service of God and of "the other."[46]

NOTES

1. World Council of Churches (WCC) Library and Archives, Geneva, box 428.3.24.
2. Ehrenström to John Bennett, April 9, 1948, WCC Archives, box 24.162.
3. WCC Archives, 428.3.23.
4. "Experience at the Geneva Session of the CHR has indicated that a consultant's position is much strengthened if he brings into the discussions of the Commission the reactions of his constituency." Report on Second Session [of the CHR], December 1–7, 1947, p. 9. WCC Archives, box 428.3.24.
5. Mrs. Roosevelt was unhappy with the State Department in these months. On March 30, replying to Malik's anxiety at the rumor that she was resigning, she said she had wished the president to feel free. And on May 16 she wrote "in deep concern" a furious letter to the secretary of state: She had not been kept informed of U.S. decisions re Palestine; U.S. action has "created complete consternation in the UN"; and "more and more other delegates seem to believe that our whole policy is based on antagonism to Russia and that we think in terms of going it alone rather than in terms of building up a leadership within the UN." Franklin D. Roosevelt Library, box 4588.
6. National Council of Churches Records, Federal Council of Churches Records, Presbyterian Historical Society, Philadelphia, RG 18, box 67, folder 5.
7. WCC Archives, box 428.3.23.
8. Dulles to Mrs. Roosevelt, June 15, Roosevelt Library, box 4588.
9. WCC Archives, box 428.3.23.
10. It is striking how few NGOs were present in 1948 and how eccentric was their character. In Category A were world UN associations (Eichelberger), the American Federation of Labor, and Christian trade unions. In Category B were the CCIA (both Nolde and Prentice), three Jewish organizations, five women's organizations, and the Red Cross, out of twelve listed.
11. WCC Archives, box 428.3.24.
12. See appendix K.

13. WCC Archives, box 428.1.02.

14. WCC Archives, box 428.3.23.

15. At the CCIA executive meeting (August 17, 1948), it was decided to invite Malik to become a CCIA vice president. Nolde asked him and he accepted, though this was only formalized in February 1949.

16. The Soviet government had decreed a boycott of the Amsterdam Assembly, so Orthodox participation was only partial. The major confrontation of the Assembly was between Dulles and Josef L. Hromadka, a Czech theologian who had taught at Princeton Seminary through the war years. Writing to Mrs. Roosevelt on August 2, Dulles rather airily dismissed the likelihood of Amsterdam becoming "anti-Russia" or political, beyond "recognizing the fact that social and political institutions that reflect an atheistic and materialist creed are not acceptable to Christians as the basis for their own functioning as citizens" (Roosevelt Library, box 3281). The Vatican took considerable pains (in contrast to later WCC assemblies) to ensure that there was no Roman Catholic presence at Amsterdam or direct coverage of its proceedings.

17. The report of the Assembly's Section IV is in *The Church and the International Disorder* (London: SCM Press, 1948), 221–32, and the declaration is reproduced in appendix L.

18. WCC Archives, box 428.3.24.

19. September, Roosevelt Library, box 4588.

20. Roosevelt Library, box 4588.

21. Indicative of suspicions at that time is an exchange between the State Department and the U.S. embassy in Paris. On September 30, a memo was sent expressing anxiety about René Cassin, the representative of France and principal jurist of the CHR—that "he is manifesting fellow-traveller tendencies" and the "crypto-Communist habit of directing criticism against the US while maintaining silence on worst features of Soviet regime." There is specific reference to the Congress of Democratic Jurists at Prague and its "obviously anti-American resolutions" which Cassin had declared "would furnish him a precious aid" at the CHR. On October 5, Sandifer of Mrs. Roosevelt's staff was sent a memo to suggest he look at the September 30 airgram. Mrs. Roosevelt annotates the letter: "I do not think he is a Communist, but he does try to conciliate." Roosevelt Library, box 4653.

22. Schomer claimed that it was he who introduced his old friend Malik to Visser 't Hooft during this session in Geneva. In addition, he also suggested that credit regarding Article 16 in that session should also be given to Dr. Alford Carleton, one of Schomer's missionary colleagues. Personal communication.

23. Schomer had followed Malik to Freiburg to study under Heidegger but, like Malik, left after experiencing Heidegger's personal commitment to Nazism. Later, as a Congregational pastor in New Jersey, Schomer sent a petition from his church to support the Cleveland Conference resolutions at UNCIO in 1945. When Schomer was president of Chicago Theological Seminary, he walked in the front rank at Martin Luther King's right hand toward the bridge in Selma, Alabama (personal communication).

24. Harvard Divinity School, Cambridge, Mass., MSS and Archives Collection, Howard Schomer Papers, box bMS 551/4 (3).

25. One of Malik's principal concerns in his early speeches in the CHR was his proposal that the UN should devote resources to making the "great books" of world civilization available in a program of general education for students of all members of the UN, but especially for those of the less developed nations. Library of Congress (LC), Washington, D.C., Malik Papers, box 208.

26. Albert Verdoodt, professor emeritus at the University of Louvain la Neuve, Belgium, was Cassin's assistant during his foundation of the Institute of Human Rights at Strasbourg. He recounts that Cassin (a Jew, whose father was a Catholic) always spoke warmly of the contribution made by Christian NGOs to the Universal Declaration (personal communication). See Philippe de la Chapelle, *La Declaration Universelle des Droits de l'Homme et le Catholicisme* (Paris: Librairie Générale de Droit et de Jurisprudence, 1967).

27. Nolde discusses Article 1 at length in his November report (p. 7). He raises the question of the word "God." It is clear that the Vatican had pressed very strongly for such a reference and, after the passage of the Universal Declaration, comment in the *Osservatore Romano* damned the whole future of the CHR for this omission. Though Mrs. Roosevelt confessed that she would have liked such a reference, Nolde was very relaxed about the issue. He made the persuasive case that "the Declaration is intended to affirm that man has the right to believe as he sees fit; it is not intended to declare what man should believe."

28. There had been a distinctive formulation of human rights at the inter-American conference at Bogotá in the spring.

29. The Saudi Arabian delegate was constantly pressing other Muslim countries to take a stand against any freedom to change religion.

30. WCC Archives, box 428.3.24.

31. WCC Archives, box 428.3.23.

32. WCC Archives, box 428.3.23.

33. Roosevelt Papers, box 4588.

34. WCC Archives, box 428.3.24.

35. WCC Archives, box 428.3.25.

36. WCC Archives, box 428.3.24.

37. Before he left Paris on November 13, Nolde wrote Malik about his travel plans; he expected to return from New York on November 26, but would be prepared to come earlier if "required by developments in connection with the Declaration of Human Rights." He gives Malik his cable address in New York, with alternative messages: "COME IMMEDIATELY" or "PRESENCE NOT NECESSARY." LC, Malik Papers, box 193.

38. Mrs. Roosevelt's Diary, Roosevelt Library, box 4719.

39. WCC Archives, box 428.3.24.

40. LC, Malik Papers, box 210.

41. Roosevelt Library, box 4653.

42. See appendix M.

43. In a talk at Montclair Presbyterian Church, Oakland, Calif., July 28, 1991.

44. Paolo Freire, *The Pedagogy of the Oppressed* (Harmondsworth: Penguin Books, 1972).

45. The program lists those CCIA commissioners so far appointed. LC, Malik Papers, box 193.

46. A grounding of the ethos of human rights in concern for "the other" became well established in late-twentieth-century Protestant theology. See Georges Casalis, Walter Hollenweger, and Paul Keller, eds., *Vers une église pour les autres* (Geneva: World Council of Churches, 1966); John Wild, "The Rights of the Other as Other," *Drew Gateway* (Madison, N.J.), winter 1969, 81–106; Eric Fuchs and Pierre-André Stucki, *Au nom de l'autre: Essai sur le fondement des droits de l'homme* (Geneva: Labor et Fides, 1985); and Jean François Collange, *Théologie des droits de l'homme* (Paris: Editions du Cerf, 1989).

CHAPTER 11

◆

Conclusion: Faith and Human Rights Need Each Other

A NUMBER OF ASSERTIONS can be made with some degree of confidence to conclude this study. Other fascinating reflections that have arisen have to be more tentative. Some of these are fundamental. They require the attention of philosophers, political scientists,[1] jurists, theologians, sociologists, and students of religions[2] and of international affairs working within or across their various disciplines.

This, however, has had primarily to be a historical treatment. So it remains to summarize what turns out to have been the case. This is above all that—contrary to received opinion—the churches of the Protestant ecumenical movement played a significant role in giving the international settlement after World War II in the United Nations its "soul" in human rights. It was their intention.

The dynamic of the Protestant ecumenical movement's commitment to midwifing a quite new kind of postwar order in international affairs came from its roots in Christian mission. The three worldwide associations (and that word itself is significant in this context)—the YMCA, YWCA, and World Student Christian Federation—that provided its leadership had strong links to those Protestant mission-societies that traced their tradition back to the freshly global mission consciousness of eighteenth-century Evangelicals. John Wesley famously claimed the whole world as his parish. Around 1900, at the moment when "Christian civilization" and "Progress" seemed launched on a happily married life together, these mission societies were emboldened to see as imminent the possibility of converting to Christianity the mass populations of other world faiths.[3] There was also at that time a parallel conviction among Western educated elites (whether Christian or not) of their imperial[4] vocation to shape a new world civilization.[5]

These, together with contemporary "philosophies of history" (including the rival Socialist International) and the impact of a technological science that promised "abundance for all," lent formidable energy to the readiness of a group of Christians to embrace and shape a one-world future, even to glimpse the Kingdom of God. Our present-day usage of the adjective "underdeveloped" is rooted in that generation's sense of a normative process at work for all peoples, who for the present are at different stages.

As that heady prospect faded after World War I, a remarkable mutation of the old territorial concept of "Christendom" was floated by J. H. Oldham and Jacques Maritain, and then developed by others. Within secular states, an organically related bundle of principles might be established and given statutory constitutional expression, and there should be no limit to their rapid extension to include the whole world. Christians and others—society's "best minds"—could probably agree upon and then define whatever is required to protect human social well-being. The UN's Universal Declaration of Human Rights of 1948 was seen as such a bundle of desiderata. Once these had been established in a regime worldwide, Christian communities would be liberated to live out every aspect of their faith. They would neither expect nor desire any privileges not equally available to other faiths, and there would be no question of coercing "the other," or of self-consciously "Christian" territories. Such an outcome would be the triumph of the public half of Oldham's missionary vision for "Christendom." What remained would be the churches' task of education, persuasion, and exemplification of "the Christian way."

Many ecumenical leaders hoped that the Universal Declaration, as it developed into binding covenants in the 1970s, would become justiciable by a world court with sufficient police powers at its disposal. It is worth noting that salient features of the original organization plan for the UN included provision for the Security Council to dispose of and use overwhelming military force, and the assumption that candidate member states would be held to their profession of human rights. At least until now, and it is hard to see change in the immediate future, the UN's commitment to state sovereignty has in practice excluded its commitment to such active monitoring of the Universal Declaration in general, or of its Article 18 in particular.

The Protestant, Anglican, and, to an extent, Orthodox ecumenical movement contributed enormously to the events that led up to the United Nations General Assembly proclaiming in December 1948 that its Universal Declaration of Human Rights was defining, with unparalleled authority, what had in its 1945 founding charter been left indeterminate. This declaration was deemed to be what the states that ratified the charter had in mind as the constituting "soul" of the new order of international affairs they created. To exclude this contribution is a historical travesty.

A principal object of this book is to remedy that exclusion. What a half-century ago began as willful ignorance—the anticlericalism of the 1789 tradition of the "rights of man"; the takeover of human rights by legal professionals; the unacceptability of "religion" as a category of discourse to representatives of the Soviet bloc; a period when the UN staff played down achievements by nongovernmental organizations of any kind; and the "forgetting" of its own history by the World Council of Churches—has become a tradition of ignorance on all sides. The passage of time will merely confirm this tradition, unless there is public reappraisal.

NOLDE'S CONTRIBUTION

The successful outcome of the struggle for global human rights institutions in the period 1944–48 was influenced to a surprising degree by the part one person, Dr.

O. Frederick Nolde of Philadelphia, was able to play. In 1942 he had been an unknown outsider, even in his own church's national life. His transition to national and international leadership in public affairs in six years could hardly have happened apart from the breaking of molds, which was only possible in the crises of wartime. A handful of intellectually able lay and ordained figures in key positions—notably Dulles, Barnes, Johnson, Warnshuis, Oxnam, and Mackay—committed energy to forming a common mind on the postwar world, and became a core resource group for his activity. But though the American ecumenical-movement churches as such provided indispensable support, they had no real conception that this unfamiliar kind of political commitment on their part (in collaboration with other nongovernmental groups) would push open doors into the big world outside. And in only a general sense were the core group's goals theirs.[6]

Nolde's work added a priceless element of practical application to Oldham's by now little-known seminar-type advocacy of a global "Christendom."[7] Perhaps Beveridge's "Welfare State" in postwar Britain is the other example.

The mission societies had given Nolde executive license to become a political operator in the run-up to the San Francisco conference with the specific limited aim of securing religious liberty. By that they had principally in mind freedom for missionaries (including foreign nationals) to preach at will anywhere in the postwar world and for their hearers to be free to convert to Christianity without penalty. Nolde shrewdly, and even courageously, refused to follow that route. His was not the normal contemporary interpretation of the last verse of Saint Matthew's Gospel.

While active in the sphere of his church's religious education programs, he concluded that the culture around him in the 1930s had changed. Men and women no longer became active Christians by intense conversion experiences but through a process of education. It was therefore, he argued in 1944, the conditions for education across the nations of the world that had to be addressed by mission societies, rather than the conditions for preaching by foreigners. And any formal inequality between the governments of sending and receiving churches was becoming outdated and offensive. So the only politically possible way forward—which happily corresponded with the best missiological judgment—was to place religious freedom firmly and ineradicably in the context of other human rights and to campaign for that whole bundle.

It was only in the summer of 1944, when Nolde had been brought in to take forward the ideas being explored in the Joint Committee for Religious Liberty, that this approach jelled in his mind and became the mainspring of his achievements in 1945 and 1948. His first two memoranda to the State Department set out this new basis for "religious liberty" in thinking about international affairs. He contends that such liberty is dependent for its fullness on rights such as freedom of assembly and access to information from any source, and also that it is the key guarantor of other rights. He makes a distinction between two unequal families of rights; that political, intellectual, and religious freedoms have a special character. Such rights involve the freedom for a person or community to strive for a goal or to receive a vocation from God.[8] These latter have to be given prerogative recognition.

The position Nolde advanced was that acceptance by states of the principle of freedom to change religion as a human right could only follow (and then only with difficulty) wholehearted acceptance of his policy by the churches. Religious liberty did in fact, he argued, depend on these other human rights, and in turn its peculiar weight and intimacy (as relating to God) had the capacity to give the whole package authority, even when confronted by the power of states. Nolde's brief from the mission societies would, he believed—with the optimism of the academic—be fulfilled in the ensuing provision of a level playing field everywhere in the world for the best and truest faith to win by convincing argument in interreligious dialogues and by personal attraction to Christian models. The global ethos future for Christian faith would thus remain to play for.[9]

It was a common factor among so many of those who campaigned for human rights that they were deeply concerned for humanistic education. The name of John Locke is a classic instance. However, perhaps the most relevant model would be the nineteenth-century Danish bishop N. F. S. Grundtvig, whom Paul Limbert followed in his work with the national YMCA in the United States. Grundtvig's folk high schools were built on the premise that all of a community's young adults—in his case small farmers' sons in their late teens already with experience of life at work— had a right to own their nation's particular traditions and be given the social resources necessary for the development of their public responsibilities as citizens. These schools were decidedly not an education into Greece and Rome, or into purely technical skills; but "education for life" lived then and there. They related to self-evidently relevant issues that were involved in both religious growth and citizen participation in democratic public life. In the mid-twentieth century, an educational institution came to be expected to live as a community-oriented and morally explicit "good society." Any Grundtvigian understanding of national community could not endure any repeat of the 1930s Depression, when an underclass within it—itself an abomination—could not escape a level of poverty that destroyed self-respect. This was dehumanizing.

EFFECTIVE OR UNIVERSAL?

It was less unclear then than it has since become how the tensions inherent in applying this model from Protestant Europe to all the cultures of the world—for instance, to the scheduled caste of Dalits in India—could be resolved. The keen interest in Soviet education policy, with its intention to mold a new man for a new society, is evidence that the Western educational world in the 1930s itself favored a degree of social engineering and (in Nolde's phrase) "planned outcomes." So it would be quite wrong to suppose that the "right to blossom" proposed for individuals by Maritain and others was "value free" in the 1960s sense, or anything but bracing. It involved both stimulus for action (couch potatoes have limited rights) and intense concern that action should be, in the words of the book of Deuteronomy, in the direction of "choosing life" as signposted by good authority.

The transposing of models of scientific progress in the twentieth century to high culture and to religion was a fundamental error. Many understood that there had been an astonishing acceleration in the increasing, defining, and circulation of understanding—through the provision of journals for every kind of discipline and subdiscipline. With academic centers of knowledge set up in cities around the world, and a clear acceptance that any hypothesis was open to contrary demonstration from whatever reputable source, it seemed the way was clear for universal endorsement of what could be counted as best. World sports institutions developed in parallel. There was no scope in these for Gresham's Law, that bad money drives out good. Such fundamental models of academic life lay behind Nolde's vision for religious liberty as a condition for successful Protestant mission on the world scene.

For the moment, at any rate, there is little evidence that inherited cultural allegiances or personal belief systems change through study of alternatives or academic debate—though there needs to be a substantial caveat regarding their internal mutation. And what of course Nolde and his associates could not foresee was the present intense resistance of state authorities worldwide to the very idea of the comparative assessment of faith systems in public—even in an academic context. The risk of culturally destabilizing community conflict, especially after conversions, is thought to be too great. The practice of "establishment" of tradition-defined communities rules!

As well as new ideas on the subject of Christian mission in the postwar world—derived from his Committee on Religious Liberty and ultimately from Oldham's reinterpretation of Christendom—Nolde was also at the cutting edge of new expectations in the churches' contact with the outside world of media and politics. These, culminating in the setting up of the Commission of the Churches on International Affairs (CCIA) in 1946, owed their inspiration largely to the experience of Walter Van Kirk and John Foster Dulles. Their mark was the discipline—painful to many church leaders—of taking effectiveness seriously. It takes more than good ideas to change things. This new realism owed much to Dulles's long-term commitment to having carefully designed structures available for the churches (should they so wish) to engage with government at every level. Nolde was an apt pupil in insisting on total clarity in specifying the task he was being asked by the churches to perform and by what authority. He also took care to master his briefs and to deliver them competently.

By making it possible to have a recognized person attached to the UN on their behalf, the member churches of the World Council of Churches (WCC), together and individually, had access to the postwar "global order" institutions from their foundation. Without the prior establishment of the CCIA, the Protestant churches (through Nolde) could not have made a contribution to the UN's Universal Declaration of Human Rights. It is clear, too, that the early WCC leaders welcomed the CCIA as the germ of a Protestant institution that, however relatively insubstantial, could play a global diplomatic role akin to that of the Vatican. The WCC realized that in most nations on the six continents, the small Protestant churches were of little consequence to their governments' delegations at the UN or, of course, to the secretary general and his staff.

Another observation on the undoubted effectiveness of the ecumenical movement's mobilization behind setting up a human rights–based world organization after World War II relates not to its use of structures newly apt for the task, but to its dependence on a self-conscious American tradition of "Christendom"—this time in its sense of a territorial folk culture. The Protestant church-related (but not necessarily practicing) populations of North America proved capable of being aroused by the word picture of a new and better postwar world that their religious leaders canvassed with such energy. At the critical political moment, they gave them the support that their elected representatives in government could scarcely resist. The word "crusade" was used, especially by Methodists (perhaps the closest of the FCC denominations to the mass of the population). It is a word with long centuries of association with disciplined action by a folk "Christendom" to pursue political goals. This says something about the way in which world-order projects of a certain kind could still draw on a national Christian identity in the "chosen people" tradition of vocation. It is not clear whether a similar project could now draw on such an energetic response from electorates that are both more privatized in their religious horizons and have a more religiously pluralist vocabulary. This also points up the often neglected fact that the currency of language in which any political leadership can be exercised normally depends on the character of a population's common religious tradition. Many such religions, denominations, or ideologies have given little help in the past to politicians looking for support in promoting internationalist or human rights policies.

Other factors in different communities' perceptions of what to them is the core of "human rights" derive from national myth. For instance, it was apparent at the end of World War II that the word "freedom" was the entry password to human rights for Americans, but that for Australians it was "fairness." Subsequently, East and South Asians preferred "harmony." It is hard to know what tribal peoples would make, if told about them, of their rights as humans—for example, to annual holidays. For many of them, it might be hard to conceive what remained in their lives not covered by their own understanding of freedom of religion.

In the decade after 1945, before the massive incursion into UN affairs of the newly independent ex-colonial states, this contextual character of the human rights package was less obvious. Certainly Protestant leaders in the 1930s tended to assume that if the faith vocabulary used by Christian churches on six continents was the same, and those churches became significant players in their own states, a common creed would bring in a new era of shared life understandings on which world peace could be built. The leaders of the British Commonwealth, as its member states gained independence, thought likewise on the basis of parliamentary institutions. As did, from the point of view of the commissars, the Politbureau in Moscow. These assumptions have not been borne out. Debates in the Human Rights Commission were perhaps too abstractly philosophical, if not doctrinal.

One of the major ways in which the WCC surprised its member churches as they emerged from World War II was the glimpse it offered of a genuinely multicentered international organization. At its foundation in 1938, its leaders had been a very top-down metropolitan group, drawn from Western Europe and the North American quadrilateral, Chicago–Toronto–Boston–Washington. The invitation to the three delegates from Australia and New Zealand to attend the Princeton Round Table in 1943 may have gone out as to the provinces, but they brought to it a distinctive regional experience and took back from it an invigorated self-confidence. This fed in directly to the determination of Australia at San Francisco to assert the role of smaller nations in the UN and to demand a world seeking to proclaim and protect human rights. Nolde's ability to call on correspondents across world cultures for his questionnaire in 1948 on the draft Universal Declaration was something of a first. It was not long after that the WCC insisted on making apartheid in South Africa its focus of concern.

FAITHS AND THE "GOOD SOCIETY"

Ernest Burgmann was one of the two Australians invited in 1947 to contribute thoughts on human rights to the document that UNESCO was preparing as from the "philosophers of the world" to help the Commission on Human Rights in its task of drawing up the Universal Declaration. He disclaimed any particular interest in human rights. They were "the effective myth" of nineteenth-century industrializing capitalist societies, and "that tide has spent itself." But, he continued, in a realistic (and creative) vein: "If we cannot find a basis for human rights in what men are by nature, we might be more successful if we consider what they hope to become. There might be some possible agreement on the point at which they hope to arrive." The requirement for a human rights world is a common vision; only then will we "be able to make a 'Declaration of Human Rights' with confidence." We are, again, at Nolde's prerogative tier of "conative" rights, to protect the individual's right to strive for a goal. It may be that lawyers and the officers running religious organizations are not best placed to do this. For such a vision to be effective, it "must speak to the heart of man, and at the same time satisfy the rational judgement of the thinking minority."[10]

Burgmann was emphatic that a roof over their heads and regular meals were most human beings' precondition for any further venturing into a human rights world. That is not implausible. The conversation he imagines about a common vision for the future of all humankind has to include at least the three discussants that did play their part in the preparation of the Universal Declaration. One was the traditional bundle of Enlightenment civil rights that has now largely captured the phrase "human rights" in media discourse. Another was concern for the physical conditions required for human "blossoming," the rights propounded both by the Soviet bloc and, following Maritain and the tradition of "social Catholicism," by the Latin Americans. The other, the prerogative (in Nolde's word, "conative") right for an individual (or a community) to strive for a goal, could in Protestant tradition be taken as a vocation received from God in conscience. As the Universal Declaration showed, these three voices are not forever condemned to be incompatible.

Career diplomats for centuries had denied the possibility of any such "common vision." National interests, faith stances, and political cultures were deemed to be "sovereignties" inherently and enduringly in active mutual contradiction.[11] So Eleanor Roosevelt's expression of a global ethos, "a Magna Carta for all Mankind," was, by all the wisdom of the past, a dangerous fantasy. But under the shadow of the Berlin airlift, the diplomats in Paris on the evening of December 10, 1948, sensed that "all peoples and all nations" do yearn for a world of free communication and mutual solidarity across state, faith, race, and gender boundaries. Could a new diplomacy representing a new "global ethos" find a practical alternative to threats of nuclear war? If so, it would surely be worth striving to advance, even if its full achievement would have to wait. Just as structuring power and justice has taken place over time in any human culture, whether political or religious, so the nations might not need to despair of structuring a "global order."

Certainly the price of giving up on that hope has not diminished since 1948. For either a faith or a nation not to locate itself in a global dimension in the twenty-first century means that it must feed off its fears of "the other." The kind of world signalled in the Universal Declaration requires continuing support from powerful institutions if it is to be built into experienced reality. Individual well-wishers in the comfortable suburbs of Western cities will not be enough. Faith communities now have a global presence, and can offer (if they will) the prayer, teaching, and public and private actions that, in an irreplaceable way, might sustain and carry forward the "neo-Christendom" model of universal human rights.[12]

POSTSCRIPT

It is sensible to acknowledge four issues that marked the period after the Second Assembly of the World Council of Churches in Evanston in 1954. First, the CCIA continued to press the claims of human rights in international affairs, but no longer as a principal player. What in the 1940s had seemed an imminent climax to the Universal Declaration of 1948 was a UN covenant that would, for the states ratifying it, bring the obligation to carry it into effect. It became a casualty of the cold war. But in 1966, shortly before Nolde's retirement, agreement was reached on two separate covenants.[13] Since then, there has been a sequence of important UN human rights documents, in the preparation of which the CCIA has continued to press its contributions, though no longer so focused on religious liberty.

Second, the developments in thought and practice that took place in Roman Catholic teaching in the 1950s, when they broke surface in the pontificates of John XXIII and Paul VI at the Second Vatican Council, produced a period of remarkably close alliance with the WCC in action for religious liberty, social justice, and peace.

The pontificate of John Paul II has been marked by consistent reaffirmation of the Vatican Council's commitment to human rights.

Third, a particularly creative contribution to global human rights thinking has come from multireligious India, after its constitutional shaping by Jawaharlal Nehru as a secular state of a particular kind. Many of the antidiscrimination issues of the Universal Declaration arise there in an acute form.

Fourth, referring back to the early and forceful opposition of the American Anthropological Association to the inclusion of human rights in the UN Charter after San Francisco, regional cultures—such as the old East Germany,[14] and in particular world faiths such as Islam[15]—continue to provide evidence for the intractability of cultures in the face of attempts to impose a universal framework felt to be in some fundamental sense alien. This is true even if such a frame for living claims to offer greater well-being or monetary wealth.

Ideologies—including those of economic globalization—and faith systems mean that different cultures give weight to different articles. It is only too evident that many rights in the Universal Declaration—repeatedly said at the time to be in indissoluble harmony—are dead letters in many, if not most, societies. It is a regularly rehearsed and professionally staffed tradition that is the foundation for a culture's ethos, and only cultures can produce public squares. Much contemporary "religion" has no organized public voice capable of being used in this way.[16] This is alarming. It will remain a huge—and probably unattainable—task for the Office of the UN Commissioner for Human Rights and for local community educators to achieve a full spectrum of integrated human rights in a widely experienced (if still not yet universal) global order, if they cannot derive effective assistance from organized religions.

Finally, to give Nolde the last word, he drafted a paragraph of the WCC's 1954 Evanston assembly report that he came to see as the credo of his international career. He himself chose to use it several times, and it seemed natural to have it printed on the booklet for his memorial service. Confronted by the ruin of so much that had been hoped for less than ten years before at the San Francisco conference, it expressed a more than personal courage:

"This troubled world, disfigured and distorted as it is, is God's world. He rules and over-rules its tangled history. In praying, 'Thy will be done on earth as it is in heaven,' we commit ourselves to seek earthly justice, freedom and peace for all men. Here as everywhere Christ is our hope. . . . The fruit of our efforts rests in His hands. We can therefore live and work as those who know that God reigns, undaunted by all the arrogant pretensions of evil, ready to face situations that seem hopeless and yet to act in them as men whose hope is indestructible."

NOTES

1. A number of recent writings by political scientists have shown keen interest in the question of whether there is a necessary relation between political democracies and "reli-

gion," however that is to be defined. In Western culture, the word "religion" has its linguistic root in a society-wide "holding together." Where there is no allowance of the possibility of a shared community in faith, how may a society find the touchstone for its "holding together"? Alan Ryan—in *John Dewey and the High Tide of Liberalism* (New York and London: W. W. Norton, 1995)—sees Dewey, a self-proclaimed "religious humanist," attempting to meet "the predicament of modern man" by looking to high art to replace "the Christian God" as the necessary "consummatory experience." See also Larry Siedentop, *Democracy in Europe* (London: Allen Lane, 2000), where in the chapter "Europe, Christianity and Islam" he establishes the alienness to many cultures of a "myth" of human rights directly rooted in the traditions of Christian Europe; and Raymond Geuss, *History and Illusion in Politics* (Cambridge: Cambridge University Press, 2001), especially in his account of human rights in the context of democracy.

2. The changing criteria of interpretation of world faiths are seen in the life work of Wilfred Cantwell Smith (1916–95), the Canadian theologian of religions who taught at Harvard. See K. Cracknell, ed., *Wilfred Cantwell Smith: A Reader* (Oxford: Oneworld, 2001).

3. Warnshuis, from his post in Shanghai, was naturally affected by the excitement of the 1911 revolution in China. Sun Yat Sen and many leaders were Christians; Christian teaching of God was given a place in state schools, and "there was even a moment when the new central Government under Yuan Shih-Kai showed an embarrassing disposition to make Christianity the authorized religion of China." Norman Goodall, *Christian Ambassador: A Life of A. Livingston Warnshuis* (Manhasset, N.Y.: Channel Press, 1963), 61–64.

4. Dr. B. Stanley, Director of the Henry Martyn Centre, University of Cambridge, writes: "There is a need for voices who will protest against the undiscriminating use of the terms 'imperialist' and 'colonialism' as smear words in mission studies. Imperialism is to my mind an ever-present reality of the human condition, not something to be conveniently confined to a particular period or segment of humanity" (personal communication).

5. Cp. "If you need a 19th-century counterpart for the neoconservative movement led by Donald Rumsfeld [et al.] look at the idealistic imperialists produced by Balliol and other Oxford colleges from the 1850s. . . . The British empire-builders of the third quarter of the 19th century spotted their chance for what they believed would be the re-ordering of mankind for its betterment." Andrew Roberts, "Americans Are on the March," *The Times* (London), April 12, 2003, 19.

6. Warnshuis wrote to Fairfield (with copies to Barnes, Nolde, and Decker) on November 26, 1946, that the Joint Committee on Religious Liberty ought to be allowed to die on Nolde's departure. His position was that any committee's usefulness depended on its executive secretary. Considering himself as the father of the committee, he wrote: "The Religious Liberty Committee was appointed to make a study. After floundering around for some time it found a leader in Bates and got something done. At times the Committee itself did some group thinking. Later its mandate was broadened and extended and it has served as a platform for Nolde. The Committee has added very little to Nolde's thinking, but it has accomplished a great deal." Union Theological Seminary, Burke Library, Warnshuis Papers, VII–wallet 122.

7. See Hugh McLeod and Werner Ustorf, eds., *The Decline of Christendom in Western Europe 1750–2000* (Cambridge: Cambridge University Press, 2003).

8. See appendix F, section 3. Nolde wrote: "Two different types of freedom are here included. In the first place there are rights in terms of action or function in society; such as freedom of speech, of press, and of public meeting. In the second place, rights in terms of objectives or areas of conviction are implied in religious worship and political belief."

9. Nolde was invited to give the Rauschenbusch lectures in 1965 at Colgate-Rochester Divinity School. There he proposed that Rauschenbusch's thinking on church and state "must now be[come] an interpretation of church and international affairs."

10. National Library of Australia, Burgmann Papers, box 11, folder titled "UNESCO."

11. Cf., the viewpoint expressed by Philip Jenkins in *The Next Christendom: The Coming of Global Christianity* (New York: Oxford University Press, 2002).

12. This conviction has been argued by Dr. Rowan Williams, the archbishop of Canterbury: "Only a morally robust UN can, realistically, draw up and help to realize the elements of a democratic compact. For this the contribution of religious communities will be essential." He spoke at a fundraising dinner in Connecticut for the Anglican Observer to the UN, under the title "Internationalism and Beyond" on June 19, 2004 (Lambeth Palace press office, www.archbishopofcanterbury.org).

13. The International Covenant on Civil and Political Rights and the International Covenant on Economic, Social, and Cultural Rights were both adopted by the General Assembly of the UN in 1966. The latter has not been ratified by the U.S. government.

14. In the summer of 2003, there was a sudden outbreak of nostalgia in the territory of the old German Democratic Republic for "the slower swaddled life of Communism," which is the theme of the film success of the year, *Goodbye Lenin*. See Roger Boyes, *The Times* (London), July 23, 2003, 18.

15. There is a substantial literature on the questions posed by Islam to human rights. It is not sufficiently realized that all the Islamic states except Saudi Arabia voted in favor of the Universal Declaration, and that positive contributions have been made by Islamic participants in recent UN (and European Union) conferences. However, an important point was made by Antony Beevor, *The Times* (London), March 29, 2003, 22: "The Islamic world, by instinctively rejecting the competition of international markets for spiritual and cultural reasons, is increasing the divide created by economic globalization." See the two volumes edited by J. Witte and J. van der Vijver, *Religious Human Rights in Global Perspective: Religious Perspectives* and *Legal Perspectives* (The Hague and London: M. Nijhoff, 1996).

16. See Patrick West, *Conspicuous Compassion* (London: Institute for the Study of Civil Society, 2004). In the London *Times* of January 31, 2004, he wrote that a major premise of secular Enlightenment thinking, that religion and superstition will decline with "progress," has been shown mistaken in post-Christian Britain. On the health of current phenomena associated with "the compassionate crowd . . . both humanists and apologists of organized faiths can agree. The challenge now is to decide whether we can really achieve a rational, atheist world in which unreason and mystery are banished, or whether this is an impossible dream, likely only to leave a spiritual void that will be filled by . . . self-centred, ersatz religion of the crowd." It now seems entirely plausible, both that "the religious" is a given in the human psyche, and that the proposal by Dietrich Bonhoeffer, a principal theological voice in WCC circles during World War II, of "religionless Christianity" cannot function apart from its roots in a religious bloodstream.

Appendix A

Extracts from the Report of the WCC-in-Formation Conference: "The Churches and the International Crisis" at the Hotel Beau Séjour, Geneva, July 1939 (13 pp.).

Source: World Council of Churches Library and Archives, Geneva, box X.

II. THE INTERNATIONAL ORDER

B. *The Application of Christian Principles*

In the world of international affairs, as we face it today, certain principles seem to us to stand out as clear applications of the Christian message.

1. *Political power should always be exercised with a full sense of responsibility.* All government involves the exercise of power, and there is therefore nothing unchristian or unethical about the nature of power in itself. But wherever there is power there is temptation to use it selfishly and carelessly, without due regard for the needs and interests of those who are affected by it. Such irresponsible use of power is definitely unchristian.

This temptation is particularly insidious in two fields of public affairs:—in international relations, especially relations between a strong state and weaker peoples, because in this sphere there is no constitutional limitation upon the exercise of power, and in economic relations, where there is also often a great disparity between the strength of the parties concerned. International economic relations,—where conditions often allow of an easy abuse of power, and where control over raw materials, capital movements and access to markets may be very unequal,—are a particularly dangerous field and call for the attention of Christians, both as citizens and participants in the modern economic system.

2. *All human beings are of equal worth in the eyes of God and should be so treated in the political sphere.* It follows that the ruling power should not deny essential rights to human beings on the ground of their race or class or religion or culture or any such distinguishing characteristic.

3. From these two principles there follows a third:—*the duty of the ruling power to develop equality before the law,* from what may be a passive and a merely formal equality, *into a political system,* which carries with it positive rights and duties. The function of the Christian ruler is so to use his responsibility as to render those, over whom his power extends, themselves more fully responsible, thereby adding to their human dignity and enabling them better to fulfil their social duties as men and Christians. . . .

4. Certain principles also stand out, in the light of recent experience, in regard to *the political structure needed for the conduct of world affairs.*

The chief of these is that *no true government can exist without law, and that no law can exist without an ethos,*—that is to say, *a sense of obligation in the conscience of the members of the community.* . . .

5. It must be made clear to the people of our respective states, that if Christian principles of national conduct are to be made effective *there must be some form of international organization which will provide the machinery of conference and cooperation.* . . .

6. . . . For the present international relations are carried on between independent states, and the same sense of social obligation that has been developed within national limits has not been extended to the relations of states. The immediate task in this field is *to improve the ethos of inter-state relations,*—to bring influences to bear upon what has been left, by a long tradition, in a jungle outside the bounds of law, of morality, of courtesy and decent human feeling. International relations at least need not and must not be definitely anti-Christian. . . .

[Rules of] neighbourliness would find [their] most natural and helpful expression in a willingness to consider the standpoint of other peoples and *to meet the reasonable needs of a changing world.* At the same time we must recognize that the rule of law cannot become a reality so long as the way is known to be open for resort to violence. It is for the international community to remove this insecurity by providing *an effective deterrent against the use of force.* For this purpose it is not sufficient for nations to renounce the use of violence on their own part. They have also a duty as good neighbours to take their share of the responsibility for maintaining good order in the international community. The full discharge of this responsibility will require that the collective will of the community shall be used *to secure the necessary changes in the interest of justice, to the same extent that it is used to secure the protection of nations against violence.* As to the use of force in this connection we are not agreed.

7. In the field of economic relations we consider that it is both necessary and possible to place *international economic life* upon a more assured basis. . . .

But it is upon personal and national attitudes that the success of such policies depends. Responsibility for one's own country and people (if considered from a very large viewpoint), must give rise to a feeling of the common responsibility of all the national economies for one another and of the responsibility of the whole of mankind for the whole earth. All peoples have an interest in the wise use of the resources of individual countries and in the planning ahead for the benefit of future generations. We do not wish to decide between the relative merits of a free and a planned economy, or to take our stand with either individualism or socialism or State captitalism. . . . It is a duty of Christians to contribute by every appropriate means in their power to such a development, both in their private conduct and in the working out and support of national and international standards, designed, not merely to abolish flagrant injustices, but also to ensure that those engaged in the economic process are not treated as mere instruments of production, but as responsible human agents engaged in tasks which call out their best powers. A case in point is the present-day colonial question. [See Appendix for development of this question.] . . .

8. We are impressed by the fact that difficulties are often allowed to become acute before they are dealt with. We suggest that by international agreement there might be brought into being some continuing international machinery charged with the duty of detecting international difficulties at their incipient stage and when the problem is still of such proportions that it could be more easily dealt with.

APPENDIX

There exists a widespread feeling in many countries that the task of colonial government is no longer one of exclusive national concern or national interest, but that it must be regarded as a common task of mankind, to be carried out in the interests of the colonial peoples by the most appropriate forms of organization. This would call for a transfer of government from the exclusive national sphere to that of international collaboration for the benefit of colonial peoples. . . .

1. [I]ndigenous peoples must not be treated as pawns of international policy;

2. [T]he paramount aim of the Governments concerned must be the moral, social and material welfare of the native population as well as native autonomy as comprehensive as the conditions of each territory allow, to the end that ultimately the population of the area may be able to assume responsibility for its own destiny;

3. [N]ative institutions, and in particular the systems of land tenure, [should] be used and developed;

4. [M]issionary work [should] be freely allowed.

Appendix B

Extracts from *A Message from the National Study Conference on the Churches and a Just and Durable Peace*, convened at Ohio Wesleyan University, Delaware, Ohio, March 3–5, 1942 (31 pp.), Section II, "Guiding Principles," pp. 10–14.

Source: National Council of Churches Records, Federal Council of Churches Records, Presbyterian Historical Society, Philadelphia, RG 18, box 28, folder 9.

1. WE BELIEVE that moral law, no less than physical law, undergirds our world. There is a moral order which is fundamental and eternal, and which is relevant to the corporate life of men and the ordering of human society. If mankind is to escape chaos and recurrent war, social and political institutions must be brought into conformity with this moral order.

2. WE BELIEVE that the sickness and suffering which afflict our present society are proof of indifference to, as well as direct violation of, the moral law. All share in responsibility for the present evils. There is none who does not need forgiveness. A mood of genuine penitence is therefore demanded of us—individuals and nations alike.

3. WE BELIEVE that it is contrary to the moral order that nations in their dealings with one another should be motivated by a spirit of revenge and retaliation. Such attitudes will lead, as they always have led, to renewed conflict.

4. WE BELIEVE that the principle of cooperation and mutual concern, implicit in the moral order and essential to a just and durable peace, calls for a true community of nations. The interdependent life of nations must be ordered by agencies having the duty and the power to promote and safeguard the general welfare of all peoples. Only thus can wrongs be righted and justice and security be achieved. A world of irresponsible, competing and unrestrained national sovereignties whether acting alone or in alliance or in coalition, is a world of international anarchy. It must make place for a higher and more inclusive authority.

5. WE BELIEVE that economic security is no less essential than political security to a just and durable peace. Such security nationally and internationally involves among other things the use of material resources and the tools of production to raise the general standard of living. Nations are not economically self-sufficient, and the natural wealth of the world is not evenly distributed. Accordingly the possession of such natural resources should not be looked upon as an opportunity to promote national advantage or to enhance the prosperity of some at the expense of others. Rather such possession is a trust to be discharged in the general interest. This calls

for more than an offer to sell to all on equal terms. Such an offer may be a futile gesture unless those in need can, through the selling of their own goods and services, acquire the means of buying. The solution of this problem, doubtless involving some international organization, must be accepted as a responsibility by those who possess natural resources needed by others.

6. WE BELIEVE that international machinery is required to facilitate the easing of such economic and political tensions as are inevitably recurrent in a world which is living and therefore changing. Any attempt to freeze an order of society by inflexible treaty specifications is bound, in the long run, to jeopardize the peace of mankind. Nor must it be forgotten that refusal to assent to needed change may be as immoral as the attempt by violent means to force such change.

7. WE BELIEVE that the government which derives its just powers from the consent of the governed is the truest expression of the rights and dignity of man. This requires that we seek autonomy for all subject and colonial peoples. Until that shall be realized, the task of colonial government is no longer one of exclusive national concern. It must be recognized as a common responsibility of mankind, to be carried out in the interests of the colonial peoples by the most appropriate form of organization. This would, in many cases, make colonial government a task of international collaboration for the benefit of colonial peoples who would, themselves, have a voice in their government. As the agencies for the promotion of world-wide political and economic security become effective, the moral, social and material welfare of colonial populations can be more fully realized.

8. WE BELIEVE that military establishments should be internationally controlled and be made subject to law under the community of nations. For one or more nations to be forcibly deprived of their arms while other nations retain the right of maintaining or expanding their military establishments can only produce an uneasy peace for a limited period. Any initial arrangement which falls short of this must therefore be looked upon as temporary and provisional.

9. WE BELIEVE that the right of all men to pursue work of their own choosing and to enjoy security from want and oppression is not limited by race, color or creed. The rights and liberties of racial and religious minorities in all lands should be recognized and safeguarded. Freedom of religious worship, of speech and assembly, of the press, and of scientific inquiry and teaching are fundamental to human development and in keeping with the moral order.

10. WE BELIEVE that in bringing international relations into conformity with the moral law, a very heavy responsibility devolves upon the Unites States. For at least a generation we have held preponderant economic power in the world, and with it the capacity to influence decisively the shaping of world events. It should be a matter of shame and humiliation to us that actually the influences shaping the world have largely been irresponsible forces. Our own positive influence has been impaired because of concentration on self and on our short-range material gains. Many of the major preconditions of a just and durable peace require changes of national policy on the part of the Unites States. Among such may be mentioned: equal access to natural resources, economic collaboration, equitable treatment of

racial minorities, international control of tariffs, limitation of armaments, participation in world government. We must be ready to subordinate immediate and particular national interests to the welfare of all. If the future is to be other than a repetition of the past, the United States must accept the responsibility for constructive action commensurate with its power and opportunity.

11. WE BELIEVE that a supreme responsibility rests with the Church. The Church, being a creation of God in Jesus Christ, is called to proclaim to all men everywhere the way of life. Moreover, the Church which is now in reality a world community, may be used of God to develop His spirit of righteousness and love in every race and nation and thus to make possible a just and durable peace. For this service Christians must now dedicate themselves, seeking forgiveness for their sins and the constant guidance and help of God.

12. WE BELIEVE that, as Christian citizens, we must seek to translate our beliefs into practical realities and to create a public opinion which will insure that the United States shall play its full and essential part in the creation of a moral way of international living. We must strive within the life of our own nation for change which will result in the more adequate application here of the principles above enumerated as the basis for a just and durable world order.

13. WE BELIEVE that the eternal God revealed in Christ is the Ruler of men and of nations and that His purpose in history will be realized. For us He is the source of moral law and the power to make it effective. Amid the darkness and tragedy of the world of today we are upheld by faith that the kingdoms of this world will become the kingdom of Christ and that He shall reign forever and ever.

Appendix C

Extracts from the Minutes of the First Full Meeting of the Joint Committee on Religious Liberty, May 6, 1942.

Source: National Council of Churches Records, Federal Council of Churches Records, Presbyterian Historical Society, Philadelphia, RG 18 Box 67, folder 2.

Present:

Representing the Federal Council of Churches: Messrs. Fischer, Mackay [elected chairman], and Van Dusen. Representing the Foreign Missions Conference: Messrs. Wasson and Padelford. Ex officio: Miss [Inez] Cavert and Messrs. Barnes and Johnson [FCC]; and Messrs. Bates and Warnshuis [FMC].

    Absent: Dr. John S. Badeau, representative of the FMC.

Basis of "Rights"

Consideration must be given to the fundamental question—"What is the basis for claiming these 'rights' when a government seeks to control education, etc., for the maintenance of state? For example, the government of Egypt permits "nothing interfering with law and order." The same condition prevails in Moslem lands, Roman Catholic countries, etc. Panama has a minister in control of religious cults.

    Has every individual the right to disseminate? At what point does religious liberty become social anarchy? What a government does in the face of such problems grows out of the historical background and cultural situation. One cannot say: "Here are principles which all reasonable men will accept," because what they will accept depends entirely on the cultural situation.

    Then does it become a question of under what conditions a Christian testimony can be borne which will not be disruptive of their religious life in the minds of Mohammedan leaders, for example.

    Is it not true that juridically a right is a claim recognized by a substantial authority? Frequently allusion is made to something that is simply a claim, which is not capable of clear definition except where recognized by a competent authority in the area under discussion. There are many instances where a natural or religious "right" is intended rather than a right given by law. . . .

Distinctions

There is a distinction between religious liberty and freedom in Christ. The latter has nothing whatever to do with the issue of religious liberty as it is constantly being considered.

There is a distinction between missionary freedom, which is not a universal right, and religious liberty. . . .

Charter of Religious Liberty connected with World Organization

To what extent do we wish to make the matter of rights or religious liberty a separate issue from that of general liberties? Much might be said for including religious liberty in the whole field of civil liberties. In this connection, the objection was raised that this might tend to limit religious liberty to one aspect, that is, freedom from constraint.

With regard to the inclusion of provision for religious liberty in a peace treaty, it must be kept in mind that such a treaty will not be made in a Protestant, or even a Christian frame. Moreover, the fact that America is a secular country must be taken into account. The principles will not flow from Christian assumptions, because those assumptions are not universally accepted.

What conception of religious liberty are we in our Protestant Christian traditions prepared to stand for or consider? That is, we must explore our own philosophy of religious liberty.

Do we want to say anything to international negotiators, whether of a general peace treaty or bilateral treaties—regarding religious liberty? What do we think now in the light of experience? What do we mean by "religious liberty"? What would we conceive to be an ideal scheme of religious liberty that ought to be considered in connection with peace?

There may be a transition period. If this is so, what should be suggested to the occupational authorities with regard to religious liberty?

Perhaps the religions of the world should have some meeting on this question similar to international conferences on labor—the voice of labor is expected to speak within the various countries.

Should this question of religious liberty and what it means and ought to mean be answered by governments or by religious bodies?

Is not our immediate objective to try to get a formulation by Christians of principles of religious liberty that is so fundamentally sound that it will appeal to governments of different countries?

Mention was made of the fact that the Shotwell group—an influential group—have already used the term, "An International Bill of Rights," and have already taken up the matter of religious liberty. They are about to do further detailed study on this now and have asked the church groups for their counsel. Advantage should be taken of this opportunity. . . .

Appendix D

The "Six Pillars of Peace," Formulated by the Commission to Study the Bases of a Just and Durable Peace Instituted by the Federal Council of the Churches of Christ in America.

Source: As in recommendation (a) of the "general endorsement" by the Delaware Conference 1942 of the Commission to Study the Bases of a Just and Durable Peace's Thirteen "Guiding Principles" (Appendix B), "to crystallize public opinion on these basic issues" (February 23, 1943). Document enclosed with a letter from Sumner Welles to Franklin Delano Roosevelt, Roosevelt Papers, box OF 213.

STATEMENT OF POLITICAL PROPOSITIONS

I. The peace must provide the political framework for a continuing collaboration of the United Nations and, in due course, of neutral and enemy nations.

II. The peace must make provision for bringing under international supervision those economic and financial acts of national governments which have widespread international repercussions.

III. The peace must make provision for an organization to adapt the treaty structure of the world to changing underlying conditions.

IV. The peace must proclaim the goal of autonomy for subject peoples, and it must establish international organization to assure and to supervise the realization of that end.

V. The peace must establish procedures for controlling military establishments everywhere.

VI. The peace must establish in principle, and seek to achieve in practice, the right of individuals everywhere to religious and intellectual liberty.

Appendix E

Statement on Religious Liberty, adopted by the Federal Council of the Churches of Christ in America, March 21, 1944, [and] The Foreign Missions conference of North America, April 12, 1944.

Source: Mackay Papers, Box 40, Special Collections, Princeton Theological Seminary Libraries.

We recognize the dignity of the human person as the image of God. We therefore urge that the civic rights which derive from that dignity be set forth in the agreements into which our country may enter looking toward the promotion of world order, and be vindicated in treaty arrangements and in the functions and responsibilities assigned to international organizations. States should assure their citizens freedom from compulsion and discrimination in matters of religion. This and the other rights which inhere in man's dignity must be adequately guarded; for when they are impaired, all liberty is jeopardized. More specifically, we urge that;

> The right of individuals everywhere to religious liberty shall be recognized and, subject only to the maintenance of public order and security, shall be guaranteed against legal provisions and administrative acts which would impose political, economic, or social disabilities on grounds of religion.
>
> Religious liberty shall be interpreted to include freedom to worship according to conscience and to bring up children in the faith of their parents; freedom for the individual to change his religion; freedom to preach, educate, publish, and carry on missionary activities; and freedom to organize with others, and to acquire and hold property, for these purposes.

To safeguard public order and to promote the well-being of the community, both the state, in providing for religious liberty, and the people, in exercising the rights thus recognized, must fulfil reciprocal obligations: The state must guard all groups, both minority and majority, against legal disabilities on account of religious belief; the people must exercise their rights with a sense of responsibility and with charitable consideration for the rights of others.

Appendix F

Statement on Religious Liberty, Memorandum No. 2, June 12, 1944.

Source: National Council of Churches Records, Federal Council of Churches Records, Presbyterian Historical Society, Philadelphia, RG 18, box 66, folder 24.

Memorandum indicating relationships between religious liberty and civil rights.

(1) *An absolute distinction between rights that are religious and rights that are civil is impossible.*

(2) *A relative distinction between rights that are religious and rights that are civil can be drawn.*

(3) *A more adequate distinction can be made between rights which have to do with the actions or functions of man in society and rights which have to do with man's objectives or areas of conviction.*

The complete text, intended to establish a necessary relationship between freedoms of function and freedoms of conviction, would then read:

> *To permit the exercise of religious, intellectual and political liberty, states shall assure their people freedom of conscience, of speech, and of press; freedom of organization and of public meeting; freedom to acquire and hold such property as may be necessary to their corporate activity; and freedom of access and exposure to the cultures, ideas, and beliefs of other peoples and freedom of cultural exchange.*

In the third paragraph of the *Statement on Religious Liberty*, the functional freedoms are *particularized* to indicate their relationship specifically to freedom of religion. In the form given in this Memorandum, the functional freedoms are generalized to show their relationship to three areas of human conviction—religious, intellectual, and political.

Appendix G

Extracts from the Report of Commission II, "The Peace Strategy of the Churches."

Source: This report was produced for consideration by the Commission to Study the Bases of a Just and Durable Peace's National Study Conference in Cleveland, January 1945. Members of Commission II were largely drawn from the Midwest (especially from Chicago). Its chair was Walter Horton, professor of theology, Oberlin College. The original document is in the collections of the National Council of Churches Records, Federal Council of Churches Records, Presbyterian Historical Society, Philadelphia, RG 18, Cleveland Conference box, pp. 24–27.

VII. *The World Mission of the Church as Related to World Order*

Reconstruction is not only a European or Asiatic problem, it is a world problem challenging all the united resources of the world church. How can the total strength of the world church be brought to the aid of all points of need in the world, so as to meet this challenge? How can the World Mission of the Church revise its methods and aims so as to contribute to world reconstruction and world order more consciously and effectively than at present?

(1) The term "foreign missions" should be dropped out of the vocabulary of the Christian Church and the term "world missions" substituted. This is because the problems dealt with are no longer exclusively foreign. Moreover, the word "foreign" signifies an alienation which we would like to avoid. The word "missions" also needs to be deepened and enlarged for a large portion of our constituency thinks of it solely in terms of securing converts to Christianity from non-Christian religions, whereas it should denote a world church deploying its forces all around the globe in a common Christian program.

(2) The whole missions movement springs from an aroused and rejuvenated Christian faith. Missionary zeal flags unless the people of the churches feel that the world needs to be saved from darkness. Well, the world today is lost in darkness—both at home and abroad—and it needs to be saved by the redemptive truths of Christianity in every department of its life. This is the task of world-wide missions. As Christianity once conquered pagan Roman civilization, it now must penetrate and reform our contemporary world paganism—even in conventionally Christian countries.

(3) While our conviction is strengthened that Christianity can fulfill its destiny only as a world religion, it must keep free from all subserviency to political or economic imperialism. No use of force or special privilege is justifiable in its promotion. Christianity must win out by its own genuine appeal, according full liberty and equality of opportunity to all other forms of religion.

(4) We must reckon with the peril of a resurgence of literalism and unintelligent, even superstitious, forms of Christianity following in the wake of the world war. We need, therefore, to emphasize the implications of world Christianity as something much larger than mere proselytizing. Our goal is not even fully expressed as the building of Christian churches and institutions. We must aim at nothing less than a Christian world order—social, economic and political in every land. Christian churches and institutions must become "energizing centers," reservoirs of good-will, for creating a devotion and loyalty to God transcending allegiance to individual governments and thus providing a basis for building a genuine world order. These *local* centers would be stimulated and guided by the *National* centers (similar to Sigtuna in Sweden) which the World Council of Churches is hoping to found in many parts of the world, related finally to an *international* center from which leaders could be sent out wherever needed most.

(5) Such a world Christianity must be largely indigenous in methods and leadership. We of the West, particularly, must be through with our attitudes and assumptions of superiority, and substitute ecumenical for denominational emphases. Sectarian names and differences must decrease and ecumenicalism must increase, both at home in the promotion of world-wide Christian projects and abroad in their operation.

(6) All this carries with it important implications as to the selection, training, and servicing of Christian missionaries. They must not only be soundly Christian in their personal lives and convictions and unquestionably devoted to Christian spiritual and moral standards, but they will also need to be equipped with an adequate understanding of the implications of Christian principles for community life and interracial and international relationships. They will need advance training in the cultural and religious background of countries to which they are sent. More attention must be paid to reinforcing them on the field by traveling seminars or bringing them home for periods of genuine study on furlough.

(7) While the World Mission of the Church has other important objectives beside the creation of world order and world peace, the whole enterprise would take on added strength and dignity if it were all consciously and deliberately related to that high purpose. We therefore endorse the suggestion of the Maritime Baptists of Canada, in their report on "The Church and the Problem of Peace", that the World Church set up a permanent organization of some sort to mobilize all its resources to deal with the long term problem of peacemaking—especially with those moral, social and cultural factors in peacemaking which are so directly related to the Church's World Mission. The best form of such an organization might be a commission of the World Council of Churches, working in close cooperation with existing organizations such as The Church Peace Union and The World Alliance for International Friendship Through the Churches. . . . By this type of global thinking and planning, it may be that the modern Church can "hold the world together" on a planetary scale, as the early Christians held the Roman world together long ago.

[Note: The final sentence of section 4, pp. 25–26, was a late insertion into the commission's draft. It foreshadows the setting up (financed by John D. Rockefeller) of the Ecumenical Institute at the Château de Bossey outside Geneva as early as 1946.]

Appendix H

Letter on Human Rights in the Charter of the United Nations, Submitted to the U.S. Secretary of State, Edward R. Stettinius Jr., May 2, 1945, San Francisco.

Source: Printed version in O. Frederick Nolde, *Free and Equal* (Geneva: World Council of Churches, 1968), pp. 77–78.

Dear Mr Stettinius,

The undersigned consultants to the Delegation of the United States of America earnestly urge upon the Delegation that it sponsor the following amendments to the Dumbarton Oaks Proposals:

(1) New purpose to be added to Chapter I of the Dumbarton Oaks Proposals:
   "To promote respect for human rights and fundamental freedom."
(2) New principle to be added to Chapter II of the Dumbarton Oaks Proposals:
   "All members of the Organization, accepting as a matter of international concern the obligation 'to defend life, liberty, independence and religious freedom, and to preserve human rights and justice in their own lands', shall progressively secure for their inhabitants without discrimination such fundamental rights as freedom of religion, speech, assembly and communication, and to a fair trial under just laws."
(3) Addition to Chapter V, Section B, 6 after "economic and social fields":
   "of developing and safeguarding human rights and fundamental freedoms."
(4) Addition to Chapter IX, Section D, I, after "social commission":
   "a human rights commission."

Principles involved

The ultimate inclusion of the equivalent of an International Bill of Rights in the functioning of the Organization is deemed of the essence of what is necessary to preserve the peace of the world.

(a) The dignity and inviolability of the individual must be the cornerstone of civilization. The assurance to every human being of the fundamental rights of life, liberty and the pursuit of happiness is essential not only to domestic but also to international peace.
(b) The conscience of the world demands an end to persecution and Hitlerism has demonstrated that persecution by a barbarous nation throws upon the peace-loving nations the burden of relief and redress.

(c) It is thus a matter of international concern to stamp out infractions of basic human rights.

(d) Therefore in the language of Judge Manley O. Hudson of the Permanent Court of International Justice: "Each state has a legal duty . . . to treat its own population in a way which will not violate the dictates of humanity and justice or shock the conscience of mankind."

RELEVANCY TO THE CONFERENCE

(a) It is fully realized that the primary objective of this Conference is to devise the structure of the new world organization.

(b) Nonetheless, it would come as a grievous shock if the constitutional framework of the Organization would fail to make adequate provision for the ultimate achievement of human rights and fundamental freedoms.

(c) The Atlantic Charter, the Four Freedoms, the Declaration of the United Nations and subsequent declarations have given mankind the right to expect that the area of international law would be expanded to meet this advance toward freedom and peace.

(d) Sponsorship of this project by the American Delegation would win the enthusiastic support of the American people, and speaking particularly for the organizations we represent, would command their hearty approval.

CONCLUSION

We therefore urge upon the American Delegation that in this vital field it take a position of leadership.

Appendix I

Extracts from Concluding Remarks of J. H. Oldham and John Foster Dulles at the Final Session in Girton College of the Meeting to Set Up the Commission of the Churchs on International Affairs, Cambridge, August 7, 1946.

Source: From the account in the World Council of Churches Library and Archives, Geneva, box 428.0.01.

Remarks by J. H. Oldham (pp. 5–6):

[Dr. Oldham] wondered whether at the close of his career he was not witnessing the birth of something that would mark an advance comparable to that which he witnessed in his early days and in which he was a participant. In both cases it hinged on a technical device. He thought they could not too often be reminded that the technical is part of God's will, and that vast spiritual issues might depend on the right technical arrangements. In the early case it was due to the initiative of John R. Mott, a great man and Christian, who persuaded the World Missionary Conference in Edinburgh to take what was then a new step in setting up for the first time a Committee with a Secretariat. At that time such a thing did not exist. But when new machinery was set up all sorts of things became possible that before were not possible at all. It was possible to consider questions which could not find a place on the agenda of the individual mission board because they concerned all the members collectively, and the very fact of setting up machinery made it possible for large and important questions to receive attention. The direct effect of that example led to the establishment of the Faith and Order movement and the Conference on Life and Work, and the example was followed eight years later in the political field by the setting up of a League of Nations with a secretariat. In that matter the Churches led the way. . . .

Remarks by J. F. Dulles (pp. 9–12):

This Conference had been essentially one which looked ahead, but he thought all of them at times during it had looked back. He himself had looked back frequently to the Paris Peace Conference of 1919 which came at the close of the first World War. Thinking back upon that conference he was shocked at the complete absence of any Christian influence whatsoever upon the working of that conference. That was not because there were no Christians at that Conference—the delegates to the Paris

Peace Conference were in the main Christian gentlemen and in their personal lives were probably fully as Christian as any of those dealing with international problems today and he was almost certain that they were more gentlemanly. Sometimes a thought had been expressed in the Conference Room that it was sufficient for the Churches to achieve their purpose if they included among their membership persons who occupied important office. The assumption was that if a Christian gentleman became Secretary of State or the delegate to a Peace Conference that in itself would bring Christian insight to bear upon the work of that conference. That was not the case.

The Churches could not rely upon influencing the world by the mere fact that foreign affairs were conducted by persons who were Church members. The reason was obvious. It was that when people acted in a corporate representative capacity they assumed certain responsibilities, as they believed, to others and felt a trustee duty primarily. If you were a director of a bank and sat on the board of affairs of that company, your primary job was to take decisions which would benefit that company and its shareholders. . . .

The Paris Peace Conference was a shocking affair because none of the people at that conference, or the Church groups, attempted to exercise the slightest influence upon the outcome of it. It was only gradually in the post-war period that it began to be realised that the Church did have a task and a responsibility beyond that of merely trying to have as many members as possible and trusting that that would automatically carry the Christian tradition into the affairs of the world. . . .

[Mr. Dulles] thought that what was done in Geneva in 1939 in the few days before the second world war made a real contribution to keeping alive the Church and its united life during the period when otherwise the world was broken up into fragments. Through the work that was carried on, largely through Geneva and Dr. Visser 't Hooft, there was kept alive throughout the war this sense of ecumenical fellowship and the unity of Christians which not even war could dissipate. That was an invaluable thing to have kept alive because it had provided a foundation upon which to build. . . .

He did not suggest that they should not oppose war because of the destruction of property and life, but the Christian approach was a different one. War was a great breeder of ill. It was the thing which above all bred hate and lust and cruelty, which were the things which Christ fought about and which His Church must always fight against. And it was because war was a great creator of evil that the Churches were bound to do something about it. Therefore they had taken a decision. They did not need to calculate the chances of success because they were doing the thing which had to be done, and they were doing it intelligently, deliberately, after an appraisal of the circumstances and having calculated the way to proceed.

He did not know whether they would succeed or fail, but he did know that in going forward upon the path they were taking they were taking the only path that a living Church could take, and they went forward united together in fellowship in the spirit which was attributed to Ulysses when he set out in his mission, to strive, to seek and not to fail.

Appendix J

Letter from O. Frederick Nolde to Mrs. Eleanor Roosevelt, December 10, 1947.

Source: World Council of Churches Library and Archives, Geneva, box 428.3.23.

Geneva, 10 December 1947

Dear Mrs. Roosevelt,

Forgive me if I point out that the form provisionally accepted for the second sentence of the article on freedom of conscience and religion contains only *worship, belief, and teaching.* Of these, belief will be deleted for it already is covered in the first paragraph [*sic*].

This limited view of the expressions of conscience and religion is contrary to our American tradition and supports a position foreign to our own.

First, it implies that in the expression of conscience and religion, the individual must act alone. There is no reference to community or corporate reality.

Second, there is no room for conscience to speak or act in relation to the needs and problems of society. Worship and teaching may be construed in the narrow 'religious' sense. Works of mercy and contributions to an improved society are ruled out. One might cite, as a single example, that religious organizations hold consultative status with the Economic and Social Council on the assumption that they have something to contribute to a society of order and justice.

Third, the practices of some religious groups [e.g., Quakers] are not embraced in the term worship. Accordingly, a third category of observance needs to be added.

If the two specifics 'worship and teaching' are mentioned in the article, the others should also be set forth; namely, observance, community, or association, and practice or action. It is not sufficient to place these in the comment, for they are not interpretations but additional aspects of freedom of conscience.

I hesitate to approach you again on this matter and am writing to take as little of your time as possible. However, the issue is vital. I am confident that I express the desire and hope of a substantial majority of the American people in all faiths, as well as of people in all parts of the world.

Respectfully yours,
O. Frederick Nolde

Appendix K

Extract from the Report of the Drafting Committee to the Commission on Human Rights, May 21, 1948.

Source: World Council of Churches Library and Archives, Geneva, box 428.3.24.

Declaration (p. 6):

Article 16

1. Individual freedom of thought and conscience to hold and change beliefs is an absolute and sacred right.
2. Every person has the right, either alone or in community with other persons of like mind and in public or private, to manifest his beliefs in teaching, practice, worship and observance.
(*Note*: The representative of the Soviet Union proposed to replace Article 16 by the following text (unofficial translation):
"Every person shall have the right to freedom of thought and freedom to practise religious observances in accordance with the laws of the country and the dictates of public morality.")

Articles 17 and 18

I. Text submitted by the United Nations Conference on Freedom of Information
Everyone shall have the right to freedom of thought and expression; this right shall include freedom to hold opinions without interference and to see, receive and impart information and ideas by any means and regardless of frontiers.

Appendix L

Extracts from the Declaration on Religious Liberty, Adopted by the World Council of Churches and the International Missionary Council in the Netherlands, September 1948.

Source: Printed version in O. Frederick Nolde, *Free and Equal* (Geneva: World Council of Churches, 1968), pp. 79–81.

An essential element in a good international order is freedom of religion. This is an implication of the Christian faith and of the worldwide nature of Christianity. Christians, therefore, view the question of religious freedom as an international problem. They are concerned that religious freedom be everywhere secured. In pleading for this freedom, they do not ask for any privilege to be granted to Christians that is denied to others. While the liberty with which Christ has set men free can neither be given nor destroyed by any government, Christians, because of that inner freedom, are both jealous for its outward expression and solicitous that all men should have freedom in religious life. The nature and destiny of man by virtue of his creation, redemption and calling, and man's activities in family, state and culture establish limits beyond which the government cannot with impunity go. The rights which Christian discipleship demands are such as are good for all men, and no nation has ever suffered by reason of granting such liberties. Accordingly:

The rights of religious freedom herein declared shall be recognised and observed for all persons without distinction as to race, colour, sex, language or religion, and without imposition of disabilities by virtue of legal provisions or administrative acts.

(1) *Every person has the right to determine his own faith and creed. . . .*

(2) *Every person has the right to express his religious beliefs in worship, teaching and practice, and to proclaim the implications of his beliefs for relationships in a social or political community. . . .*

(3) *Every person has the right to associate with others and to organise with them for religious purposes. . . .*

(4) *Every religious organisation, formed or maintained by action in accordance with the rights of individual persons, has the right to determine its policies and practices for the accomplishment of its chosen purposes. . . .*

In order that these rights may be realised in social experience, the state must grant to religious organisations and their members the same rights which it grants to other organisations, including the right of self-government, of public meeting, of speech, of press and publication, of holding property, of collecting funds, of travel, of ingress and egress, and generally of administering their own affairs.

The community has the right to require obedience to non-discriminatory laws passed in the interest of public order and well-being. In the exercise of its rights, a religious organisation must respect the rights of other religious organisations and must safeguard the corporate and individual rights of the entire community.

Appendix M

Extracts from the Universal Declaration of Human Rights, December 10, 1948.

Preamble

... Now, Therefore, the General Assembly proclaims this *Universal Declaration of Human Rights* as a common standard of achievement for all peoples and all nations, to the end that every individual and every organ of society, keeping this Declaration constantly in mind, shall strive by teaching and education to promote respect for these rights and freedoms and by progressive measures, national and international, to secure their universal and effective recognition and observance, both among the peoples of Member States themselves and among the peoples of the territories under their jurisdiction.

Article 18

Everyone has the right to freedom of thought, conscience and religion; this right includes freedom to change his religion or belief, and freedom, either alone or in community with others and in public or private, to manifest his religion or belief in teaching, practice, worship, and observance.

Article 19

Everyone has the right to freedom of opinion and expression; this freedom includes freedom to hold opinions without interference and to seek, receive and impart information and ideas through any media and regardless of frontiers.

Bibliography

Acton, Lord. *Lectures on Modern History.* London: London: Macmillan & Co., 1906.

Allen, Roland. *Missionary Methods: St Paul's or Ours?* London: R. Scott, 1912.

American Anthropological Association. "Statement on Human Rights." *American Anthropologist* 49 (1947): 539.

American Law Institute. *Statement of Essential Human Rights.* New York: American Law Institute, 1944.

Aulén, Gustav. *Christus Victor.* London: Society for the Promotion of Christian Knowledge, 1931.

Baltzell, E. Digby. *Sporting Gentlemen: Men's Tennis from the Age of Honor to the Cult of the Superstar.* New York and London: Free Press, 1995.

Bates, M. Searle. *Religious Liberty: An Inquiry.* London and New York: International Missionary Council, 1945.

Beach, Harlan P., and Charles H. Fahs, eds. *World Missionary Atlas.* New York and London: Institute of Social and Religious Research, 1925.

Bell, George. *Christianity and World Order.* Harmondsworth: Penguin Books, 1940.

———. *The Kingship of Christ: The Story of the World Council of Churches.* Harmondsworth: Penguin Books, 1954.

Blanshard, P. *American Freedom and Catholic Power.* Boston: Beacon Press, 1949.

Booth, Alan. *Not Only Peace: Christian Realism and the Conflicts of the Twentieth Century.* London: SCM Press, 1967.

Boyle, Kevin, and Juliet Sheen. *Freedom of Religion and Belief: A World Report.* London and New York: Routledge, 1997.

Brickman, William W. *Pedagogy, Professionalism, and Policy: History of the Graduate School of Education at the University of Pennsylvania.* Philadelphia: Graduate School of Education, University of Pennsylvania, 1986.

Brown, Callum. *The Death of Christian Britain.* London: Routledge, 2001.

Brown, Colin. *Forty Years On: A History of the National Council of Churches of New Zealand 1941–1981.* Christchurch: National Council of Churches, 1981.

Burgess, Faith. "The Public Face of Mount Airy." In *Philadelphia Vision: Mt Airy Tradition.* Philadelphia: Lutheran Theological Seminary, 1991.

Casalis, Georges, Walter Hollenweger, and Paul Keller, eds. *Vers une église pour les autres.* Documents of the World Council of Churches Study Department on Mission. Geneva, 1966.

Christendom. Journal for the American Committee of Life and Work and then of the World Council of Churches, 1935–48 (New York). Became *the Ecumenical Review* (Geneva).

Clements, Keith. *Faith on the Frontier.* Edinburgh and Geneva: T. and T. Clark, 1999.

Collange, Jean François. *Théologie des droits de l'homme.* Paris: Editions du Cerf, 1989.

Counts, George S. *Dare the School Build a New Social Order?* New York: John Day Co., 1932.

Cracknell, Kenneth, ed. *Wilfred Cantwell Smith: A Reader*. Oxford: Oneworld, 2001.

Crockett, Peter. *Evatt: A Life*. Melbourne and Oxford: Oxford University Press, 1993.

Dawson, Christopher. *The Making of Europe*. London: Sheed & Ward, 1932.

Dulles, Avery. *John Foster Dulles: His Religious and Political Heritage*. Lafayette: University of Southwestern Louisiana Press, 1994.

Dulles, John Foster. *War, Peace, and Change*. New York: Macmillan, 1939.

Edwards, David. *Christians in a New Europe*. London: Collins, 1990.

Eliot, T. S. *The Idea of a Christian Society*. London: Faber & Faber, 1939.

Engel, Frank. *Christians in Australia: Times of Change 1918–1978*. Melbourne: Joint Board of Christian Education, 1993.

Fey, Harold E. *A History of the Ecumenical Movement 1948–1968*. London: Society for the Promotion of Christian Knowledge, 1970.

Foreign Relations of the United States, Diplomatic Papers 1945. Vol. I, General: The United Nations. Washington, D.C.: U.S. Government Printing Office, 1967.

Freire, Paolo. *The Pedagogy of the Oppressed*. Harmondsworth: Penguin Books, 1972.

Fuchs, Eric, and Pierre-André Stucki. *Au nom de l'autre: Essai sur le fondement des droits de l'homme*. Geneva: Labor et Fides, 1985.

Gaer, Felice, ed. *To Reaffirm Faith in Fundamental Human Rights*. New York: American Jewish Committee, 1995.

Gairdner, W. H. T. *Edinburgh 1910: An Account and Interpretation of the World Missionary Conference*. Edinburgh: Oliphant, Anderson & Ferrier, 1910.

Geuss, Raymond. *History and Illusion in Politics*. Cambridge: Cambridge University Press, 2001.

Glendon, Mary Ann. *A World Made New: Eleanor Roosevelt and the Universal Declaration of Human Rights*. New York: Random House, 2001.

Goodall, Norman. *Christian Ambassador: A Life of A. Livingston Warnshuis*. Manhasset, N.Y.: Channel Press, 1963.

Gorringe, T. J. *A Theology of the Built Environment*. Cambridge: Cambridge University Press, 2002.

Grubb, Kenneth. *Crypts of Power*. London: Hodder and Stoughton, 1971.

Gutek, Gerald L. *The Educational Theory of George S. Counts*. Kent, Ohio: Kent State University Press, 1970.

———. *George S. Counts and American Civilization: The Educator as Social Theorist*. Macon, Ga.: Mercer University Press, 1984.

Haller, William. *Foxe's Book of Martyrs and the Elect Nation*. London: J. Cape, 1963.

Hempenstall, Peter. *The Meddlesome Priest: A Life of Bishop Burgmann*. St. Leonards, N.S.W.: Allen & Unwin, 1993.

Hocking, William Ernest, ed. *Re-Thinking Mission: A Laymen's Inquiry after One Hundred Years*. New York and London: Harper and Bros., 1932.

Hoffman, Edward. *The Right to Be Human*. Los Angeles: J. P. Tarcher, 1988.

Holmes, M., and D. Garnsey, eds. *Other Men Laboured 1896–1946: 50 years with the SCM in Australia*. Melbourne: Australian SCM Press, 1946.

Hoopes, T., and D. Brinkley. *FDR and the Creation of the UN*. New Haven, Conn.: Yale University Press, 1997.

Hudson, Darril. *The World Council of Churches in International Affairs*. Leighton Buzzard, U.K.: Faith Press for the Royal Institute of International Affairs, 1977.

Humphrey, John P. *Human Rights and the United Nations: A Great Adventure*. Dobbs Ferry, N.Y.: Transnational Publishers, 1984.

Johnson, F. Ernest. "Religious Liberty." *Christendom* 9, no. 2 (1944): 181–94.

Johnson, M. Glen. "The Contributions of Eleanor and Franklin Roosevelt to the Development of International Protection for Human Rights." *Human Rights Quarterly* 9, no. 1 (1987): 19–48.

Kennedy, W. R. *The Shaping of Protestant Education.* New York: Association Press, 1966.

Kirk, Linda. "Eighteenth-Century Geneva and a Changing Calvinism," in Stuart Mews, ed., *Religion and National Identity.* Oxford: Basil Blackwell, 1982, pp. 367–80.

Korey, William. *NGOs and the Universal Declaration of Human Rights: "A Curious Grapevine."* New York: St. Martin's Press, 1998.

Kraemer, Hendrik. *The Christian Message in a Non-Christian World.* London: Edinburgh House Press, 1938.

————. *Theology of the Laity.* London: Lutterworth Press, 1958.

Lauren, Paul Gordon. *The Evolution of International Human Rights: Visions Seen.* Philadelphia: University of Pennsylvania Press, 1998.

Limbert, Paul M. "The YMCA and Public Affairs," typescript, 1941. Kautz Family YMCA Archives, Minneapolis.

————. *Reliving a Century.* Asheville, N.C.: Biltmore Press, 1997.

Longley, Clifford. *Chosen People: The Big Idea That Shapes England and America.* London: Hodder and Stoughton, 2002.

Macaulay, Wilson. "To Princeton and Back (Notes from the Moderator General's Diary)." *The Messenger* (Melbourne), October 1943 to June 1944.

MacMillan, Margaret. *The Peacemakers.* London: John Murray, 2001.

Mansfield, Joan. "The Christian Social Order movement 1934–51." *Journal of Religious History* (Sydney) 15 (June 1988): 109–27.

————. "The Social Gospel and the Church of England in New South Wales in the 1930s." *Journal of Religious History* (Sydney) 13 (December 1985): 411–33.

Maritain, J. *Human Rights and Natural Law.* New York: Scribners, 1943.

————. *Humanisme intégral.* Paris: F. Aubier, 1936. Engl. trans., *True Humanism.* London: G. Bles, 1938.

McLeod, Hugh, and Werner Ustorf, eds. *The Decline of Christendom in Western Europe 1750–2000.* Cambridge: Cambridge University Press, 2003.

Morsink, J. *The Universal Declaration of Human Rights: Origins, Drafting and Intent.* Philadelphia: University of Pennsylvania Press, 1999.

Moyes, John. *American Journey.* Sydney: Clarendon Publishing Company, 1944.

Nelson, E. Clifford. *The Rise of World Lutheranism: An American Perspective.* Philadelphia: Fortress Press, 1982.

Nolde, O. Frederick. "Christian Community and World Order." In *Toward World-Wide Christianity,* ed. O. Frederick Nolde. New York: Harper, 1946 and 1969.

————. *Christian World Action: The Christian Citizen Builds for Tomorrow.* Philadelphia: Muhlenberg Press, 1942.

————. *The Churches and the Nations* (with foreword by W. Visser 't Hooft). Philadelphia: Fortress Press, 1970.

————. "The Commission on Human Rights: Possible Functions." *Annals of the Academy of Political and Social Science* (Philadelphia), January 1946.

————. "The Department of Christian Education in the Theological Seminary: A Type Study of the Lutheran Theological Seminary at Philadelphia." Ph.D. diss., University of Pennsylvania, Philadelphia, 1929.

————. *Free and Equal.* Geneva: World Council of Churches, 1968.

————. "Freedom of Religion and Related Human Rights." In *The Church and International Disorder,* ed. World Council of Churches. London: SCM Press, 1948.

————. *Freedom's Charter* (with introduction by Eleanor Roosevelt). New York: Foreign Policy Association, 1949.

————. *A Guidebook in Catechetical Instruction.* Philadelphia: Board of Publications, United Lutheran Church in America, 1932.

————. *Power for Peace: The Way of the United Nations and the Will of Christian People.* Philadelphia: Muhlenberg Press, 1946.

———. "Religious Liberty and Missions." In *Christian World Missions,* ed. William K. Anderson. Nashville: Commission on Ministerial Training, Methodist Church, 1946.

———. *Truth and Life: The Meaning of the Catechism.* Philadelphia: United Lutheran Publishing House, 1937.

———. *Yesterday, Today, and Tomorrow: A Course of Study for Pre-Confirmation Classes.* Philadelphia: Board of Publications, United Lutheran Church in America, 1936.

Nurser, J. S. "A Human Rights 'Soul' for a Secular World of 'Faiths': A Contradiction, or Just a Paradox?" in *Political Theology* 6, no. 1 (in press): 51–65.

———. "The Ecumenical Movement Churches, Global Order, and Human Rights 1938–1948." *Human Rights Quarterly* 25, no. 4 (November 2003): 841–81.

———. "Faith and Human Rights." *Sewanee Theological Review* 44 (2000–1): 13–26.

———. "Human Rights: The Future for a Re-Visioned Christendom." In *The Idea of Human Rights: Traditions and Presence,* ed. J. Halama. Prague: Protestant Theological Faculty of Charles University, 2003.

———. *The Reign of Conscience: Individual, Church, and State in Lord Acton's History of Liberty.* New York: Garland Press, 1987.

Oldham, J. H. *Christianity and the Race Problem.* London: Student Christian Movement, 1924.

———. *The Resurrection of Christendom.* London: Sheldon Press, 1940.

Oldham, J. H., and W. Visser 't Hooft. *The Church and Its Function in Society;* vol. 1 of *Church, Community, and State.* London: G. Allen & Unwin, 1937.

Paton, David M., ed. *Reform of the Ministry.* London: Lutterworth Press, 1968.

Post-War World. CJDP Newsletter. New York.

Proskauer, Joseph. *A Segment of My Times.* New York: Farrar, Straus, 1950.

Rabben, Linda. *Fierce Legion of Friends.* Hyattsville, Md.: Quixote Center, 2001.

Reeves, Marjorie, ed. *Christian Thinking and Social Order: Conviction Politics from the 1930s to the Present Day.* London: Cassell, 1999.

Robbins, Keith. *History, Religion, and Identity in Modern Britain.* London: Hambledon Press, 1933.

Roosevelt, Franklin D. *The Public Papers and Addresses of FDR,* vol. 13. New York: Harper, 1950.

Rothblatt, Sheldon. *The Revolution of the Dons.* London: Faber, 1968.

Rouse, Ruth. *The World's Student Christian Federation.* London: SCM Press, 1948.

Rouse, Ruth, and S. C. Neill, eds. *A History of the Ecumenical Movement 1517–1948.* London: Society for the Promotion of Christian Knowledge, 1954.

Ryan, Alan. *John Dewey and the High Tide of Liberalism.* New York and London: W. W. Norton, 1995.

Shafer, Luman J. *The Christian Alternative to World Chaos.* New York: Round Table Press, 1940.

Shotwell, James T. *The Faith of a Historian.* New York: Walker, 1964.

———. *The Long Way to Freedom.* New York: Bobbs-Merrill, 1960.

Siedentop, Larry. *Democracy in Europe.* London: Allen Lane, 2000.

Stettinius, Edward R. *Diaries of Edward R. Stettinius,* ed. T. M. Campbell and G. C. Herring. New York: New Viewpoints, 1975.

Tambaram Conference. *The World Mission of the Church.* London and New York: International Missionary Council, 1939.

Tappert, Theodore G. *History of the Lutheran Theological Seminary at Philadelphia 1964–1964.* Philadelphia: Lutheran Theological Seminary, 1964.

Tawney, R. H. *Religion and the Rise of Capitalism.* London: John Murray, 1926.

Teihard de Chardin, Pierre. *The Phenomenon of Man.* Engl. trans. London and New York: Harper, 1959.

Temple, William. *Christianity and the Social Order.* Harmondsworth: Penguin Books, 1942.

Toynbee, A. J. "Religion: What I Believe, and What I Disbelieve." In *Experiences.* London and New York: Oxford University Press, 1969.

———. *A Study of History.* 10 vols. London: Oxford University Press, 1934, 1939, 1954.

Traer, Robert. *Faith in Human Rights: Support in Religious Traditions for a Global Struggle.* Washington, D.C.: Georgetown University Press, 1991.

Van Dusen, H. P. *The Spiritual Legacy of John Foster Dulles.* Philadelphia: Westminster Press, 1960.

Van Kley, Dale. *The Religious Origins of the French Revolution.* New Haven, Conn.: Yale University Press, 1996.

Vidler, A. R. *Christ's Strange Work.* London: Longmans, Green and Co., 1944.

Visser 't Hooft, Willem. *The First Six Years 1948–54.* Geneva: World Council of Churches, 1954.

———. "An Impression of the World Missionary Conference." *International Christian Press and Information Service*, Geneva, January 1939.

———, ed. *The Ten Formative Years 1938–48.* Geneva: World Council of Churches, 1948.

Ward, W. R. *The Protestant Evangelical Awakening.* Cambridge: Cambridge University Press, 1992.

Warneck, Gustav. *Outline of a History of Protestant Missions.* Engl. trans. Edinburgh (n.p.), 1901.

Walzer, M. *The Revolution of the Saints.* London: Wiedenfeld and Nicolson, 1966.

Wells, H. G. *The Outline of History*, 1st ed. London: George Newnes, 1919–20.

West, Patrick. *Conspicuous Compassion.* London: Institute for the Study of Civil Society, 2004.

Wild, John. "The Rights of the Other as Other." *Drew Gateway* (Madison, N.J.), winter 1969, 81–106.

Witte, John, and John D. Van der Vijver. *Religious Human Rights in Global Perspective: Religious Perspective.* The Hague and London: M. Nijhoff, 1996.

Woodhouse, A. S. P. *Puritanism and Liberty.* London: Dent, 1966.

Woody, Thomas. *New Minds, New Men? The Emergence of the Soviet Citizen.* New York: Macmillan, 1932.

World Council of Churches. *The Church and International Disorder.* London: SCM Press, 1948.

Yocum, A. D. *An Analysis of Education as Conduct Control.* Philadelphia, 1923.

Zeilstra, Jurjen A. *European Unity in Ecumenical Thinking 1937–1948.* Zoetermeer: Uitgeverij Boekencentrum, 1995.

Index